BLOOD THAT CRIES OUT
FROM THE EARTH

BLOOD THAT CRIES OUT FROM THE EARTH

The Psychology of Religious Terrorism

James W. Jones

OXFORD

UNIVERSITY PRESS

OXFORD

UNIVERSITY PRESS

Oxford University Press is a department of the University of Oxford.
It furthers the University's objective of excellence in research, scholarship,
and education by publishing worldwide.

Oxford   New York
Auckland   Cape Town   Dar es Salaam   Hong Kong   Karachi
Kuala Lumpur   Madrid   Melbourne   Mexico City   Nairobi
New Delhi   Shanghai   Taipei   Toronto

With offices in
Argentina   Austria   Brazil   Chile   Czech Republic   France   Greece
Guatemala   Hungary   Italy   Japan   Poland   Portugal   Singapore
South Korea   Switzerland   Thailand   Turkey   Ukraine   Vietnam

Oxford is a registered trade mark of Oxford University Press
in the UK and certain other countries.

Published in the United States of America by
Oxford University Press
198 Madison Avenue, New York, NY 10016

© Oxford University Press 2008

First issued as an Oxford University Press paperback, 2012.

Library of Congress Cataloging-in-Publication Data
Jones, James William, 1943–
Blood that cries out from the earth :
the psychology of religious terrorism/James W. Jones.
p. cm.
Includes bibliographical references and index.
ISBN 978-0-19-533597-2 (hardcover); 978-0-19-993364-8 (paperback)
1. Terrorism—Religious aspects.
2. Terrorism—Psychological aspects.   I. Title.
BL65.T47J66 2008
201'.763325—dc22   2007034721

9 8 7 6 5 4 3 2 1

Printed in the United States of America
on acid-free paper

Dedicated to all the victims of religious violence and terrorism

Cain rose up against his brother Abel and killed him. Then the Lord God said to Cain, "Where is your brother?" Cain said, "I do not know. Am I my brother's keeper? And the Lord God said, "What have you done? Listen, your brother's blood is crying out to me from the earth."
—Genesis 4:8–10

Terrorists are containers into which one can project one's unconscious hostility.
—J. Victoroff (2005), quoting L. DeMause

PREFACE

This is a work in progress. It may look like a finished project with its printed text bristling with references and its bibliography. But that is an illusion—in Freud's sense. For Freud, an illusion was a wish. This book carries with it my wish to be done with this terrible topic. In the early months of the year 2001 I completed a book entitled *Terror and Transformation: The Ambiguity of Religion in a Psychoanalytic Perspective.* Because it had the word "terror" in the title and came out around the time of 9/11, I have been swept up into a vortex of discussions about religion and terrorism, a topic I find extremely foreign to my experience and very aversive. Also, like many in the New York metropolitan area, 9/11 still casts a longer shadow over my life (in ways that I still find hard to talk about) than the World Trade Towers ever cast when they stood erect over lower Manhattan. As much as I wanted to escape from these discussions, I have been unable to, and that has resulted in this book.

Sections of this book were previously published in *The Psychoanalytic Review,* 2006, volume 93, and are used here with the permission of the National Psychological Association for Psychoanalysis and the editor, Dr. Michael Eigen.

There are many, many people to whom I owe the deepest debt of gratitude for their contributions to my thinking and writing about this topic. This book simply would not have been possible without their aid. On that bright, clear, and bitter fall morning, now known as 9/11, Kathleen Bishop and I were taking our usual morning walk when a stranger shouted to us from his car that the World Trade Center was under attack. "He must be crazy," we said to each other. But we went back to her house and turned on the TV in time to see the first tower fall. And then the second. There we sat together in shock as bodies dropped from the sky on TV like birds interrupted in flight. Then my daughter, walking to work in Manhattan, called. At that same time, my other daughter, who was supposed to be on a plane at that very moment, was being ushered out of Newark Airport by armed National Guard. It was to Kathleen's house that she and her boyfriend found their way and stayed with us since they could not return to their home in Brooklyn. The next morning I drove by the parking lots in the train stations near Kathleen's North Jersey home. Even though no commuter trains were running on September 12, there were scattered cars in the lots. Cars of people who had left for work the morning of 9/11 and not returned that night. Or ever. Later Kathleen and I, in our roles as psychotherapists, were asked to run drop-in groups for anyone who wanted to simply have a place to come and talk. Even now I cannot think of that day or read the 9/11 Commission report of those events without tears in my eyes. Much of what I had to read for this book has meant reliving that day again and again, and that has often been retraumatizing. And reading and rereading texts that make it clear that authors want me, my family, my friends and colleagues to die painful deaths has certainly taken its toll on me. I could never have done that without Kathleen being there with me as I did so. In addition, she read the manuscript and continually encouraged me to work on it when the emotions aroused seemed paralyzing and the project seemed not worth it.

Mark Lewis Taylor, colleague and friend, contributed many careful readings and sharp and spirited debates to this project. I thank the members of the PsyBC international online seminar on psychoanalysis and fundamentalism, especially Dan Hill, the organizer, Ruth Stein, Chuck Strozier, Ana-Maria Rizzuto, Walter "Mac" Davis, Richard Koenigsburg, Mike Eigen, Don Moss, Dan Shaw, and Joel Whitebook, who also organized a faculty seminar on psychoanalysis and fundamentalism at Columbia University to which I was invited. The blunt, honest, and intellectually sophisticated discussions among this group, while conducted in a medium that was very aversive to me (online forums), deepened and broadened my thinking about this topic beyond any way I have to thank them. And our interchanges serve as a model for me of productive conversations about emotionally provocative topics among colleagues who profoundly disagree.[1]

This book began as a lecture I was invited to give after 9/11 in Sweden at Uppsala University and the University of Lund. Then it turned into a paper that was eventually published in *The Psychoanalytic Review* in 2006.

After time in Japan, it was augmented by a paper on Aum Shinrikyo. My thinking and writing about religious terrorism was further expanded by a series of conferences and seminars on the subject. Then began discussions with publishers about making this into a book. At each turn the project grew exponentially more complex, and the amount of material grew progressively more unmanageable. The emergence of a viable book from all this chaos was facilitated by the careful and consistent editorial hand of Cynthia Read at Oxford University Press. I am deeply indebted to her detailed and patient work on this text.

The several anonymous reviewers of this manuscript as it made its way through the publishing process contributed numerous helpful suggestions that have immensely strengthened this book. I have no way to thank them other than anonymously, but I want to do that here. If they should read the published book, I hope they recognize the impact of their comments.

I owe a profound debt to the faculty and staff of the Center on Terrorism at John Jay College in New York, and especially its director, Charles B. Strozier, my colleague, friend, and bourbon-consuming buddy. Chuck and his colleagues have welcomed me into their conferences and seminars on terrorism, and given me an invaluable exposure to the broader field of terrorist studies and the larger context in which the religiously motivated groups operate.

Also, my deepest gratitude goes to my colleagues at the Nanzan Institute for Religion and Culture at Nanzan University in Nagoya, Japan, especially Jim Heisig, Paul Swanson and, most of all, Manabu Watanabe. They provided me a more than comfortable guestroom and a beautiful office from which I watched the cherry blossoms bloom and fall during the month of April 2005 while I researched Aum Shinrikyo in Japan. Professor Watanabe made his considerable knowledge of that group readily available to me as well as providing gracious Japanese hospitality along with trenchant critiques of my developing ideas.

I am more than fortunate to have colleagues like all of these. Of course, most of these people who contributed so much to my thinking powerfully disagree with much of what I conclude here—they are in no way responsible for my arguments or conclusions, which, for better or worse, are mine alone.

CONTENTS

INTRODUCTION: RELIGION, PSYCHOLOGY, AND TERRORISM

This book was conceived and written by a professor of religious studies who is also a practicing clinical psychologist. Both of these interests—the clinician's concern with the dynamics of individual personalities and the scholar's knowledge of the diversity and complexity of the religious life—shaped the book. As both a clinician and a teacher of religious studies, I am interested in the psychological dynamics involved in religion and especially religiously motivated violence. And I want to know how understanding those dynamics can contribute to our general understanding of the psychology of religion. Thus this book is about religion first and terrorism second. My main goal in writing it is to contribute to our psychological understanding of religion. Of course I also hope, at this moment in history, to contribute something to our understanding of terrorism. But that is not my main agenda.

Since the beginnings of psychoanalysis with Freud's writings, psychoanalysts have applied various clinical theories—developed in the psychic struggle of patient and therapist—to understanding the passions and motivations that drive religious belief and practice (and also the rejection of religious belief and practice) and that are expressed in and through rituals, theologies, stories, and songs from the various religions of the world. Over the past several decades, this process has produced a plethora of books and articles far too numerous to review here. During this time a consensus has formed in the field of religious studies that psychodynamically informed models can bring tremendous interpretative gain to our understanding of religious phenomena (for reviews see Jones, 1991, 2002).

A religion is, among other things, a complex of relationships: with a divine figure, with a teacher or leader, with a sacred text or set of symbols, with a set of ideas, with a community of co-religionists. Such relationships embody certain patterns, and these patterns often reflect and repeat relational patterns in other areas of a devotee's life: a search for an authority figure or the rejection of all authority, a deep longing or attachment or a drive to keep aloof and distant from others, a need for absolute certainty or a fear of any commitments. These and many other patterns reverberate through the gods that are believed in or rejected, the dogmas of Christianity and the speculations of the Upanishads, the meditational disciplines of Zen and the philosophies of the skeptics. From the standpoint of relational psychoanalysis, the accepting or rejecting of the gods, the longing for a savior, the lure of a spiritual discipline, the attraction of a purely materialistic worldview, or the call of martyrdom all carry certain interpersonal themes, thoughts, and affects. It is the task of a contemporary psychodynamic inquiry to analyze those patterns and the cognitions, affects, and behaviors that carry them.

As a clinician, I listen for repeating themes and patterns in the patient's life, not just in his or her behavior but also in ways of thinking and feeling. Listening to the patient's history, it is often apparent that these patterns, some of which do mischief in the person's life, have their roots in early interpersonal encounters and experiences. When I read religious texts or study religious practices, there, too, patterns repeat. It is that method of interpretation, which I have refined and used for several decades both in working with religious patients and in studying and teaching religious texts and practices, that I apply here specifically to understand religiously motivated terrorism, again by listening for the psychological–religious themes that echo in the writings and statements of terrorists.

From the perspective of a scholar of religious studies, there is a certain irony in the present moment. The rise of religiously motivated terrorism has provoked many people into thinking about religion to an extent that probably would not have happened without it. In my many years of studying and teaching about religion, I have never seen such a rash of academic seminars and conferences on fundamentalism, religion and violence, apocalypticism, and related topics as in the last 6 years. This has been paralleled, I suspect, by an equal increase in programs and articles on these topics on radio and television and in the popular press. All the good works done by religions in the last 50 years—the marches of Martin Luther King Jr. and the Southern Christian Leadership Council, the speeches of the Dalai Lama, to say nothing of the thousands of soup kitchens, food pantries, and other service projects run by religious congregations—never provoked this level of scholarly discussion about the nature of religion. But the bombings of American embassies and bases around the world by Muslim militants, the fanatical rhetoric of the Jewish settlers in the occupied territories, the suicide bombings in Israel and Europe by Islamicists, the rise to power of the extreme religious right in the United States, and the 9/11 attacks on the World Trade Center by the jihadists have provoked a flurry of seminars, conferences, journal articles, and books designed to answer basic questions about the nature of religion. The scholar of religion detects a certain irony here. It has taken an upsurge of fanaticism and terrorism to bring religion into public view and scholarly discussion.

I am not proposing a general theory of terrorism here but rather asking what a psychological, primarily psychodynamic, exploration of religious terrorism might tell us about that phenomenon and about the psychology of religion in general. Reading the literature on the topic of terrorism, I am struck by the paucity of discussion about both of these factors—the psychodynamics of religious terrorists and the religious aspect itself. In part this lack is because most of the mainstream, scholarly literature is written by social psychologists, not clinicians, and by political scientists rather than scholars of religion or psychologists of religion. This book is one small contribution to filling in that gap in the discussion.

I construct my argument in several stages, First, I briefly present some of the current social psychological models of terrorism in general (chapter 1). The second chapter focuses primarily on the Muslim jihadists and compares the major themes of their writings with those of other world religions. This will introduce the central psycho-religious themes found in religious terrorism (chapter 2). Next I illustrate these central themes with two very different groups that merge religion and violence: the Japanese cult Aum Shinrikyo, which is based in Buddhism and whose members released the toxic sarin gas in the Tokyo subway, and the extremely apocalyptic elements, based in Christianity, of the religious right in the United States (chapters 3 and 4). Throughout the book there will be examples from other religious movements as well. Then I draw together the most important themes from this material and present some of the interpretative light that a clinical psychoanalytic theory might shed on them (chapter 5). Finally, I conclude by mentioning some of the implications of my presentation for understanding the psychology of religion (chapter 6).

We must keep in mind that there is no one psychology of religious terrorists. Most likely the motivation and psychology of Chechen suicide bombers defending their homeland is rather different from that of the Japanese students seeking spiritual renewal who joined Aum Shinrikyo, and they are different still from those who murdered American doctors and nurses at women's health clinics. And the psychology of the leaders of terrorist groups may be rather different from that of the followers and members. The character structure of the main 9/11 hijackers who were primarily educated, adult men who had lived on their own and in the west for years is surely radically different from the uprooted and unformed adolescents recruited into and constantly watched over after their initiation by militant Palestinian groups. It must be emphasized, although this should be obvious, that, like religion itself, religiously motivated terrorism is a multidimensional, multidetermined phenomenon (Baumeister & Vohs, 2004; Hafez, 2006b; Marsella, 2005). No one theoretical lens will reveal the whole picture. Only multiple perspectives can help us understand it. Political scientists, journalists, social psychologists, students of religion, and clinicians have all written about the topic. All these perspectives are necessary to understand religiously motivated terrorism; none is sufficient in itself, although their proponents sometimes claim they have the key to understanding religiously motivated terrorism. But if scholars of religion have learned nothing else in the last 100 years of religious studies, they have certainly discovered that no one unitary explanation for religious behavior can ever be sufficient. The perspective articulated here, like any perspective, is one piece of a much larger puzzle.

Besides the complexity of the phenomenon, another reason for insisting on the importance of multiple perspectives in understanding religiously motivated terrorists concerns the possible misuse of psychology. Shortly after 9/11, I heard an Israeli psychologist interviewed on a New York radio station. He explained his understanding of the dysfunctional family situations from which he said Palestinian suicide bombers came. He went on to claim that these suicide bombers showed all kinds of symptoms of psychopathology. In the next chapter we will consider whether there is actually any evidence to support this claim. That is not my point here. This psychologist's subtext was clearly that because psychopathology was the cause of suicide terrorism, there was no need to consider other possible causes, including any possible political and legal grievances on the part of the Palestinians. I consider this a misuse of psychology. I do not want any of the psychological accounts presented in this book to obscure other factors that also contribute to religiously motivated terrorism, especially political, social, and religious grievances on the part of the communities from which they come. There is also a religious version of this maneuver that functions in exactly the same way. To demonize religiously motivated terrorists as simply evil doers or demonic agents makes them easy to dismiss. Exhibiting certain psychological motivations or committing heinous acts does not mean that religiously motivated terrorists lack legitimate political grievances. While the terrorists are almost always marginal in relation to the larger religious communities and traditions from which they come, they also frequently articulate widespread grievances and feelings present within these communities. But terrorists act on these grievances in ways never justifiable, especially within the religious traditions they claim to represent.

Given my insistence on the multidimensional nature of religion and of religious terrorism, I am not interested in taking sides in a controversy in the literature over whether external pressures or processes internal to the group or individual dynamics are more salient in turning a religious group violent. For personal reasons, some individuals are more attracted to or more easily recruited by fanatical groups than others, and often an interactive system operates between the group and the larger society whereby the perceived hostility of the outside world, sometimes generated by the group's own actions, causes a group to feel more threatened and to withdraw more into itself and perhaps also to increase its criticisms of the larger society which, in turn, fuels further opposition, which in turn fuels more defensive moves on the part of the group. Such cycles ended in disaster in cases like Jonestown, Waco, and Aum Shinrikyo (see Reader, 2000; Wessinger, 2000, for different positions on this issue).

Even if many groups like The People's Temple, the Branch Davidians, or Aum Shinrikyo turned violent in part in response to the perceived attacks upon them by the larger society, or even if Islamic militants are responding to perceived threats by western culture, the question remains as to whether there are some dynamics inherent in these religions (or perhaps inherent in all religions) that lead to violence. Certainly there are social conditions that contribute to religious violence. But the current upsurge of religious violence is not only a response to modernity, secularity, or the decline of tradition or spiritual presence. So-called New Age movements can also be seen as a response to these social factors, and they are almost uniformly profoundly nonviolent. Something else is at work in those groups that turn violent. The thesis of this book is that one of the many additional factors involves the psychologies of those religious devotees that turn to terrorism. But again, I see this as a supplement to and not a substitute for all the other perspectives on religiously motivated terrorism.

In the months following 9/11, I often heard demagogues on the radio say that psychologists (like me) who seek to understand the psychology behind religiously motivated violence simply want to "offer the terrorists therapy." The idea that one must choose either understanding or action—that one cannot do both—is an idea that borders on the pathological and represents the kind of dichotomizing that the proceeding chapters demonstrate is part of the terrorist mindset. Such dichotomized thinking, wherever it occurs, is a part of the problem and not part of the solution. So that I am not misunderstood on this point, the reader should remember that I worked for 2 years in the psychology department at a hardcore, maximum security prison. I certainly did offer the rapists and killers and muggers therapy. But I never thought of that as a substitute for just and vigorous law enforcement. And I have also worked as a psychologist with police officers and veterans. *Understanding an action in no way means excusing it; explaining an action in no way means condoning it.*

It is a symptom of how fractious and volatile the discourse around terrorism—and especially religious terrorism—has become that I must state the obvious and say as unequivocally as possible that, despite the fact that all the religions of the world have done it, the use of violence against civilians and noncombatants is condemned in all the world's religions. And to my mind the targeting of noncombatants, civilians going about their daily lives, and children can never be justified no matter how lofty or sacred the cause is held to be. Nothing in the coming pages should be read to say anything other than that.

There is, however, a deeper issue here. Understanding others (even those who will your destruction) can make them more human. It can break down the demonization of the other that some politicians and policymakers feel is necessary to combat terrorists. The proceeding chapters show that the demonization of the other is a major weapon in the arsenal of the religiously motivated terrorist. Must we resort to the same tactic—which is so costly psychologically and spiritually—in order to oppose terrorism? Or can we counter religiously motivated terrorists without becoming like them?

BLOOD THAT CRIES OUT FROM THE EARTH

CHAPTER I

RELIGION AND TERRORISM

The Need for a Multidimensional Model

HOW MIGHT WE BEGIN TO UNDERSTAND RELIGIOUS TERRORISM psychologically? This is the first question we must confront. But this one question is really many questions: what do we know about the psychology of terrorism in general? How might a general understanding of terrorism apply to the specific case of religious terrorism? Is religious terrorism a special case or just another variation on the general theme of terrorism?

WHAT IS RELIGIOUS TERRORISM?

I am sitting around a table at a conference at the Center on Terrorism in New York City with 20 experts discussing the question, what is terrorism? From this discussion involving 20 people, more than 30 definitions emerge. A quick perusal of relevant texts leads to the same conclusion: there is no one agreed-upon definition of terrorism. For example, after an extensive review of conflicting definitions, Hoffman (2006) defines terrorism as "the deliberate creation and exploitation of fear through violence or the threat of violence in the pursuit of political change" (40). Title 22 of the United States Criminal Code defines terrorism as "premeditated, politically motivated violence perpetuated against non-combatant targets by subnational groups or clandestine agents, usually intended to influence an audience" (section 2656f/d). Martha Crenshaw wrote in 1981, long before 9/11, that terrorism is "the premeditated use or threat of symbolic, low-level violence by conspiratorial organizations" (379). The United Nations Panel on Threats, Challenges, and Change defined terrorism as an action "that is intended to cause death or serious bodily harm to civilians or non-combatants, when the purpose of such an act, by its nature or context, is to intimidate a population or compel a government or international organization to do or abstain from doing any act" (2004: 52). The report of the Club de Madrid summit on "Democracy, Terrorism, and Security" calls for a precise definition of terrorism so that such groups could not "evade the frank term for what they were actually doing" and offered the following: "terrorism is the pursuit of political ends by . . . violence against civilians and non combatants where the purpose is sowing fear in that population" (Club de Madrid, transcription of the plenary session, March 9, 2005). The common cliché has it that "one's person's terrorist is another person's freedom fighter." Such a cliché can make for powerful polemics but is virtually useless for scholarly analysis. However, this cliché does underscore that any definition of terrorism is deeply contextual. This obviously makes a consensus definition of terrorism very difficult (Horgan, 2006).

Some years ago I taught an introductory course in religious studies. The goal was to introduce students to the diversity of religious traditions throughout the history of *Homo sapiens*. A subtext for the course was to investigate whether we could arrive at a definition that would cover all the groups and practices that humankind had labeled "religious" at one time or another. After 15 weeks we had utterly failed at that task. There is simply no single definition that will encompass all the phenomena that human beings have called religious. So arriving at a definition of "religious terrorism" would seem to involve combining the unknown with the obscure.

Some themes, however, emerge from all these definitions of terrorism. As distinct from justifiable warfare, terrorism involves the targeting of civilians, noncombatants, or those not directly involved in the conflict. Unfortunately, when religion enters the picture, it tends to eradicate in the minds of religiously motivated terrorists any real distinction between combatants and noncombatants, the guilty and the innocent. In the mind of many religiously motivated terrorists, as we shall see, anyone who is not a co-religionist is presumed guilty and available for killing. Another theme that emerges from virtually all definitions of terrorism is that it "is a form of political action" (Club de Madrid, 2005: 13). Perhaps the insistence on the centrality of the political in defining terrorism results from the fact that, to date, most studies of terrorism have been authored by political scientists and policy experts. However, we will question here the extent to which a singular emphasis on political motives helps in understanding religiously motivated terrorism. In addition, most definitions emphasize the terrorist goals of intimidation and creating fear. This is important for our purposes because experiences of fear and intimidation are profoundly psychological, and we know something about the psychology of fear and intimidation. Another element that is often mentioned in definitions of terrorism is that the actions are symbolic. This is a major dimension of religiously motivated terrorism (Juergensmeyer, 2000). So, at a minimum, a terrorist act must be violent, must be directed at those the observer (if not the perpetrator) considers innocent or noncombatant, must inspire fear and terror, and is often symbolic in some sense.

Also, I have argued elsewhere that, in general, religion involves denoting something—a person, a text, an institution, an experience, a part of nature—as "sacred" (Jones, 2001, 2002). This category of "the sacred" has become common in the field of religious studies as a defining characteristic of things labeled religious (see references in Jones, 2002). So as a working definition of religious terrorism, I propose that it involves the use of violence, often in symbolic but deadly actions, in the service of sacred goals or values. It will be the burden of the rest of this book to elaborate what this means in practice and how it might be understood psychologically.

THE ONE THING WE KNOW FOR SURE: TERRORISM IS A COMPLEX PHENOMENON

How much do we really know about terrorism? The short answer is "a lot" and "a very little." Horgan (2006) concludes his book by saying that "we are still nowhere near an agreed *understanding* of terrorism" (159, emphasis in original). "Terrorism" is more often an epithet or a bit of propaganda than a useful category for increasing understanding. There is general agreement that terrorism is not an end in itself or a motivation in itself (except perhaps for a few genuinely psychotic lone wolves). No movement is only a terrorist movement; its primary character is more likely political, economic, or religious. Terrorism is a tactic, not a basic type of group.

We must also question the purpose of our attempts to understand terrorism. Part of the confusion over the understanding of terrorism results from the more basic confusion of not knowing what we want our explanations of terrorism to *do* for us. Before we undertake to explain terrorism, we should be clear as to what we want this explanation to accomplish. Many hope that understanding terrorism will help predict future terrorist actions. Others hope that it will help devise effective counter-terrorism strategies. Will a clinical psychological understanding of religious terrorism like that articulated here aid in those goals?

In the next chapter I list some of the psycho-religious characteristics of religious groups that turn to violence. Groups with these characteristics are potentially dangerous. But I know from my work in forensic psychology that predicting violent behavior in any specific case is very, very complicated and rarely successful. And dramatic acts of violence that change the course of history—the assassination of the Archduke Ferdinand that was the catalyst for World War I, the taking hostage of the American embassy in the Iranian revolution, the 9/11 attack—are rarely predictable.[1] So no claim is made here that this model will enable us to predict with any certainty when specific individuals or groups may turn to terrorism. That is not my goal.

As for counter-terrorism, it is an important strategic principle that one should know one's enemy. We succeeded in containing the expansiveness of the former Soviet Union in part because we had a detailed and nuanced understanding of the Soviet system (see Lustick, 2007, for a discussion of the success of these anti-Soviet policies in relationship to the war on terror). In the last chapter of this book I argue that understanding some of what is at stake religiously and spiritually for religious groups that engage in terrorism can help devise ways of countering them. So a religious–psychological understanding can be an important part of the response to terrorism. But this book is oriented primarily toward the goal of understanding religion; predicting and countering terrorism are multidisciplinary tasks beyond the scope of this one volume.

The one concept that almost all contemporary scholars of terrorism agree on is that terrorism is multidimensional. Therefore, attempts to comprehend it must be profoundly multidisciplinary. For example, Reich (1998), in the introduction to his collection of essays on the origins of terrorism, emphasizes terrorism's complexity and the need for multiple fields to contribute to our understanding. Relying on only one discipline is to demand too much of a single, limited perspective. All the authors of the essays in that collection would agree with Kellen (1998), who writes, "There are essential differences among types of terrorists. The Palestinian terrorists are different from the Irish, and the West German terrorists are 'more different' yet" (46). Al-Qaeda, Aum Shinrikyo, and the fanatical religious right in America could all be added to that list. The working group on the psychology of terrorism of the Club de Madrid (2005) suggests that

> we should be discussing terrorisms—plural—and terrorist psychologies— plural—rather than searching for a unified theory explaining all terrorist behaviour. . . . There is not a "one size fits all" explanation. . . . To comprehend this complex phenomena fully requires an inter-disciplinary approach, incorporating knowledge from political, historical, cultural, economic, ideological and religious scholarship. (7)

The Club de Madrid organized their discussions of the causes of terrorism into five areas (psychology, politics, economics, religion, and culture), and the report of each working group begins, as the one on psychology did, with an insistence that "terrorism is not a monolithic phenomena but rather quite diverse" (Club de Madrid, 2005: 13). All of these five factors are crucial for understanding terrorism, but this book is devoted to only one—religion.

Mohammed Hafez (2006a, 2006b), in his writings on suicide attacks, suggests that three levels of analysis are necessary to understand terrorist acts and especially suicide bombing: individual motivations, organizational goals and strategies, and cultural catalysts. Organizationally we must understand "the strategic and tactical considerations of militant organizations waging asymmetric warfare"; we must also attend to "the political context most propitious for the emergence of extreme violence"; and individually we must understand "the discursive practices that inspire individuals to engage in self-sacrificial terror" (Hafez, 2006a: 170). According to Hafez, these three domains work synergistically to produce the conditions that result in suicide bombing. Such a perspective argues that organizational strategizing requires a religious reframing of such actions and the creation of a cult of martyrdom through ritual. Without these religious motivations, far fewer people could be recruited as human bombs; without organizational planning, inspired individuals could not carry out these acts.

> In the case of Palestinians, suicide bombings would not have been possible if reason and faith were not sewn together into a logic of liberation and personal redemption. Rationality alone would not have inspired people to make the ultimate leap toward a "heroic" end; and religion alone would not have inspired organizations to plan, prepare, and perpetrate suicide attacks. Suicide bombings were choices inspired by reason and faith. (Hafez, 2006a: 181)

By inspiring and motivating individuals, religion plays its most significant role in suicide terrorism, according to Hafez.

> The last will and testaments of suicide bombers . . . frame self-sacrifice as an opportunity for redemption and a test of one's identity, courage, and faith. Suicide bombers insist that "martyrdom operations" are necessary to fulfill one's commitment to God and the Prophet Muhammad who urged Muslims to fight persecution and not fear death. Suicide bombings are portrayed not as a strategic tool or innovative tactic that is better than all the other strategies and tactics. . . . Instead, their comments are almost exclusively focused on the religious imperative to engage in jihad and the need to embrace martyrdom to achieve liberation, end injustice, seek vengeance, or fulfill one's duty to country and God. (Hafez, 2006a: 175)

For example, one bomber wrote that "love for jihad and martyrdom has come to possess my life, my being, my feelings, my heart, and my senses. My heart ached when I heard the Qur'anic verses, and my soul was torn when I realized my shortcomings and the shortcomings of Muslims in fulfilling our duty toward fighting in the path of God almighty" (Hafez, 2006a: 175).

Religion, then, is one part of the complex mix that is contemporary terrorism; a mix that "cannot be reduced to individual motivations, organizational strategies, or societal contexts" (Hafez, 2006b: 8). This book treats only one aspect of this complex mix—the psychology of the individual's religious motivations. This is, however, clearly an important aspect, for the deeper causes of terrorism "mainly concern worldviews held by the terrorists, such as the bipolar view of good versus evil, the notion of us against them, seeking the pleasure of God, and salvation from hell in the afterlife" (Bin Hassan, 2006: 532). In this book, for heuristic purposes I isolate the religious factor, but it clearly cannot be separated completely from many other factors. So one agreed-upon aspect of contemporary terrorism is that it is multidimensional—Horgan calls terrorism "an extremely heterogeneous phenomenon, ever changing, and as a *tactic* open to newer types of movements (Horgan, 2006: 31, emphasis in original)—with religious motivation being one factor among many.

WHAT DO WE KNOW ABOUT THE PSYCHOLOGY OF TERRORISM? A BRIEF INTRODUCTION

The most shocking conclusion of many of the studies of genocide and terrorism is that most extraordinary acts of inhumanity are committed by very ordinary people. As much as we may want to resist it, Hannah's Arendt's famous phrase "the banality of evil," coined in reference to the Nazi leader Adolf Eichmann, appears to apply to most perpetrators of genocide and terror. They are ordinary people, just like you and me. Or, conversely, all of us have the potential to be agents of extraordinary evil. Theologians have said this for centuries. Now many social psychologists are coming to the same conclusion.

No serious contemporary study has found any evidence for diagnosable psychopathology in those who commit acts of terror and genocide (see, e.g., the review in Horgan, 2006). This has been found true of the vast majority of those who participated in carrying out the genocidal policies of the Third Reich; for the most part they had no overt psychopathology and were simply ordinary citizens functioning in an extraordinarily evil system. After reviewing all the literature on the perpetrators of genocide, the social psychologist James Waller (2002) concluded that all the evidence supports "the reality of the propensity of ordinary people to commit extraordinary evil" (121). He could find no evidence that the actual perpetrators of genocide, taken as a whole, displayed any particular psychopathology or character disorder (for a similar conclusion, see also Atran, 2003a; Horgan, 2006; Post, 1984; Reich, 1998; Victoroff, 2005). Pape (2005), in his extensive review of suicide terrorists, reported that "what stands out is that, to a striking degree, the most deadly suicide terrorists have been almost ordinary people" (220). McDermott (2005), in his meticulously researched study of the 9/11 hijackers, concluded that his inquiry "yields a truly troubling answer: the men of September 11 were, regrettably, I think, fairly ordinary men" (xvi).

The two most widely cited social-psychological experiments in the literature of genocide—Milgram's obedience to authority and Zimbardo's prison experiments—support this conclusion. In the early 1960s, Stanley Milgram recruited a cohort of 40 ordinary men from New Haven, Connecticut, some professionals with advanced degrees, others laborers or middle managers. He brought them into a university laboratory and told them to inflict increasing electric shocks on a subject in response to the subject making mistakes on a word association test as part of a conditioning experiment. The subject was, in fact, part of the experiment and did not receive any actual shocks. In response to the white-coated experimenter's requests, the majority of the recruited participants inflicted increasingly severe shocks on the subject as a punishment for his wrong answers to questions. Even when the subject portrayed signs of severe distress or cried out, 65% of the participants were willing to inflict what they were told was a near-fatal shock to the subject in obedience to the experimenter's commands. Significantly less than half the participants were willing to defy the experimenter at all. Over the years, Milgram's findings have been replicated time and time again in a variety of different settings and countries. In every variation of the experiment, at least some participants were fully compliant with the experimenter's orders (Bass, 1999; Milgram, 1974).

However, there was always a cohort (sometimes larger or smaller) who consistently refused to go along with the experimenter's commands. The research suggests that proximity is an important variable here. The closer the participants were to the victim physically (seeing him, hearing his screams, etc.), the more likely they were to protest and even to disobey. So the capacity to empathize with victims or potential victims may be an important factor in countering blind obedience (Eisenberg, Valiente & Champion, 2004). In the proceeding chapters we will see that religion is a very ambivalent force here. On one hand, throughout history, religions have encouraged empathy and compassion toward the outsider and the other. On the other hand, we will find many examples of religions that discourage and undermine any such empathy. These are the religions that often give rise to terrorism.

While often cited as an analogue for genocide and terrorism, Milgram's obedience experiments get at only one aspect of the larger phenomenon. There is more to acts of genocide and terrorism than obedience (Miller, 2004). In the coming pages I describe many other factors such as the demonizing of the opponent, the fascination with violence, and the sacralizing of one's cause that play crucial roles in religiously motivated terrorism, factors that were not addressed in Milgram's experiments.

There is another aspect of Milgram's experiment that I find extremely important but that I have never seen commented on because it is so taken for granted that it is invisible. The experiment is conducted in a scientific context. The first setting was a laboratory filled with scientific equipment in a building associated with Yale University; the experimenter wore a white lab coat; and the process was overtly described as part of a scientific experiment. Would the experiment have gone the same way if, for example, the building was attached to a mosque or a church and not a university; if the leader wore the robes of a Muslim ayatollah or a Catholic cardinal; if the process was described as developing a new way to convert heretics? My guess is that far fewer would have gone along with the requests.

In our culture, things done in the name of science are rarely questioned, whereas things done in the name of religion or art, for example, often are. Why? In part because we idealize science, we feel our lives are dependent on scientific progress, and that science is a source of security and truth. While referred to as a test of obedience to authority, most commentators discuss the aspect of obedience and overlook the dimension of authority. Yet Milgram's experiment reveals an aspect of obedience that is crucial to understanding terrorism—it is almost always carried out in relation to an idealized object. In Milgram's case that idealized object was science. In the case of religiously motivated terrorism, that idealized object can be a divine being, a sacred text or set of beliefs, a holy institution, or a revered teacher or leader. Again, the proceeding chapters contain many such examples.

In 1971 at Stanford University, Philip Zimbardo recruited a cohort of typical male college undergraduates and randomly assigned one group to play the role of prisoners and the other to play the role of prison guards. He set them up in a mock prison setting. Anyone with noticeable psychological problems was screened out; only those most mature and stable participated. Given the random assignments, both groups were basically similar. Within days, a third of those assigned to be guards became increasingly cruel, sadistic, and tyrannical toward the prisoners, whom they knew were really just fellow undergraduates like themselves. Only two of the guards engaged in any humane treatment of the mock prisoners. This experiment thus demonstrated how easy it is to elicit cruel and sadistic behavior, even from those not otherwise inclined or socialized in that direction, and suggested that the potential for cruelty is there in all of us. In the mock prison, the brutality escalated so rapidly that the 2-week experiment was stopped completely after 6 days (Zimbardo, Maslach & Haney, 1999).

Neither experiment is exactly analogous to terrorism. As a matter of fact, there are some significant differences between these experimental conditions and religiously motivated terrorism. For example, religious terrorism is often characterized by a theologically informed campaign of demonizing the potential victims, and there are almost always economic, political, or cultural conflicts associated with religiously sponsored killing. Neither of these factors played any role in Milgram's or Zimbardo's experimental conditions. However, both experiments strongly suggest that ordinary people, with no particular history of violence, can be relatively easily recruited into roles in which they are willing and able to inflict severe pain on their fellow human beings. What, then, are the psychological processes that transform ordinary citizens into agents of genocide and terrorism?

Waller (2002) offers what he sees as a comprehensive model of the social-psychological factors that permit ordinary people to become perpetrators of extraordinary evil. His model suggests four such factors. The first two are "dispositional factors"—they refer to characteristics of the perpetrators themselves. The first factor Waller calls "our ancestral shadow." Here he draws on the theories of evolutionary psychology to argue that all of us have certain genetic predispositions shaped by natural selection. To the evolutionary psychologist, human nature is not a blank slate. Rather, among our inherited traits as *Homo sapiens* are tendencies toward ethnocentrism, xenophobia, and the drive for social dominance. Under the right circumstances, these traits can make us susceptible to committing vicious deeds. As we shall see, religious leaders and institutions are particularly adept at playing on and manipulating these inherited inclinations toward ethnocentrism and us-versus-them thinking. This is clearly one of the ways that religion can contribute to terrorism and genocide.

Waller's second dispositional factor involves the ways in which these inherited traits are shaped by culture to make us even more potentially available for heinous actions. Among the significant cultural belief systems are religious beliefs about the role of authority, which may generate an external locus of control, as well as about the dichotomy between the in-group and out-group and the demonizing of those considered outside the true fold. Religious beliefs often serve as justifications for killing. In addition, there are other, secular authoritarian cultural teachings, traditions, and institutions (especially the family and state) that shape our behavior. By reinforcing ethnocentrism and scapegoating outsiders, these cultural and ideological forces, religious and secular, can facilitate a moral disengagement through which we cease to see a horrific deed as immoral and may redefine and relabel otherwise abhorrent actions (such as killing innocent noncombatants) into something justified and even meritorious. McDermott (2005) writes that 9/11 "is a story about the power of belief to remake ordinary men; it is the story about the dangerous power of ideas wrongly wielded" (xvi).

According to Waller's model, these two individual factors interact with two contextual or situational factors to transform the ordinary, upstanding citizen into an agent of murder and terror. The third factor in his model, a situational factor, is "a culture of cruelty." This involves the individual, already predisposed in this way by his genetic inheritance and his religious and cultural training, to be directly trained as a killer or terrorist. Through escalating commitments (in which an individual is gradually introduced and desensitized to more heinous acts) and a ritual initiation, the individual's conscience is gradually numbed or repressed when inside a culture of violence. Initiation into such violent groups allows for a diffusion of responsibility, creates an ethos of deindividuation in which individuals can act with anonymity, and makes them subject to an almost irresistible peer pressure. The result is what Waller calls the "merger of role and person," which is aptly illustrated by Zimbardo's prison experiment. Thus a culture of cruelty comes to overwhelm and sublate the individual and his conscience. Many religious groups, we will see shortly, have become potential or actual cultures of cruelty in this sense.

This is where most of the current psychological discussion is located. Most recently published psychologically oriented articles focus primarily on the group processes and induction procedures by which individuals are recruited to perform terrorist actions (Atran, 2003; Moghaddam, 2005; Moghaddam & Marsella, 2004; Post, Sprinzak & Denny, 2003). The stated assumption of this literature is that group dynamics alone can transform a normal individual into a terrorist (Zimbardo, 2004). Milgram's and Zimbardo's classic experiments and the commonly asserted finding that there does not seem to be any common personality or psychopathological traits exhibited by terrorists appear to point in this direction.

However, not every member of a society from which terrorism arises joins a terrorist group, and not every member of a terrorist cell actually engages in a terrorist operation, nor did every subject in Milgram's experiments comply with the experimenter's demands. Merari (1998) writes in this regard concerning one form of terrorism "the simple fact that most terrorists—Shi'ite, Japanese, Irish, or German, regardless of the conditions under which they have lived and fought—have neither committed suicide nor tried to do so attests to the importance of personality characteristics in the phenomenon of suicide terrorism" (202). So it seems most prudent to conclude with Victoroff (2005), who writes after an extensive review of the literature that "terrorist behavior is probably *always* determined by a combination of . . . factors . . . the much-cited claim that no individual factors identify those at risk for becoming terrorists is based on completely inadequate research" (34, emphasis in original).[2] I return to this point in chapter 5.

Also, these social influence and social process models apply best to tight-knit terrorist groups where there is a structured process of recruitment, initiation, training, and eventual deployment (this is the kind of process described by Horgan and in most of the essays in Reich's collection and that of Moghaddam and Marsalla). Here the type of group dynamics that Bandura, Milgram, Zimbardo, Horgan, and others emphasize are certainly strong factors. But we will discover throughout this study that contemporary terrorism is more likely the result of rapidly evolving leaderless groups or self-starters in which there is little overt recruitment and much of the training is done over the Internet or in small cliques. In such loose confederations of like-minded people, classical models of social influence may lose some of their explanatory power.

Waller's fourth factor concerns what is done to the victim. As a prelude to genocide and terrorist acts, the intended victims or targets undergo what Waller calls a "social death." In the context of dichotomized, us-versus-them thinking, potential victims are dehumanized—labeled as beyond the pale of human compassion and empathy. Potential victims are often blamed for their victimization. One way or another they are said to deserve what they get. Throughout this book we will see many powerfully effective ways that religion can dehumanize and delegitimize opponents. Religion may be, in fact, one of humanity's most powerful means to the social death of the other.

Along this line, Albert Bandura (1998, 2004) has written at length about the role of what he calls "moral disengagement" by which individuals become desensitized to the heinousness of their actions. Again, the point is that the vast majority of people who commit terrorism or genocide are normal people who are not psychopathological. Normal people have inhibitions against killing other human beings. These inhibitions have to be overcome or disengaged in order for normal people to become terrorists and killers. According to Bandura (1998), some of the mechanisms by which a human being's tendencies toward empathy and compassion are disengaged are the "redefinition of harmful conduct as morally justified," "sanitizing language," "diffusion of responsibility within a group," "minimizing the harm done," and "dehumanizing the victims and blaming them for the harm done to them." Bandura emphasizes that people need a moral justification before they will engage in reprehensible actions. He argues that "the conversion of socialized people into dedicated fighters is achieved not by altering their personality structures, aggressive drives, or moral standards. Rather it is accomplished by cognitively redefining the morality of killing" (Bandura, 2004: 124). Bandura (2004) points out that religion has a long and bloody history as one of the major vehicles for providing that moral justification of mass bloodshed. Hafez notices precisely this role of religion in his studies of Palestinian human bombs. His words apply to all religiously motivated terrorists:

> Discursive practices that transform accepted religious ethics and symbols into vehicles for mobilizing violent militants are necessary for individual moral disengagement. Self-regulatory mechanisms that inhibit people from killing and maiming others must be overcome before one can engage in extreme violence. Moral disengagement is the process by which these cognitive codes are deactivated by transforming immoral conduct into ethical imperatives. Religious reframing can enable moral disengagement by imbuing acts of extreme violence with meaning, purpose, and morality. It transforms cruel terror into sacred missions in the minds of terrorists. (Hafez, 2006a: 169)

Redefining the morality of killing is only one of the links in the chain of radicalization by which ordinary people turn into terrorists. Another is the adoption of a euphemistic language that hides the horror of certain deeds, such as calling the killing of innocent civilians "collateral damage" or referring to soldiers tragically killed by mistake as victims of "friendly fire." In addition, group activities provide a diffusion of agency so that no one has to feel the burden of responsibility for a terrible act. Dehumanization of the victim is, as Waller and others pointed out, another crucial mechanism by which terrorism and genocide become normalized.

Bandura (2004) emphasizes that these psychological processes happen gradually. Individuals and groups may not set out to become violent but may gradually evolve in that direction—something that happened with Aum Shinrykio and that Sprinzak (1998a) describes happening to the "Weathermen" in the 1960s. The process may also be part of trajectory by which alienated Muslim youth in Europe become jihadists. The processes Bandura enumerates usually take place through extensive training in an authoritarian milieu. This is the traditional way a group becomes violent. But more current examples such as the formation of radical jihadist cliques in Europe suggest that this process may also occur more spontaneously, without the heavy hand of a group leader or trainer, but rather through reading religious literature on one's own, listening to sermons on tape or over the Internet, and discussions with friends (see, e.g., Khosrokhavar, 2005; Kirby, 2007; Sageman, 2004). No contact with a leader or trainer is necessary. In any case, Bandura describes the cognitive-psychological dimensions of the conversion experience by which formerly quiet and peaceful people become terrorists. As discussed in the proceeding chapters, religion can be a powerful site of this conversion, engaging all of these mechanisms of cognitive transformation.

TERRORISM: RELIGION AND/OR POLITICS?

The preceding discussion raises the larger and hotly contested question of the relation between religion and politics in international religious terrorism. This question has been raised explicitly by Robert Pape (2005) in his carefully researched book about suicide terrorism, *Dying to Win*. A careful analysis of his argument helps illuminate some of the various relationships between religious and political concerns in international terrorism. Pape's basic thesis is that "At bottom, suicide terrorism is a strategy for national liberation from foreign military occupation by a democratic state" (Pape, 2005: 45). Thus he accentuates the role of political factors—national liberation movements—in the genesis of suicide terrorism. Pape's focus is slightly different from mine. He is writing only about suicide terrorism, whereas here I am focusing on the role of religion in fomenting terrorism, suicidal and otherwise. Pape does not deny the role of religion. Quite the reverse. He claims "Religion plays a role in suicide terrorism" but he goes on to say that role is "mainly in the context of national resistance" (166).

When using Pape's data to draw conclusions about motivation, it is important to recognize that he is using a critical incident database, which encodes incidents of suicide bombing in statistical terms describing its effects, the number of people involved, and so on. This gives us a tremendously broad range of data that is not very deep. There is no ideographic material; no interviews are included in such databases. Such data tell us nothing about motivation or the individual's reasons for their action.[3] Motivational factors can be interfered, of course, but they are inferences based on the context, confederates' pronouncements, and so on. Hafez, who has dealt directly with human bombers in Palestine, comes to a very different conclusion about their primary motivation:

> For individuals, religious appeals that equate self-sacrifice with martyrdom are instrumental in motivating suicide attacks. Suicidal violence is not framed as an optimal strategy based on the constraints of the political environment or rational calculation of costs and benefits, but rather as an act of redemption and religious obligation in the context of persecution and injustice. The religious framings of Hamas and Islamic Jihad . . . [combine] symbolic narratives with ritual and ceremony to foster a culture of martyrdom that legitimate and venerate self-sacrifice. This culture of martyrdom is the principal means through which it generates high rates of volunteerism for suicide missions. (Hafez, 2006: 180)

Pape's studies also clearly show the impact of religion on suicide terrorism. Religion runs through the history of suicide terrorism. Historically, religion is implicated in the beginnings of suicide terrorism. The earliest suicide campaigns were all religiously motivated—Jewish zealots, Muslim assassins, Japanese kamikazes (Pape, 2005: 11). And in the present day, Pape's detailed statistical analysis appears to show that religion is a necessary (but not sufficient) ingredient for a campaign of suicide terrorism. He writes, "The nationalist theory of suicide terrorism predicts that suicide terrorism would occur in tandem with only one of the combinations of independent variables—that is, when there is *both* a religious difference and a [nationalistic] rebellion" (99, emphasis added). Thus Pape "develops a theory of the causes of suicide terrorism, contending that nationalistic rebellion and religious difference . . . are the main conditions under which the foreign occupation of a community's homeland is likely to lead to a campaign of suicide terrorism" (101). He claims that this combination of factors predicts virtually all contemporary campaigns of suicide terrorism. Indeed, "religion matters, but mainly in the context of national resistance" (116). My task in this book is to discuss in some detail exactly how religion matters and from whence it derives its power to matter so much. This is not necessarily a disagreement with Pape but rather a difference of focus.

Again, my concern here is with religiously motivated terrorism in all its forms, not just with suicide bombers. Clearly Pape's analysis would shed little light on Aum Shinrikyo or American apocalyptic Christianity and its turn toward violence. Both Asahara and the Christian militants felt their societies were in decline. In that sense contemporary Japan and the United States were felt to be occupied by demonic, foreign forces of secularism and materialism. But the enemies are their fellow-citizens and, in many cases, co-religionists, not invading armies from other countries.

Some further points must also be made about Pape's basic thesis. For example, regarding al-Qaeda, he writes, "Overall, the analysis of al-Qaeda's suicide terrorists shows that its most lethal forces are best understood as a coalition of nationalist groups seeking to achieve local change in their home countries, not as a truly transnational movement seeking to spread Islam or any other ideology to non-Islamic populations" (Pape, 2005: 116). Having downplayed the role of religion in al-Qaeda, he then says almost immediately,

> The politics of religious difference is central to al-Qaeda's campaign of suicide terrorism against the United States. Throughout virtually all the statements, interviews, sermons and books by Osama bin Laden and other al-Qaeda leaders over the past decade, the United States is portrayed as a religiously motivated "Crusader" on an aggressive mission to subdue, occupy, and transform Muslim societies. (Pape, 2005: 119)

Pape ends by quoting bin Laden's "declaration" where he writes that Muslim youths "have no intention, except to enter paradise by killing you . . . They stand tall to defend the religion" (Pape, 2005: 124). This makes religion sound quite central to al-Qaeda's mission of terror. Repeatedly, bin Laden in his statements and his *fatwa* attacks the presence of the United States in Saudi Arabia, but this is not because of U.S. occupation per se but primarily because of the perceived religious threat to the holy sites and to Islam (54). Pape acknowledges this when he writes, "Although he also believes that the United States is interested in oil, bin Laden most strikingly characterizes the United States as the leader of a Christian-Jewish alliance that is mainly motivated by religious aims" (119; see also 120ff. for more on the centrality of religious motivations to al-Qaeda).

Moghadam (2006) makes the same point when he writes regarding the statements of the Al Qaeda leaders that "their remarks point instead at the centrality religion plays in al Qaeda's ideology and mission" (722). Hoffman (2006) concurs, writing that for al Qaeda "the religious motive is overriding; and indeed, the religious imperative for terrorism is the most important defining characteristic of terrorist activity today" (82; see also Khosrokhavar, 2005).

Pape (2005) takes pains to explain that suicide terrorism is not simply the result of Islamic extremism (a point I certainly agree with): "the effects of religion that matter do not lie mainly in Islam or any other single religion or culture" (166). He goes on to describe the influence of religion in ways that parallel much of what we have already seen. For Pape, religion serves to (1) reduce the room for compromise (territorial rights can be negotiated and compromised, but religious differences cannot be); (2) enable demonization through differences (90); and (3) legitimize martyrdom (89–92). But his main argument is that a religious difference between occupying forces and those occupied is crucial for suicide terrorism. "We cannot measure quantitatively how much these [religious] mechanisms increase the likelihood of suicide terrorism. What we can say is that the presence of a religious difference tends to promote suicide terrorism in ways that a language difference would not" (92). Pape seems to think of religion as primarily a marker—perhaps the most powerful marker—of cultural difference (in this case between occupying forces and their victims), analogous to language or other cultural customs that can mark difference.

In some places, Pape seems to suggest that religion is primarily a tool in the hands of actors who are basically politically motivated: "the history of disputes that have escalated to suicide terrorism involves primarily the clash of two religions. . . . Religious difference routinely enabled terrorist leaders to gain significant public support for suicide terrorism by painting the conflict in stark zero-sum terms, demonizing the opponent, and gaining legitimacy for martyrdom" (Pape, 2005: 126). To a student of religion, these claims—that religion is primarily a marker of cultural difference and a rhetorical device used by political leaders—seem like a rather superficial understanding of the role of religion in human life and, as I am arguing here, in religiously motivated terrorism.

Pape seems to go back and forth over the importance of religion. He writes that "Under the circumstances of foreign occupation . . . religious difference can inflame nationalist sentiments in ways that encourage mass support for martyrdom and suicide terrorism" (Pape, 2005: 88). This seems to imply that nationalism is the independent variable and religion just serves it. But many of Pape's examples, as well as many throughout this book, suggest that religion may provide its own, independent motivations, separate from purely political ones.

Take for example, Sri Lanka, which is often cited as an example of a purely secular suicide terrorist campaign; the Tamil Tigers are often described in western accounts as a Marxist-Lennist group. Pape rightly emphasizes that the genesis of this conflict lies in a religious division within Sri Lanka and the fear on the part of the Tamil minority that the Sinhalese majority will impose its Buddhist religion on them. He writes that the conflict has escalated to the point of suicide attacks because "The Tamil community has come increasingly to believe that the Sinhalese government is deliberately pursuing policies that seek to stamp out core attributes of Tamil national identity, and that Buddhist religious forces are the driving force behind this program" (Pape, 2005: 140). This reached its climax and spurred the suicide attacks when, in 1972, the Sinhalese government adopted a new constitution that accorded Buddhism "the foremost place" and directed the state "to protect and foster it" (141). Although the Tamil Tigers are clearly concerned with preserving Tamil culture, their Hindu religion is a central part of that culture and so "the most prominent factor driving Tamil community support for individual self-sacrifice is fear of Buddhist extremism" (145).

Regarding Tamil Tiger martyrs, their "heroic death founded with the fire of Tamil nationalism has given birth to a new set of terms, almost all derived from the ancient Tamil religion of Saivism; indeed within the North and East, Tamil nationalism has the appearance of a new religious movement . . . People bedeck these 'shrines of Martyrs' with offerings of flowers and oil as they normally do their temples or holy shrines" (quoted in Pape, 2005: 149). Another has written, "The LTTE [that is, the Tamil Tigers] selectively revives religious concepts relating to a martyr cult . . . the LTTE sacralizes its aim . . . by declaring it to be a holy aim" (quoted in Pape, 2005: 150). The LTTE word for martyrdom "is rooted in the Hindu religion and means the voluntary abandonment of life in the very act of taking life, in the act of killing . . . a rather specific Indian form of martyrdom [with] roots in the last section of the Bhagavadgita" (Pape,

2005: 150). Michael Roberts (2005), in a detailed study of the Tamil Tigers, calls attention to the detailed ritualizing and symbolizing (which are deeply rooted in Tamil Hinduism) that is a part of the Tigers' world and calls the claim of their secular character a "popular misunderstanding." His research shows instead how their practices "are deeply rooted in the lifestyles and religious practices of Tamils in India and Lanka" (Roberts, 2005: 493).

So several of Pape's examples of national resistance in fact seem more centered on religion: al-Qaeda's concern with the desecration of Muslim holy places, the Tamil's fear of a militant Buddhist hegemony in Sri Lanka, and Sikhism, which is a religion whose campaign of suicide terrorism began when one of its main temples was attacked by Hindu troops (Pape, 2005: 161). Suicide terror campaigns may frequently be resisting foreign encroachments, but these encroachments are often resisted because they are seen as threats to religion.

In addition, of the three suicide terrorists whom Pape discusses in depth, two are clearly motivated by religion: Atta "who became a committed fundamentalist" (Pape, 2005: 225) and who trained in Afghanistan in al-Qaeda camps where "recruits were not admitted to the camps unless they were already devout" (223), and a member of Hamas whose training involved between 2 and 4 hours per day studying the Koran, meditating in a cemetery, and who is described as "devout" (232). Regarding the third suicide terrorist, the Tamil Tiger young woman who killed Rajiv Ghandi, Pape does not discuss her religious convictions or lack of them, but the LTTE clearly has its roots in religion (Roberts, 2005).

In most, if not all, of the instances Pape mentions, national identity and religion are so intertwined that separating them is virtually impossible. Pape sometimes appears to stretch to make his point. For example, he writes, "Al-Qaeda appeals to national identities on three levels—Arabian, pan-Arab, pan-Muslim" (Pape, 2005: 95). It is not clear in what sense pan-Muslim is a national identity because there are Muslims of almost every national and ethnic heritage. Pan-Muslim is clearly a religious rather than a national-territorial designation. Going back and forth again over the role of religion, Pape acknowledges this when he writes "the association between foreign occupation and suicide terrorism does not mean that religion plays no role. . . . Since national and religious identities often overlap, distinguishing the main motive for particular suicide terrorist campaigns may seem excessively difficult" (46–47). He argues that national resistance takes precedence over religion as a cause because terrorist groups target those who occupy their nations rather than simply opposing religionists. Also his survey suggests that individual suicide attackers are about evenly divided between the religious and the secular: "Of the 384 attackers for whom we have data, 166, or 43 percent were religious, while 218, or 57 percent were secular . . . Suicide terrorism is not an overwhelmingly religious phenomenon" (210). I suspect that many of those counted as secular were members of the Tamil Tigers, which may be ideologically secular but whose movement, we have seen, was rooted in a religious conflict and characterized by religious ritual and devotional practices (Roberts, 2005; see also Moghadam, 2006, who refigures Pape's data and comes to the opposite conclusion).

My point is not that religion is the primary or only motivation for suicide or other terrorist campaigns. Rather, I want to insist that terrorism, even religiously motivated terrorism, is a multidetermined, multifactorial phenomenon. My disagreement with Pape is not that he insists on the importance of national resistance to occupation in suicide terrorism. Clearly, national resistance can play a major role. For me, one of the things that mars Pape's account is his tendency to insist on a single motivation: "In fact, every suicide campaign from 1980 to 2003 has had as a major objective—or as its central objective—coercing a foreign government that has military forces in what they see as their homeland to take those forces out" (Pape, 2005: 42). This insistence on only one factor—the strategic one— weakens his argument. As Hafez (2006a) writes on precisely this point,

> In the case of Palestine suicide bombers, a careful reading of their statements suggests multiple motivations that are invariably infused with religious and normative inspirations, not strategic or tactical considerations. . . . If the strategic logic of suicide bombings is abundantly obvious, why do militant organizations exert a great deal of time, effort, and resources to honor and venerate the "heroic" deeds of their martyrs? (168)

Pape's charts and statistics illustrate that religion also functions as an independent variable in suicide terrorism. On that we agree. Religion is not the only cause of suicide terrorism, but it is one cause. My task here is to elaborate how religion functions to promote terrorism in all its forms, not just suicide attacks. In addition, Pape points to the connection between religion and nationalism in religiously motivated terrorism. But religion not only joins with nationalism, in many cases it also transforms nationalism by sanctifying the national cause and idealizing and divinizing the nation or the race. This sacralizing of the nation, and not just simple nationalism, is a feature of Aum Shinrikyo, American apocalyptic Christianity, and bin Laden's pronouncements, among others.

Pape's focus is entirely on suicide terrorism in the service of national liberation. As virtually all current investigators of international terrorism (e.g., Atran 2005b; Hoffman, 2006; Khosrokhavar, 2005; Moghadam, 2006; Sageman, 2004) point out, religiously motivated terrorism has undergone a major metamorphosis in the last decade: a metamorphosis away from local conflicts to global ones and from close-knit, hierarchical cells to loosely organized, autonomous cohorts.

> Terrorist actions are now chiefly executed by self-forming cells of friends that swarm for attack, then disappear or disperse to form new swarms. Independent studies . . . show that more than 80 percent of known jihadis currently live in diaspora communities, which are often marginalized from the host society and physically disconnected from each other . . . most jihadis follow kin and colleagues more than they do orders from afar. These difficult-to-penetrate social networks consist of about 70 percent friends and 20 percent family. (Atran, 2006b: 135)

Terrorism, like so many other aspects of life, has been globalized. Local conflicts and resistance fighters can be made to fit Pape's model; but they are no longer the primary face of contemporary terrorism. The Internet changed all that. As I argue in the coming chapters, it is impossible to exaggerate the role of the Internet on contemporary terrorism, something virtually every current author acknowledges (e.g., Atran, 2005b, 2006b; Atran & Stern, 2005; Hoffman, 2006; Kirby, 2007; Moghadam, 2006; Weimann, 2006). For example, the U.S. invasion of Afghanistan destroyed (at least temporarily) al-Qaeda's training camps and base of operations. That put an end to al-Qaeda as a top-down, tightly managed organization. That might have meant the end of al-Qaeda, except that at exactly the same time, the World Wide Web was going worldwide. Now loose local confederations of radicalized Muslims throughout the world could maintain contact, exchange information, trade inflammatory images, raise funds, network, and carry out all the other activities central to terrorist planning through chat rooms, e-mails, text messages, and websites (see, e.g., Hoffman, 2006, Kirby, 2007; Weimann, 2006). The International Institute of Strategic Studies in London notes that "the counter-terrorism effort has perversely impelled an already highly decentralized and evasive transnational terrorist network to become more 'virtual' and protean and, therefore, harder to identify and neutralize" (quoted in Atran, 2003b: 1). No command and control from bin Laden and company is necessary (Atran 2006b, 2005b). Thus jidhadism and radical apocalyptic Christianity (to take just two examples) morphed into a "leaderless resistance" or a movement of autonomous "self-starters."

TERRORISM: RELIGION AS POLITICS

This mingling of religion and politics in religiously motivated terrorism, which Pape's (2005) book illustrates, underscores another important dimension of this issue with which policymakers in the West have hardly begun to come to terms. Such political religiosity, violent or simply politically militant, reveals that large numbers of people around the world (and within American society) are convinced that God has given them *the* single master plan for how societies should be organized and governed. Since these blueprints come from God, it is the true believers' sacred duty to follow them to the letter and even to impose them on the societies in which they live. And since they are a divine mandate, these master plans cannot be compromised. Liberal democracies, based on the value of individual rights and government by negotiation and compromise, have not yet begun to find a way to address these citizens and their convictions.

This is another potential contribution of religion to terrorist actions: the idea that certain devotees possess a divine mandate for their societies and for the whole world. This comes through clearly in many of bin Laden's statements. Take, for example, bin Laden's 2001 message to the Muslim youth: "The time has come when all the Muslims of the world, especially the youth, should unite and soar against the kufr [nonbeliever] and continue jihad till those forces are crushed to naught, all the anti-Islamic forces are wiped off the face of the earth and Islam takes over the whole world and all other false religions" (quoted in Hoffman, 2006: 96; see also McDermott, 2005). Bin Ladin's statements and those of other jihadists make clear that their goal is not simply defeating the West militarily or driving the "crusaders" from the Muslim holy lands. Their goal is nothing less than replacing secular governments with those that follow strict Muslim law throughout the Middle East and maybe even throughout the globe (Juergensmeyer, 2000; Lawrence, 1989; Stern, 2003).

A mujihadeen in Pakistan described the goal of jihad by saying "Our mission is to invite all of humanity to Islam, to persuade the whole world to worship only Allah. . . . Islam is not just a religion. It regulates every aspect of life, including politics. We would like to see implementation of divine laws here" (quoted in Stern, 2003: 115). Another Muslim theorist has written that the problem in Muslim countries is

> Those government officials (who claim to be Muslims but are not). . . . We are required to focus on our Islamic duties, first to apply the Law of God (the *shari'a*) and the Word of God. And there can be no doubt that the first battleground of *jihad* is the removing of those shackles of unbelief that constrain us and substituting for them an Islamic order. (quoted in Lawrence, 1989: 189)

Thus Lawrence (1989) concludes

> Judaism and Islam . . . both have long asserted, and continue to assert, the priority of communitarian goals over individual rights. Among both Sunni and Shi'i Muslims, the battle is waged in the political arena. Fundamentalists require an Islamic state since the collective good of Muslims can only be realized through conformity to the *shari'a*, and only an Islamic state can fulfill the demands of a religious society by upholding the high standards of shari'a loyalty. (121)

In the same way, the ultra-orthodox parties in Israel seek to remove the current secular government and establish in its place a government that implements strict orthodox law (Juergensmeyer, 2000; Lawrence, 1989).

The same goal of replacing secular governments with strictly religious ones is also articulated by the Christian Reconstructionist movement in the United States. The goal of Reconstructionism is turning the United States into a theocratic state characterized by the imposition of "biblical law" on all U.S. citizens. This would be the end of democracy, labor unions, civil rights laws, and public schools. Women would be confined to the home. Non-Christians would be deprived of citizenship, perhaps executed (Clarkson, 1994: 1).

Reconstructionism arose out of conservative Calvinism and seeks to make the laws of ancient Israel, as found in the books of Moses, or "biblical law" the basis for transforming society into the kingdom of God on earth. The assumption is that the Bible is the ruling law for all areas of life—such as government, education, law, and the arts—an assump-

tion shared by ultra-orthodox Jews in Israel and Muslim jihadists in regard to the Koran. One Reconstructionist theologian insists that "The
Christian goal for the world is the universal development of Biblical
theocratic republics, in which every area of life is redeemed and placed
under the Lordship of Jesus Christ and the rule of God's law" (Clarkson, 1994: 1). Central to the Reconstructionist's ideal political order
is widespread use of capital punishment. In addition to the current
list of capital crimes common in the United States, Reconstructionists
advocate the death penalty for "crimes" such as apostasy and abandoning Christianity, heresy, blasphemy, witchcraft, astrology, adultery, sod-
omy or homosexuality, incest, striking a parent, incorrigible juvenile
delinquency, and, in the case of women, "unchastity before marriage"
(Clarkson, 1994: 2).

Although most Christian Reconstructionists seek to impose their
agenda on America through democratic means and not through violent revolution or terrorist means (although their triumph would mean
the end of those same democratic principles), their teachings are often
taken up by Christian terrorists in the United States. For example, Paul
Hill (the killer of a physician in front of a women's health clinic) said,
"My worldview is based on Reconstruction principles" (quoted in Stern,
2003: 168). Hill writes that "the primary function of government is to
uphold the Moral Law with the sword" (Hill, 2003: 48). Like other
Reconstrictionists, Hill makes it clear that his agenda goes beyond simply ending abortion—he looks forward to nothing less than the transformation of American society. Hill told Jessica Stern that "Sooner or
later America will become a Christian nation. Only Christians will be
elected to public office. No false worship allowed" (Stern, 2003: 169).
So it is no surprise that Hill advocates "A consistent effort to bring civil
law into conformity with the Moral Law" (Hill, 2003: 3). Neal Horsely
(n.d.), another advocate of killing physicians who perform abortions
and creator of the Nuremburg Files, has on his website mainly pages
devoted to calling for the overthrow of the present government and
the establishment of a "Christian commonwealth" based primarily on
imposing the laws found in the books of Moses on Americans.

Again, these themes are common to the writings of many religious
terrorists across many different religious traditions. These terrorists
see their societies as ruled by antireligious leaders who may claim to
be Jewish, Christian, or Muslim but really are not. Religion is defined
in primarily legal terms, as a divine law, the "Moral Law" in Paul Hill's

(2003) writings. A divine mission to impose this law on the whole society and replace secular or hypocritical leaders with devout leaders is proclaimed. This is why religious terrorists reject the separation of church, synagogue, or mosque and the state. Their religion requires of them that all aspects of life—from laws governing capital crimes to women's clothing and children's discipline—be subject to religious control. And the prominent issues in this divine mandate are also similar across traditions: the "proper" roles of men and women, the regulation of sex, ending abortion, and prohibition of homosexuality. These laws are not just for their personal lives but for whole societies, for their God-given mission demands that they bring all of society under theocratic control. This understanding of the divine mandate is shared by Christian Reconstructionists, Muslim jihadists, ultra-orthodox Jews, and groups like Aum Shinrikyo and the Hindu nationalist party as well. Whether such a divine mission can coexist with liberal democracy may be the major religious and political debate of the twenty-first century.

RELIGIOUS TERRORISM?

Combining resources from religious studies and current thinking about terrorism, I would define religious terrorism as the use of violence, often in symbolic but deadly actions, in the service of sacred goals or values. All current scholars insist that terrorism is a complex, multidimensional, multidetermined phenomenon and that a multidisciplinary approach is necessary to understand it. All psychological studies agree that terrorists are not abnormal psychologically or diagnostically psychopathological. Thus attempts to construct a psychological profile of the terrorist personality, useful for predicting who will become a terrorist, have not been very successful. That does not mean that certain psycho-religious themes cannot be found as characteristic of religiously motivated terrorists across religious traditions. Given that most terrorists are psychologically normal, research has clearly shown that group pressures can motivate ordinary individuals to do heinous things. In the past, the focus of psychological study has been on these group processes (recruitment procedures, authority structures, moral disengagement, redefinition of killing as morally justified, etc.) shared by terrorist groups, but current terrorist cohorts appear to be smaller, looser, decentralized cliques of friends or relatives (Atran, 2006b; Sageman,

2004). This may limit (but not eliminate) the relevance of studies of more tightly knit terrorist cells. Religious terrorists from every tradition are often motivated by a political theology that fuses moral, religious, and political goals and seeks the reformation of society. So issues of national liberation, resisting domination, and economic justice are often intertwined with and sacralized by religious and spiritual motivations that cannot be ignored if contemporary terrorism is to be understood.

CHAPTER 2

JIHADISM IN COMPARATIVE PERSPECTIVE

Psychological Themes in Religiously Motivated Terrorism

IN THE LATE FALL OF 1948, A THIN, MUSTACHED, YOUNG Egyptian arrived in New York as the postwar boom was beginning. Sayyid Qutb, middle-level bureaucrat in the Egyptian Ministry of Education, came supplied with a generous stipend from the Egyptian government to study English and education in America (Wright, 2006). He was exceptionally westernized. Photographs show him in western suits and ties; he wrote of his love of European classical music; he watched Hollywood movies; and he was well-versed in the classics of Western literature (Stanley, 2003; Wright, 2006). But he had grown up in a rural village in Egypt and received a traditional Muslim education, and later in life he would write a multivolume commentary on the Koran (Berman, 2003).

Already acquainted with a form of Islamic fundamentalism before he got off the boat, his up-close experience of American culture appears to have further soured Qutb on the West (Berman, 2003; Stanley, 2003). In the 1940s, 8 years before he arrived in America, he was already inveighing against the popular music playing on Egyptian radio and the scantily clothed women in their bathing suits on the beaches of Alexandria (Terman, 2007). Qutb's writings suggest that he grew increasingly shocked by what he found in America (Wright, 2006). As a dark-skinned

man, he immediately encountered American racism. Even more shocking was the American openness about sex. He arrived as the Kinsey
report on the *Sexual Behavior of the Human Male* was hitting the popular
media with its portrayal of a society in which homosexual experiences
were not rare, adultery was common, and prostitution virtually normal.
To Qutb's chagrin, sexual matters were common topics of conversation.
While attending classes in Colorado, he was particularly scandalized by
the risqué behavior of the undergraduates, especially the coeds who
(by his report) openly flaunted their sexuality. And it was not just their
sexual openness that disturbed him; he was even more shaken by the
forwardness and assertiveness of American women, whom, he wrote later,
"[wear] bright colors that awaken primitive sexual instincts, hiding nothing, but adding to that the thrilling laugh and the bold look" (quoted in
Wright, 2006: 15). To Qutb's eyes, in 1948 America was already sinking
into debauchery and decadence; a land of spiritual emptiness where the
dollar was the only real god—"the soul has no value to Americans," he
wrote (quoted in Wright, 2006: 23).

Qutb returned to Egypt after 2 years in America convinced that the
West had nothing to offer the Arab world. The values by which the modern West lived—rationalism, the separation of religion and state, democracy, individual rights, tolerance of difference and personal freedom
(especially for women)—were not signs of progress but rather symptoms
of profound decay and disease. Instead, true progress was only possible
by a return to the past, to the golden age of early Islam, to the austere
and clear faith of the Prophet and the direct regulation of every aspect
of life by the revealed will of God (Khosrokhavar, 2005). Rather than feel
humiliated by the military, scientific, and technical triumphs of the West,
the Arab people should realize they possess the true wisdom in the sacred
Word of God. Western values—especially the separation of religion and
the state and the mixing of the sexes—were bitterly and diametrically opposed to the divine plan. The way of the modern West must be dismantled
and replaced by the purity of the divine law regulating every area of life.

Qutb believed that the immediate problem was not America, bask-
ing in its new-found wealth and power. The immediate problem was
the Arab rulers, especially in Egypt, who had contaminated the purity
of Islam by embracing Western ideas of democracy, secularization, and
political corruption. The Egypt to which Qutb returned was groaning
with poverty, disease, corrupt governance, and lawlessness. The only
group that cared about the average Egyptian was the outlawed Muslim

Brotherhood, which had established an entire counterculture of schools, mosques, hospitals, and charities. Qutb joined the Brotherhood and with his rhetorical gifts became a major polemicist, articulator, and shaper of their vision to deconstruct the fledgling and corrupt secular government of Egypt and instead impose strict Islamic law on all aspects of life (Stanley, 2003; Wright, 2006).

Qutb was imprisoned by Colonel Nassar, the ruler of Egypt, released, and then imprisoned again after an attempt on Nassar's life by the Muslim Brotherhood. He was tortured in prison, briefly released, rearrested for plotting against the government, and given the death sentence. "Thank God," he is reported to have said, "I performed jihad for fifteen years until I earned this martyrdom" (Wright, 2006: 31).

While in prison Qutb (1996) wrote and smuggled out a series of brief polemics that were bound together and published underground with the title *Milestones*. When they became openly available, they were immediately banned in Egypt; anyone caught with them could receive the death penalty. *Milestones* is now the basic text of the jihadist movement and is, in my opinion, the purest exposition of the fundamentalist viewpoint to be found in any religion.

The idea, popular in some American circles after 9/11, that jihadists hate an America they are unfamiliar with (the assumption being if they just knew America better, they would embrace it) is clearly false. Qutb spent 3 years traveling around America and living both in large cities and in a smaller rural community; Ramzi Yousef, who led the first World Trade Center attack, had lived and study in the United States for some years; and Khalid Shaikh Mohammed, the mastermind of the 9/11 attacks, reportedly attended several American universities in the 1980s and received a graduate degree in engineering in the United States. Qutb wrote from firsthand knowledge of modern America. His *Milestones* represents a trenchant, theologically grounded critique of the sterility, materialism, and amorality of the modern secular West. "Mankind today is on the brink of a precipice," Qutb begins, "because humanity is devoid of those vital values which are necessary not only for its healthy development but also for real progress. Even the Western world . . . knows that it does not possess anything which will satisfy its own conscience and justify its existence" (Qutb, 1996: 7).

Qutb thus signals that Islam's war with the West will be about values and about what gives life meaning. It will be a war of ideas first, and a war of military action second. The modern Western idea that most needed to be replaced was the separation of religion and the state—that is, the compartmentalization and limitation of religion to a special, small, private sphere of influence (Berman, 2003). Instead, Islam must "take concrete form in society" in a community whose "manners, ideals and concepts, rules and regulations, values and criteria, are all derived from the Islamic source" (Qutb, 1996: 11). Thus the first principle of the Islamic revolution must be undoing the compartmentalization of religion, its separation from other aspects of culture, and the tolerance for different viewpoints. Instead, all aspects of life must be regulated by "the Islamic source."

But such an Islamic community no longer exists. It existed once in the golden age of the Prophet. But now, it "is buried under the debris of the man-made traditions of several generations" (Qutb, 1996: 11–12). The present age, even the so-called world of Islam, is corrupt. Thus "it is necessary that the Muslim community be restored to its original form" (Qutb, 1996: 11). So the first milestone on the way to an Islamic revolution must be a return to the past, a return of the Islamic religion to its early, pristine form.

What made the first generation so pure? Qutb is clear that it is not so much the presence of the Prophet and his teachings as it is the sacred text: "The holy Qur'an was the only source from which they quenched their thirst and this was the only mold in which they molded their lives, this was the only guidance for them" (Qutb, 1996, 24). Later generations brought Greek philosophy, Persian ideas, and scholastic theologies into Islam. This mingling of the purity of the sacred text with human ideas is the main reason for the decline in Islam. The first generation was well acquainted with Roman and Greek science, philosophy, and civilization. But instead of following these human institutions, they decided to "place sole reliance on the Book of Allah" (24). The true Muslim is one who does likewise and rejects all human learning and is guided solely by the sacred text, from which "we must also derive our concepts of life, our principles of government, politics, economics, and all other aspects of life" (33). All government, science, economics, politics, thought, and behavior in every aspect of life must be made to totally conform to "the way of life demanded of us by the Qur'an" (33). The first principle of Islam is "that every aspect of life should be under the sovereignty of God "(61). Therefore "one should accept the Shari'ah [Muslim law] without any question and reject all other laws in any shape or form. This is Islam. There is no other meaning of Islam" (63). This is heart of the problem of modernity for Sayyid Qutb: the emancipation and separation of politics, science, economics, and personal relationships from religion (Berman, 2003).

Secularization was the source of all the conflicts and anxieties of the present age. That core of the modern project must be opposed at all costs. "Man should not cut himself off from this authority to develop a separate system and a separate scheme of life" but rather "follow His [God's] law in all spheres of life" (Qutb, 1996, 81). Instead of the Enlightenment idea of the right of private judgment, everyone should live "their entire lives in submission to Allah and should not decide any affair on their own, but must refer them to God's injunctions" (84).

Another reason for the decline of Islam from the first generation until now is that now people approach the sacred text out of a desire to understand it, "for the sake of knowledge itself," rather than to "find out what the Almighty had prescribed" (Qutb 1996, 27). The devout attitude toward the text is not to seek to comprehend it or "increase the sum total of knowledge" (27) but rather to simply obey it like a soldier in battle. "We must return to it with a sense of instruction for obedience and action, not for academic discussion and enjoyment" (33).

In contrast to the purity of the bygone age, the present age is decadent and immoral because it claims the right to decide matters of law and morality and religion for itself. Qutb (1996) writes bluntly,

> If we look at the sources and foundations of modern ways of living, it becomes clear that the whole world is steeped in *Jahiliyyah* [ignorance of divine guidance]. . . . This *Jahiliyyah* is based on rebellion against God's sovereignty on earth. It is now not that simple and primitive form of the ancient *Jahiliyyah*, but takes the form of claiming that the right to create values, to legislate rules of collective behavior, and to choose any way of life rests with men, without regard to what God has prescribed. (15)

All of modern culture, even its religiosity, is corrupt and worthless: "Our whole environment, people's beliefs and ideas, habits and art, rules and laws—is *Jahiliyyah*, even to the extent that what we consider to be Islamic culture, Islamic philosophy, Islamic thought, are also constructs of *Jahiliyyah!*" (Qutb, 1996, 32). Hopelessly corrupt, modern culture must be completely abolished and replaced with a new system based solely on the Koran (Qutb, 1996, 83).

How should this happen? Purely nonviolent, religious means are not enough: "the bringing about of the enforcement of the Divine *Shari'ah* and the abolition of man-made laws cannot be achieved only through preaching." (Qutb, 1996: 105). Rather, change must begin with "*Jihaad bis saif* [striving through sword] which is to clear the way for striving through preaching" (110). Qutb furiously rejects the idea that jihad is simply a defensive action in response to an attack. Rather, jihad is "an eternal state" in which the true Muslim is always engaged (116). And Qutb is clear that this continual jihad is not simply an inner struggle against sin, but it is, more often than not, an active political and military struggle to impose Islamic law on the entire world, "to establish God's authority on the earth; to arrange human affairs according to the true guidance provided by God" (127). Jihad then grows directly from the fact that "Islam has a right to remove all these obstacles which are in its path" in order to enforce "servitude to God and follow only the *Shari'ah* of God." (136). Regarding cultures that teach and establish laws and practices that interfere with the imposition of *shari'a*, "it is the duty of Islam to annihilate all such systems" (137). The claim of Islamic terrorists that jihad is the central duty in Islam is the direct result of the writings of Qutb.

Qutb's understanding of jihad was soon taken up and amplified in *The Neglected Duty* by Abd Al-Salam Faraj, one of the leaders of a group called Al-Jihad, which carried out the murder of Anwar Sadat in 1981. Like the Muslim revolutionary vanguard described in Qutb's *Milestones,* "the ultimate aim of Al-Jihad is a world governed by *shar'ia*" (Rapoport, 1998: 109).

> The title of the book *The Neglected Duty* does not refer to the lapse regarding the *shar'ia* but to a different one—namely the failure to participate in the *jihad* or holy war, which lack, the author believes, is the cause of Islam's decline and despair. Returning to the *jihad,* he maintains, is *the* essential means for reviving Islam. (Rapoport, 1998: 110)

Thus Qutb's message of the central duty and relevance of jihad is passed on to another generation of Islamic militants.

Echoes of *Milestones* can be found in bin Laden's 1996 "Declaration of War against the Americans Occupying the Land of the Two Holy Places," referring to Saudi Arabia. Bin Laden's attack on the Saudi regime for the "suspension of the Islamic Sharia law and exchanging it with man made civil law" and his insistence that "after Belief there is no more important duty than . . . Jihad against the enemy" are ideas that come directly from Qutb's writings (McDermott, 2005: 255, 256). Robert Darr recently described for me a visit to an Afghan family in which the sons insisted on the sole authority of *Shari'a* and the central duty of jihad (see also Darr, 2006). In a 2005 interview, Abu Bakar Ba'asyir, the alleged emir of the al-Qaeda–linked organization of Jemaah Islamiyah, said, "There is no better deed than jihad. None. The highest deed in Islam is jihad. If we commit to jihad we can neglect other deeds" (Atran, 2005a: 2).

In *Milestones*, we find many of the themes at the heart of religious texts of terror from around the world: (1) the complete rejection of the modern values of individual judgment and the separation of religion and the state and therefore the demonizing of secularization as the enemy of religion; (2) the insistence on a previous time of spiritual purity to which we must return, a past purity that has been corrupted by the replacement of divine revelation with human thought (Rapoport writes, "the sacred terrorists' eyes are on the past—on the particular precedents established in the religion's most holy era" [1998: 118]); (3) the centrality of law in religion and the ultimate duty to impose that law on all aspects of human life; (4) the claim that the modern age is characterized by growing decadence and immorality; (5) the strict dualism of good and evil, the godly and the unrighteous; (6) a sacred text or teacher that is seen as infallible (Hood, Hill, & Williamson, 2005); and (7) the advocacy of violence. By its continual citation of the Koran and quoting of precedents from Islamic history, as well as its insistence that jihad is a religious duty, *Milestones* graphically illustrates the ways in which Islamic militancy is a religious movement. But these concerns are not unique to the jihadists. They are paralleled in fundamentalist movements in all the other religions of the world (Kimball, 2002; Lawrence, 1989; Marty & Appleby, 1994).

As religious movements, Islamic fanaticism and all fundamentalisms and fanaticisms can be approached psychologically using the tools developed in the clinical psychology of religion. A clinical psychology of religion uses the theories and models developed in clinical practice (in my case a predominantly psychodynamic practice) to shed light on the motivations and passions of the religious devotee. Just as the psychodynamic clinician listens for recurring themes in the discourse of her patients, I am listening here for some of the recurring themes in the discourses of Islamic militants. And, as a scholar of religion as well as a clinician, I point out regions of comparison between Islamic terrorists and those from other traditions, which further illustrates and amplifies the psychological themes found here.

SHAME, HUMILIATION, AND RELIGION

Feelings of humiliation on the part of Arab populations has been one of the most frequently cited root causes of the turn to fundamentalism (Abi-Hashem, 2004; Davis, 2003; Hassan, 2001; Khosrokhavar, 2005). One Palestinian trainer of human bombers has said, "Much of the work is already done by the suffering these people have been subject to. . . . Only 10 percent comes from me. The suffering and living in exile away from their land has given the person 90 percent of what he needs to become a martyr" (Davis, 2003: 154).[1] Hafez (2006b), in his study of human bombers, makes the same point, writing "In Palestine, intense feelings of victimization underpin societal support for suicide bombings" (7). A Palestinian psychiatrist reports that "humiliation is an important factor motivating young suicide bombers" (quoted in Victoroff, 2005: 29). By one estimate, more than 90% of the recruits to militant Palestinian groups come from the villages and camps suffering the most from the Israeli presence, where the humiliation is greatest and the struggle is most intense (Post, Sprinzak & Denny, 2003: 173). Hassan (2001) reports: "Over and over I heard them [militants] say, 'The Israelis humiliate us. They occupy our land, and deny our history'" (38). In a recent lecture, Jessica Stern (2006), the author of *Terror in the Name of God,* said that in the Muslim communities, the greatest cause of terrorism is the feeling of humiliation.

A very different example of the same theme of humiliation is that, like many new religious movements, the Japanese cult Aum Shinrikyo (the group that unleashed sarin gas in the Tokyo subway and also murdered several people) regularly engaged in rituals of shaming and humiliation of its members. Members were often harangued by the guru, kept in isolation, and made to wait hours for their leader to appear while chanting over and over, "Master, please appear" (Lifton, 2000; other, even more horrific, acts of humiliation are described in Reader, 2000:137–141).

Forensic psychology has emphasized connections among shame, humiliation, and violence. Forensic psychologists cite numerous studies correlating conditions of shame and humiliation with increases in violence and crime, especially for males (Gilligan, 1996; W. Miller, 1993). For example, a psychiatrist working in prisons reports on a study that suggests that every act of violence in the prison was preceded by some humiliating event in the life of the prisoner (Gilligan, 1996). And statistics show that in the United States, at least, increases in crime exactly follow increases in the number of unemployed men.

Although often rooted in social and political circumstances, shame and humiliation are profoundly psychological, and often spiritual, conditions. By holding out an absolute and perfect ideal—whether it's a divine being or a perfect guru or master—against which all mortals inevitably fall short and by insisting on the "infinite qualitative difference" (in the words of Søren Kierkegaard) between human beings and the ideal, religions can easily exacerbate and play upon any natural human tendency toward feelings of shame and humiliation (McNish, 2004; Pattison, 2000). I would suggest the more any religion exalts its ideal, or portrays the divine as an overpowering presence and emphasizes the gulf between finite human beings and that ideal so that we must feel like "worms, not human" (in the words of the Psalms), the more it contributes to and reinforces experiences of shame and humiliation.

In addition, many writers have noted the connection between feelings of shame and disgust with the body and embodiment. One of the Muslim leaders of the 9/11 attacks wrote some years earlier in his will that no woman or other unclean person should touch his body and that his genitalia be washed with gloved hands. A classic example in the West is St. Augustine, who virtually single-handedly made the doctrine of original sin central to the Western Christian understanding of human nature. It is not coincidence that this proponent of the idea that we are born sinful and impure continually (in his book the *Confessions*) expresses revulsion at anything associated with his body. But such a theological linkage of the body with feelings of shame is (unfortunately) not unique to Augustine but can be found in the traditional texts of many religions. And even the very secular, science-fiction–based Heaven's Gate cult, whose members committed suicide in an act of violence against themselves, recommended castration for all the men in the cult.

Much psychological research suggests that there is a linkage of shame, humiliation, and violence; religion then can contribute to terrorism by creating and/or reinforcing and potentiating feelings of shame and humiliation, which in turn increase the likelihood of violent outbursts. While much of the humiliation that fuels certain acts of terrorism might begin in social and cultural conditions, fanatical religions may build upon that and establish a cycle where their teachings and practices increase feelings of shame and humiliation that intensifies aggressive feelings, and then in turn the religion provides targets for that aggression. By fomenting crusades, dehumanizing outsiders, and encouraging prejudices, fanatical religions provide ready, religiously sanctioned targets for increase in aggression.

To understand contemporary religiously motivated terrorism, it is important to emphasize that the humiliation that leads to violence does not have to be experienced directly and personally; for example, it may be the humiliation of a family member or of the whole Muslim community with which Islamic terrorists identify. The rise of mass media and the Internet throughout the Muslim world has extended the range of this identification (for examples, see Atran, 2006b; Hoffman, 2006; Khosrokhavar, 2005; Rosenthal, 2006). Mohammad Sidique Khan, thought to be the leader of the group that bombed the London underground in July 2005, said in his last video shown on television by Al Jazeera on September 1, 2005,

> Your democratically elected governments continuously perpetuate atrocities against my people all over the world. And your support makes you directly responsible, just as I am directly responsible for protecting and avenging my Muslim brothers and sisters. . . . Until you stop the bombing, gassing, imprisonment and torture of my people we will not stop this fight. (United Kingdom, 2006a: 19)

The pictures from Abu Ghraib prison in Iraq or the demolition of family homes in Palestine evoke these identifications and feelings of humiliation, which can lead directly to terrorist acts. Khosrokhavar (2005) calls this "humiliation by proxy."

This expansion of the feeling of humiliation illustrates the way in which the experience of humiliation can be embedded ideologically. A conquered, imprisoned, subjugated population experiences humiliation directly. But that is not the only source of humiliation now. An Arab citizen in Europe does not have to experience humiliation directly; mass communications can generate feelings of humiliation through empathy with fellow Muslims thousands of miles away (Khosrokhavar, 2005; Rosenthal, 2006). Religious ideology can play a major role here too. Throughout the Muslim diaspora, commentators and preachers strengthen this empathic link with co-religionists around the world, established by the mass media. The role of Muslim preachers of hate, living in England and throughout Europe, in stirring up the passions of their hearers, sometimes to the point of committing terrorist acts, has been well-documented (Khosrokhavar, 2005). On the other side, Jewish settlers describe feeling humiliated because Palestinians are living on "their

land" in the occupied West Bank (Juergensmeyer, 2000). No United
Nations mandate gave them title to that land; the "might makes right"
philosophy of conquest has been illegal in international law for a century
or more. The only claim the settlers have on the land is through religion—"that God gave us this land forever." Their feelings of humiliation
because Palestinians are living there are derived entirely from a set of
religious convictions about it being their land. Both the Muslims living in
Europe and the settlers living on the West Bank use religious ideologies
and interpretations to construct and intensify a sense of humiliation. For
another example, Asahara felt that Aum Shinrikyo was being humiliated
by the Japanese press inquiring into his activities, even though that is well
within the accepted role of the press. And some conservative American
Christians claim to feel humiliated by the separation of church and state,
the teaching of evolution, or images in the movies.

In all these instances, a set of religious beliefs generates these feelings
of humiliation on the part of many in the Muslim diaspora, in the Jewish settlements, or among the American apocalyptic Christians. The fact
that these various forms of humiliation are ideologically driven does not
mean they are not real. Quite the contrary. Such feelings of humiliation
are just as able to fuel terrorist acts as the humiliation arising from military occupation. Thus religions fuel humiliation not only by subjecting
devotees to humiliating rituals or beliefs or by playing on experiences of
humiliation by occupying powers, religions also cast an ideological net
that enables devotees to feel humiliated in circumstances when no direct
humiliation is present.

Globalization and the new world order does in fact result in a homog-
enization of societies and their economies—a McDonaldsization of the
world. With this comes the loss of local cultures and values. In ways that
are apparently hard for those in the West who benefit from globalization
to comprehend, many indigenous cultures experience this loss of local
culture as a cultural imperialism on the part of the West, and especially
on the part of the United States. Rather than a military invasion and
occupation, this is felt to be a cultural invasion and occupation. Like all
occupations by foreign powers, this one, too, can be experienced as a
humiliation. And fanatical religions can and do play on these widely held
feelings of humiliation caused by globalization's cultural imperialism.

In this sense religious fundamentalism throughout the world is not
simply, as so many commentators have insisted, a reaction against modernity (e.g., Armstrong, 2001; Lawrence, 1989). Rather, the contemporary

international rise of fundamentalism can also be seen as a response to the failure of the utopian dreams inherent in modernity—that technology and market economics would create a material paradise on earth. It has for some people. But for many around the world, modernity has not brought the promised benefits. Especially in the Muslim Middle East, the vision of a secular utopia has collapsed. Marxist–socialist parties and leaders oriented toward Western capitalism have each produced only dictatorships and misery for the common person (Stern, 2003). There are precious few examples of third-world, underdeveloped countries turned into material utopias by either market-oriented elites or Marxist cadres. The failures, as much if not more than the successes, of the ideologies of modernity (capitalism and Marxism) are the breeding ground for fundamentalism and its violent offshoots. And this analysis applies only to the physical commodities of life and does not even touch upon the spiritual vacuum left by secular modernity to which fundamentalist groups and spiritual renewal movements like many militant Islamicists, Aum Shinrikyo, or the People's Temple appeal. Aum Shinrikyo, the People's Temple, and some jihadist groups began as movements for spiritual renewal; their violent actions came as the result of the search for spiritual transformation.

A central psychological–spiritual theme in the writings of the jihadists and other religiously motivated terrorists is the feeling of humiliation. Such feelings of humiliation on the part of Muslim populations, Jewish settlers, Japanese students, and extreme right-wing American Christians provide a major part of the psychological motivation for (but never the justification of) their terrorist actions. And, as I discuss further in the final chapter, part of the response to religiously motivated terrorism must be the insistence that Muslim, Jewish, Buddhist, and Christian leaders forcefully teach that feelings of humiliation can never justify terrorist acts.

THE APOCALYPTIC VISION

One of the most common and widespread beliefs of fanatically violent religious movements, which many commentators mention, is their apocalyptic vision. Giving even a cursory history of apocalyptic movements is far beyond the scope of this book. My focus is primarily on the psychological themes implicit in such a vision. The term "apocalyptic" comes from the Greek words *apokalypto*, a verb that means to disclose, uncover, bring to light, or appear, and *apokalysis,* the noun form that means a disclosure, a revelation, or an appearance. Within Christian history, over time this general term gradually became restricted in its meaning to the appearance of Jesus at the end of time. But in its original context, at the time the New Testament, the Greek term did not necessarily have any of the violent, end-of-the-world connotations it has acquired in certain religious circles; then it meant simply any revelation or appearance. The same restriction of meaning has occurred to another Greek term commonly used in Christian apocalyptic circles—*parousia.* The term simply means "presence" but it gradually became restricted to refer to the second coming of Christ at the end of history. In the original Greek these terms simply meant the presence of God in history and in human life. In the course of Jewish and Christian history, starting with the Hebrew Bible (especially the book of Daniel) and continuing through some Jewish writings during the period before the birth of Christ and then into the New Testament, these terms gradually acquired references to the end of history and of human life as we know it and to violence and bloodshed (Collins, 1998; McGinn, 2005).

Thus, over time apocalypticism acquired a more limited reference to events at the end of history. As such, apocalypticism is an inherently religious phenomenon. It depends on the belief that some transhistorical forces or powers are in charge of history. This is as true of Marxism with its transhistorical dialectical laws as it is of apocalyptic Christianity and Islam. Apocalypticism has its roots in Judaism beginning at the third century BCE when the conquered Jewish population began to envision a violent end of the world in which their enemies would be destroyed by God and they would be restored to their rightful place as the righteous ruling nation (Collins, 1998; McGinn, 2005). Apocalypticism is thus connected to the idea of an elect and chosen people especially favored by God and destined to rule the world and a God who destroys his (apocalyptic deities are virtually always male for reasons we will discuss later) enemies. Thus, as the historian Bernard McGinn (2005) writes in his article on apocalypticism in antiquity, "the apocalyptic world view is inherently violent" (209). So apocalypticism, which is both inherently religious and inherently violent, brings religion and violence together (Beit-Hallamhi, 2002).

Although rooted in religion, such apocalypticism is found in secular revolutionary terrorist groups as well. The following description of a radical left-wing terrorist group in Germany could just as easily apply to jihadists, apocalyptic Christians, and Aum Shinrikyo.

What do the terrorists want? They want The Revolution, a total transformation of all existing conditions, a new form of human existence, an entirely new relationship of people to each other, and also of people to nature. They want the total and radical breach with all that is, and with all historical continuity. Without a doubt they are utopians. The source of their (self-proclaimed) legitimacy is the utopia they want to make real. . . . There is no voice that could call them back to reason. For them there is no connection between the vision that drives them and the existing reality. . . . They are fascinated by the magic of extremes, the hard, uncompromising either/or, life or death, salvation or perdition. . . . Any compromise they do not even regard as weakness, but as treason. They are driven by a pitiless hatred for those they look upon as their enemies, a hatred fed by a disgust with what they regard as a morbid, decadent society of sly and immoral practices and mendacious hypocrisy. (Kellen, 1988: 49–50)

My task here is to trace the functions that this apocalyptic vision of radical, total, and violent transformation serves in contemporary religiously motivated terrorist movements and to describe some of the psychological factors that make such a vision appealing.

AT WAR WITH THE WORLD

One of the most widespread beliefs of violent religious movements is their apocalyptic vision of a cosmic struggle of the forces of the all-good against the forces of the all-evil (Juergensmeyer, 2000; Kimball, 2002; Wessinger, 2000). Osama bin Laden says it clearly: there are "two adversaries; the Islamic nation, on the one hand, and the United States and its allies on the other. It is either victory and glory or defeat and humiliation" (quoted in Moghadam, 2006: 717). Virtually all religious terrorists agree that they are locked in an apocalyptic battle with demonic forces, that is, usually with the forces of secularism. We have seen how Sayyid Qutb denoted secularism and the concomitant values of individual rights and the separation of religion and law as demonic and the source of most of the misery of the modern world and demanded a jihad against it (Berman, 2003). Continuing Qutb's diatribe, the founder of Hamas told a reporter, "There's a war going on" not just against Israeli occupation but against all secular governments including the Palestinian authority because there "is no such thing as a secular state in Islam" (Juergensmeyer, 2000: 76). Hamas's arch enemy, Rabbi Meir Kahane, whose Jewish Defense League was responsible for numerous attacks on Muslims in the United States and Israel, said bluntly "secular government is the enemy" (Juergensmeyer, 2000: 55). Asahara, the founder of the Aum Shinrikyo, is reported to have shouted again and again at his followers, "Don't you realize that this is war" (Lifton, 2000: 56) and to have insisted that his group existed "on a war footing" (Lifton, 2000: 60). The Reverend Paul Hill, who shot and killed a physician in front of a family planning clinic in the United States, wrote "The battle over abortion is primarily spiritual. The conflict is between God's will and kingdom and Satan's opposing will and kingdom" (Hill, 2003: 8). Hill's actions were justified to an interviewer by his brother-in-arms, the Reverend Michael Bray, who wrote the bible of the violent anti-choice movement, entitled tellingly *A Time to Kill*, as the product of a

> Christian subculture in America that considers itself at war with the larger society, and to some extent victimized by it. . . . This subculture sees itself justified in its violent responses to a vast and violent repression waged by secular . . . agents of a satanic force . . . a great defensive Christian struggle against the secular state, a contest between the forces of spiritual truth and heathen darkness, in which the moral character of America as a righteous nation hangs in the balance. (Juergensmeyer, 2000: 36)

Juergensmeyer concludes in his investigation of religiously sponsored terrorism around the globe, *Terror in the Mind of God,* that "what is strikingly similar about the cultures of which they [religious terrorists] are a part is their view of the contemporary world at war" (Juergensmeyer, 2000: 151). Qutb and the jihadists are not alone in declaring war on the secular state.

SATANIZING THE OTHER

The demonizing of enemies is a major tactic of fanatical religious movements. Khomeini proclaimed the West the "Great Satan." Shortly before his assassination, I heard a group of ultra-orthodox rabbis on a New York radio station calling the late Israeli Prime Minister Rabin a traitor to the nation and an enemy of God who should be removed "by any means possible." Which, of course, he was when an ultra-orthodox Jewish student shot him. Militant Hindu nationalists have burned mosques and churches. In the United States, physicians have been murdered and family planning clinics bombed. As one commentator on fanatical religions wrote, such groups "paint the world in black and white, creating radical polarities between good and evil" (Ammerman, 1994: 155).

The image of oneself as a participant in a cosmic battle with the forces of evil delegitimizes one's opponents in a process Juergensmeyer calls "satanization," which he defines as "creating satanic enemies [which] is part of the construction of the image of cosmic war" (Juergensmeyer, 2000: 182). The idea of sacred warfare makes possible the idea of a satanic opponent. Enemies who embody pure evil cannot be argued with or compromised with; they can only be destroyed. And as morally or spiritually subhuman, destroying them is not an immoral act but is, rather, a moral duty. "The process of satanization can transform a worldly struggle into a contest between martyrs and demons" (Juergensmeyer, 2000: 163). Such us-against-them thinking, so central to religiously in-spired apocalypticism, can lead to what Waller calls "the social death of the victim."

With his notion of "pseudo-speciation," Erik Erikson made the same point. By "pseudo-speciation" Erikson (1969) meant that the single human race is split into ideologically driven subspecies by race or other external characteristics and then the groups are set against each other. For Erikson the most important point is that, in the words often at-tributed to the American psychiatrist Henry Stack Sullivan, "we are all more human than not." Pseudo-speciation obscures this fact by dividing this one human race into distinct racial, tribal, national, or ideological identities and attributing superior status to one group and inferior status to all others.

Drawing on Erikson, Charles Strozier (1994) underscores the crucial importance of religion in the process of pseudo-speciation.

> Part of the power of Erikson's insight is the recognition that destruction between groups can only make sense with a spiritual grounding. We can-not value ourselves and degrade and ultimately kill the other unless we call God onto our side in the struggle. In the same way, the genocidal impulse is grounded in perverse forms of idealism and deep yearnings for spiritual purification. (252–253)

The overidealization of one's own tribe, tradition, or gender in the name of religion provides a ready rational for violence against the "other," who is now seen as demonic and impure and thus having been dehumanized and having died a social death can now be slaughtered with impunity.

Religion can, thus, be a powerful force (perhaps the most powerful force) in desensitizing devotees to the humanity of the other and thus creating the moral disengagement that, as we saw in the previous chapter, is one of the major ingredients that makes terrorism and genocide possible (Bandura, 2004).

This demonizing of the other is not confined to religious groups. Sprinzak (1998a) notices it in the radical New Left movements of the 1960s in America. But in describing it, he has recourse to the religious imagery of the children of light and the children of darkness. He writes,

> Individuals who are identified with the rotten, soon-to-be-destroyed, social and political order are depersonalized and dehumanized. They are derogated to the ranks of subhuman species. Dehumanization makes it possible for the radicals to be disengaged morally and to commit atrocities without a second thought. It bifurcates the world into the sons of light and the sons of darkness, and makes the "fantasy war" of the former versus the latter fully legitimate. (Sprinzak, 1998a: 82)

Envisioning the world as a cosmic battleground between totally good forces and the forces of evil appears to be one major theme in the worldview of religious fanatics and terrorists. This belief serves what Waller calls the social death of the victim, dehumanizing the victims by seeing them as satanic. This demonizing and dehumanizing of the other is one of the most powerful ways in which religion promotes terrorism. As Juergensmeyer (2000) writes, "a satanic enemy cannot be transformed; it can only be destroyed" (217).

Aggrandizing the Self

Besides delegitimating one's enemies, the image of cosmic warfare enables its proponents to feel they are part of the army of the pure and godly, fighting in the climactic battle of history. A report on Islamic militants reports that "by belonging to a radical group, otherwise powerless individuals become powerful" (Post et al., 2003: 176). The image of oneself as a participant in a cosmic battle with the forces of evil simultaneously delegitimizes one's opponents and aggrandizes oneself. Obviously this feeds a person's grandiosity and narcissism, empowering him or her to do actions the person would never do under less dramatic circumstances. Juergensmeyer (2000) writes, "The idea of cosmic war is compelling to religious activists because it ennobles and exalts those who consider themselves a part of it. . . . They become involved in terrorism not only to belittle their enemies but also to provide themselves with a sense of power" (184). Feeling oneself a part of the army of the righteous gives a person a heightened sense of power and transforms ordinary people into actors whose actions have cosmic significance.

Juergensmeyer (2000) writes:

> For those in cultures of violence who experience both despair and defiance over what they perceive to be hopeless situations, religion provides a solution: the cosmic war. As opponents become satanized and regarded as "forces of evil" . . . the world begins to make sense. Those who felt oppressed now understand why they have been humiliated and who is behind their dismal situation. Perhaps more important, they feel the exhilaration of hope, that in a struggle with divine dimensions God will be with them and, despite all the evidence to the contrary, somehow they can win. (185)

A member of Aum Shinrikyo says of the changes that took place in him after joining the group, "To put it bluntly, I am arrogant. Rather than believing in just Asahara, I believed in myself. I had the belief that I am a great person, so I will survive" (Lifton, 2000: 95). Another referred to himself as "a warrior in the battle between good and evil" (Lifton, 2000: 82).

FOMENTING CRUSADES

This radically apocalyptic vision that dichotomizes the world into all-good and all-bad camps often goes beyond dehumanizing those seen as evil and corrupt to fomenting crusades to rid the world of them. At first this crusade may exist only in the realm of fantasy with visions and portrayals of a climactic eschatological battle in which God triumphs over his enemies. As time goes on, the focus may shift from God's activity to ours, and fanatics may come to feel that they can and should take it upon themselves to purify the world of the enemies of God. Along this line, Juergensmeyer (2000) concludes:

> I came up with a list of several conditions . . . [indicating when] any religious tradition is susceptible to becoming associated with actual acts of violence: The cosmic struggle is understood to be occurring in this world rather than in a mythical setting. Believers identify personally with the struggle. The struggle is at a point of crisis in which individual action can make all the difference. (161)

The religious terrorist grows impatient waiting for God to bring history to a close. Not content to believe and wait, he and his comrades take the apocalypse into their own hands and act to bring it about in a crusade against the evildoers and the unrighteous. For example, in 2003 a group of Christians were arrested in Israel for a plan to blow up the holy mosque on the sacred mount in the center of Jerusalem, hoping that action would precipitate a holy war in the Middle East that would lead to Armageddon. Lifton (2000) describes Asahara and the members of Aum Shinrikyo as having a "consuming hunger for Armageddon" and one member reported feeling "we should get actively involved with Armageddon soon" (58). Another member reported that Asahara not only "was pleased that such a war would come—and soon. But that he was actually trying to pull the trigger of Armageddon itself" (Lifton, 2000: 85).[2]

PURIFYING SELF AND WORLD

Beyond naked aggression or revenge, the drive for purification may also power terrorist actions. The theme of death and rebirth is common theme to almost all the world's religions. Virtually all the traditions say that some process of dying—to self-centeredness, to a false self, to antispiritual cravings—is central to spiritual transformation. Apocalyptic religion takes this theme and historicizes it. Death and rebirth are now something that can and must happen within history, in real time.

A related theme that runs through this material is the increasing spiritual and moral decline of the world, which is often pictured as sinking rapidly into moral and spiritual oblivion, a world heading for disaster. A major theme in Qutb's *Milestones* is that today "the whole world is steeped in *Jahiliyyah*" (Qutb, 1996: 15). The vanguard following the road Qutb has laid out must be prepared to "march through the vast oceans of *Jahiliyyah* which has encompassed the entire world" (17). Earlier Qutb had castigated America for its open attitude about sex and before that, while still in Egypt, he had denounced women in bathing suits, calling them "naked" and "cheap meat" (Terman, 2007; Wright, 2006). A mujahadeen told Jessica Stern, "In European countries and in America there is too much sex. We respect women. She must always be in a full purdah. In America women are treated like sheep and goats. The American president [Clinton] raped a girl the age of his daughter" (Stern, 2003: 125).

Again, this theme of decline can be paralleled in virtually all religious texts of terror. An Aum Shinrikyo member reports feeling "the world was getting worse, pushing itself towards Armageddon with its increasing evil" (Lifton, 2000: 93). The decadence of modern Western society is a theme found in almost all the writings of religiously motivated terrorists. Eric Rudolph, who bombed several women's health clinics, a gay night club, and the Olympic Park in Atlanta, wrote from prison that

> A new barbarism, a culture of death has now taken root in America. The state is no longer the protector of the innocent, promoting values that challenge the darker angels of human nature, but now it is the handmaiden of the new hedonism, supporting the citizen in a lifestyle of selfishness and decadence. It is a black, nasty decadence. . . . Rights which were created to protect life are now used to protect the killer. . . . Fundamental rights such as the right to life have now been twisted into the prerogatives of the barbarian ogre satisfying his lifestyle of self-indulgence. . . . It is the necessary adjunct to the sexual license that goes with the orgy of modern life. . . . This is not progress, this is not humanity, this is a return to barbarism and the culture of death. . . . This country promotes a culture of selfishness and death. . . . Every variety of filth is tolerated and aggressively pushed with the complete support of the state—abortion, homosexuality, pornography—but this country does not tolerate the values of life, family, and human dignity (Rudolph, 2005: 2).[3]

His brother in arms, Paul Hill (2003), argues that

> If a majority in a democratic nation loses its moral bearings (as our nation has), and its respect for human life, this majority could elect representatives for the express purpose of cruelly oppressing and murdering a helpless minority—such as the unborn. Many pro-choice citizens vote with this very object in view. The more relativistic the people in a democracy become, the further they drift from the Moral Law, the more they can be expected to elect leaders who will pass laws that permit them to indulge themselves at the expense of the helpless and the needy. . . . Governments that sanction mass murder are grossly unjust; America's government has sanctioned mass murder; we must conclude, therefore, that America's government is grossly unjust. (48–49)

These exact same sentiments were echoed by a member of the Jewish Defense League in Israel who claims, in words that could have been spoken by any American Christian Identity soldier:

America is the most asexual society. American women try to be like men. They turn men off with feminism. This is ruining the white people. While western society is dying, all the savages around the world, they are not doing this. Their women aren't feminists. They have real culture, real strength. The Muslims, they are ready to fight. They are ready to die for something. They are ready to die for their ideals. Democratic liberal societies are getting globalized, they are rotten to the core. . . . You see America getting rotten with liberalism, which is more feminine. . . . America emphasizes the individual to the extent that the individual becomes nobody. An individual grows when he gets higher and higher through education, by being with God. But without education and God you don't develop. You lead an animal life, you have no freedom of choice, you become the simple and despicable animal of the earth. . . . Judaism has the special task . . . to preserve certain values, family values. To make sure men are men and women are women. Homosexuals should be somewhere else, in Africa maybe, with those that prefer that lifestyle. (quoted in Stern, 2003: 101)

Over and over we find these same themes (many of which we saw highlighted by Qutb in the middle of the last century)—an abhorrence of the materialism and individualism of the West, its lack of spirituality, its sexualized culture, its blurring of traditional gender roles and the emasculation of its men, and its tolerance for homosexuality—in the writings of religiously motivated terrorists, whether they are living in settlements in the occupied territories on the West Bank, in the Taliban camps in Afghanistan, or in the Christian enclaves in rural America. All of them agree that there is a rottenness in the world, and especially in the West, that is crying out for purification. Things are getting so bad that only a drastic intervention can turn things around. Lifton (2000) describes Aum Shinrikyo, in a phrase that could apply equally well to many religiously motivated terrorist groups, when he writes that they were driven by "the relentless impulse toward world-rejecting purification" (204). Stern (2006) says that religiously motivated terrorism is often a "project of purifying the world through extermination." The psychodynamics of such projects of purification will be a major theme later in this book.

Apocalyptically historicized or not, the themes of purification and renewal, often linked to themes of death and rebirth, appear central in virtually every major religious tradition and are not unique to terroristic movements. Some, like the nineteenth-century French sociologist Emil Durkheim (1902/1965), have argued that the split between the pure and the impure, the sacred and the profane, is the defining characteristic of the religious consciousness. Certainly this seems especially true of fanatical religions at war with the impure and unrighteous world around them. The traditional sectarian response has been to withdraw from the sinful world and create islands of purity separate from it (e.g., the Amish). Religious terrorists are not content to simply withdraw and protect their purity, they seek to actively transform and purify the surrounding world. Asahara is described as developing a "vision of an apocalyptic event or series of events that would destroy the world in the service of renewal" (Lifton, 2000: 203).

In many religions the theme of purification is linked with the theme of sacrifice. The Latin root *sacrificium* means "to make holy." Sacrifice is a way of making something holy, of purifying it. Sacrifices are offerings to the divine and to the community. But they are a special kind of offering in that what is given is destroyed. But something is not only destroyed, it (or something related to it like the religious community) is also transformed. Something is offered; something is made holy.

The practice of sacrifice may go back to the very foundations of religion. The early Vedas in India center around various sacrificial rituals, and much of the Hebrew Torah consists of instructions for conducting sacrifices. Hinduism later gave rise to the Upanishads with their elaborate metaphysical discussions as well as to a wide range of yogic, meditational, and devotional practices. And the Hebrew prophets and later writings came to ridicule the idea that God requires blood sacrifices, insisting instead on a "broken and contrite heart" (Isaiah) and "justice, mercy, and humility" (Micah). But the theme of sacrifice did not die out entirely. It was taken up by some strands of Christianity who continued to insist, with the author of the New Testament letter to the Hebrews (apparently a conservative Jewish convert to Christianity), that "without the shedding of blood, there is no forgiveness of sins" (Hebrews 9:22). My goal in this book is to examine the psychology behind this connection between purification or redemption and the shedding of blood, since that theme appears so central to so much religiously motivated violence.

The theme of blood sacrifice is not traditional in Islam, but it often appears as part of the larger religious context from which the Muslim human bombers emerge. In reference to this theme of sanctification by self-sacrifice, Strenski (2003) writes, "The 'human bombers' are regarded as 'sacred' by their communities of reference. They have been 'made holy' in the eyes of the community that 'accepts' them and their deed. They are elevated to lofty moral, and indeed, religious levels, as sacrificial *victims* themselves or as kinds of holy saints" (8; emphasis in original).

Hafez (2006a) describes how

> Proponents of suicide bombings create posters, websites, and public exhibits to honor their "martyrs" and publicize their "heroic" sacrifice. During a visit to al-Najah University in Nablus, a place that has produced many suicide bombers, the author saw many posters and murals for "martyrs" exhibited on nearly every wall and entrance. These posters often combine the two seemingly contradictory themes of death and marriage into a coherent frame that portrays martyrdom as a vehicle for achieving eternal happiness. (177)

One suicide bomber, a civil engineering student, wrote in his will: "My last wish to you my family is that none of you should weep in my procession to heaven. Indeed, distribute dates and ululate in the wedding of martyrdom." Another wrote in his final letter to his family: "Do not be sad and do not cry for we are in heaven. . . . Receive news of my martyrdom with elation and chants to God for it is a day of celebration" (both quotes from Hafez, 2006a: 177).

Hassan (2001) reports that in Palestinian neighborhoods:

> Calendars are illustrated with the "martyr of the month." Paintings glorify the dead bombers in Paradise, triumphant beneath a flock of green birds. The symbol is based on a saying of the prophet Mohammad that the soul of a martyr is carried to Allah in the bosom of the green birds of paradise. . . . A biography of a martyr . . . tells of how his soul was borne upward on a fragment of a bomb. . . . [An Imam] explained that the first drop of blood shed by a martyr during jihad washes away his sins instantaneously. On the Day of Judgment, he will face no reckoning. On the Day of Resurrection, he can intercede for several of his nearest and dearest to enter Heaven. (39)

Scholars familiar with the hagiographic traditions of the world's religions will see many common themes here—for example, the images of Christian saints and Buddhist Bodhisattvas borne up to paradise and ensconced in the highest heavens where, purified and sinless, they can intercede for others. By their offering and sacrifice, the human bombers and other martyrs have indeed become holy. Along this line, a Palestinian militant said "It is attacks when a member gives his life that earn the most respect and elevate the bombers to the highest possible level or martyrdom" (Post et al., 2003: 179). The Tamil Tigers also refer to their suicide bombings in Sri Lanka by a word that means "to give oneself." Their actions are "a gift of the self." In joining the Tigers one takes an oath in which "the only promise is I am prepared to give everything I have, including my life. It is an oath to the nation" (Strenski, 2003:22; see also Hoffman, 2006; Pape, 2005). A Palestinian questioned by Post and his colleagues angrily rejected their appellation of suicide and told them "This is not suicide. Suicide is selfish, it is weak, it is mentally disturbed. This is *istishad* (martyrdom or self-sacrifice in the service of Allah)" (Post et al., 2003: 179). It must be noted that this understanding of martyrdom and self-sacrifice is not traditional in Islam, and it has been condemned by many leading Muslim clerics and scholars around the world. Rather, it represents a major theological innovation on the part of radical Islamicists such as bin Laden, and it requires a very selective reading of traditional Islamic texts (Davis, 2003; Khosrokhavar, 2005; Kimball, 2002; Strenski, 2003; Venkatraman, 2007).

The leader of the 9/11 attacks, Mohammed Atta, called on his comrades to "purify your soul from all blemishes" and spoke to them of-"offering sacrifices and obedience" in "these last hours" (Atta, n.d.). In this letter Atta also refers to those whom they will kill as animals being ritually sacrificed. The word Atta uses in his letter for the slaughtering of the passengers is the Arabic word referring to the butchering of animals in a ritual way. It is also the word used in a videotape in reference to the beheading of two American contractors in Iraq in 2004 (Horgan, 2006: 119). These are seen as ritual acts of sacrifice. Hafez found this same conjunction of sacrifice and purification to be part of the cultures from which the Palestinian human bombers came.

Martyrdom is seen as an attempt to redeem society of its failure to act righteously. Words expressed by revered martyrs carry a great deal of weight. Thus, many suicide bombers use their statements to express their view of how individuals and communities should act to overcome the malaise that characterizes their condition. Muhammad Hazza'a al-ghoul, a Hamas activist who blew himself up on a bus on 18 June 2002, killing 19 and injuring 74 Israelis, wrote in his last will and testament: "How beautiful for the splinters of my bones to be the response that blows up the enemy . . . not for the love of killing, but so we can live as other people live. . . . We do not sing the songs of death, but recite the hymns of life . . . we die so that future generations may live." Some urge their mothers, fathers, brothers and sisters to pray regularly (especially the dawn prayers), to wear the head covering (*hijab*), and to become from among the best Muslims on earth. Shadi Sleyman al-Nabaheen, who carried out a failed suicide mission on 19 May 2003, wrote in his last will and testament: "My dear brothers and sisters: . . . Be from among the patient and steadfast and hold tightly to the religion of God. Guide your children to the mosque and instruct them to read the Qur'an and attend the recitation lessons, and teach them to love jihad and martyrdom. (Hafez, 2006a: 176)

The discourse of the human bombers is not a martial discourse of anger and revenge but rather a spiritual discourse of redemption and purification.

Jesus and the early Christians, as well as the Jewish defenders of Massada and the Buddhists who immolated themselves during the Vietnam War, martyred themselves. The medieval inquisitors martyred their victims. Human bombers and suicide terrorists martyr both themselves and their victims. What does this mean? Why is the human bomber sacrificing his victim and usually himself?

Two examples from the history of religion may help answer this question. One of the most dramatic examples of this theme of sacrificing one's self and/or one's victim to effect sanctification and purification is found in Aum Shinrikyo and Asahara's (the founder of Aum Shinrikyo) doctrine of *poa*, which I discuss in more detail in the next chapter. This doctrine, which grows out of Asahara's interpretation of certain texts in Tantric Buddhism, claims that there is a religious duty to kill certain people in order to save them from acquiring more and more bad karma. Several scholars point to this doctrine of *poa* (the most unique element in Asahara's teaching) as the root cause of Aum Shinrikyo's sarin gas attack in Tokyo. And, while Buddhism is often portrayed in the West as a religion of peace and compassion, it too has a history and tradition of violence in the service of religious causes upon which Asahara drew. In addition, this idea of compassionate killing or killing in order to save the victim from worse karma has its roots in Buddhist tradition. Asahara is not alone here. This doctrine of *poa* is another example of the idea of blood sacrifice (either of oneself or others) leading to the sanctification of oneself or another that is central in much religiously sponsored terrorism. We will find a similar linkage of violent death and purification in the doctrines of American apocalyptic Christianity. In chapter 5 I discuss whether there is a psychological reason that inclines people to accept the idea of sanctifying oneself (and the other as well in the case of *poa*) through death.

This idea that killing is a means to redeem oneself or another is not unique to Aum Shinrikyo. Another example can be found in the history of the United States and the most prosperous religion born in the American milieu—Mormonism. In the mid-1800s, as Mormonism settled into its new home in Utah, it underwent a burst of religious enthusiasm. Among the fruits of this "Mormon Reformation" were a more strident assertion of polygamy and an intensified proclamation of the necessity of what they called "blood atonement." This doctrine directly connected bloodshed and purification and maintained the concomitant assertion that killing was necessary and justified to redeem the unrighteous—shedding their blood and making them sacrificial victims for the sake of their own salvation. This doctrine of blood atonement, which originally referred to the death of Christ on the cross, became applied more widely within early Mormonism. Juanita Brooks, the most extensive chronicler of life on the Mormon frontier, wrote that blood atonement was a "literal and terrible reality. Brigham Young advocated and preached it without compromise" (quoted in Bagley, 2002: 51). Faced with one who had committed an unpardonable sin, Brigham Young homilized, "will you love that man or woman well enough to shed their blood?" He claimed that hundreds of people could have been saved "if their lives had been taken and their blood spilled on the ground as a smoking incense to the Almighty" (Bagley, 2002: 51). The Mormon prophet went on to insist that if a sinner wished to be saved and it was "necessary to spill his blood on the earth in order that he might be saved, spill it" (51). Regarding apostates, Young told the council of Mormon leaders, "I want their cursed heads cut off that they may atone for their sins" (51). In his meticulously researched history of violence in early Mormonism, Will Bagley writes,

> Perhaps the most troubling aspect of the [Mormon] Reformation [of the 1850s] was the Mormon leadership's fascination with blood. Their rhetoric dripped with sanguine imagery, and their Old Testament theology incorporated this dark fascination in a perplexing doctrine known as blood atonement. Joseph Smith taught that certain grievous sins put sinners "beyond the reach of the atoning blood of Christ." Their "only hope [was] to have their own blood shed to atone." Strictly interpreted, the doctrine seems to have applied only to believing Mormons, but it led to the widespread belief

that the LDS [Latter Day Saints] church shed the blood of apostates "as an atonement for their sins." As the doctrine evolved under Brigham Young, it would be a powerful—and confusing—influence. Of all the beliefs that laid the foundation of Utah's culture of violence, none would have more devastating consequences. (Bagley, 2002: 50)

Brigham Young was not alone in preaching this doctrine to the first and second generation of Mormons. Jedediah Grant, known as "Brigham's sledge hammer," told his hearers that they possessed the "right to kill a sinner to save him. . . . We would not kill a man, of course, unless we killed him to save him" (Bagley, 2002: 51). "We have those amongst us," Grant said, "that are full of all manner of abominations, those who need to have their blood shed, for water will not do, their sins are of too deep a dye" (51).

Early Mormonism sought to institutionalize and ritualize blood atonement. "Brigham's sledge hammer" advised Young "to appoint a committee to attend to [cases of sinners] and then let a place be selected, and let the committee shed their blood" (Bagley, 2002: 51). John D. Lee, who was the only Mormon convicted in the bloody massacre at Mountain Meadows, wrote the "right thing to do with a sinner who did not repent and obey the Council, was to take the life of the offending party, and thus save his everlasting soul. This is called Blood Atonement" (52). Many historians who have carefully researched the Mountain Meadows massacre (see, e.g., Bagley, 2002; Krakauer, 2004), in which more than 100 men, women, and children were slaughtered in a brutal and gory rampage, conclude that the Mormon hierarchy and its doctrine of blood atonement were directly responsible.

What Bagley (2002) calls "early Mormonism's peculiar obsession with blood and vengeance" (379) continued even into the twentieth century. In 1902, Brigham Young's grandson brutally butchered a woman, claimed to be a prostitute, and wrote "Blood Atonement" on the wall in his father's apartment (Bagley, 2002). In 1984 in Utah, a young mother and her 15-month-old baby were slain in a blood-splattered slaughter in their own home. Two of her brothers-in-law, members of a fundamentalist Mormon group who wanted to return to the early days of Mormonism (including polygamy and blood atonement), were convicted of the crime (Krakauer, 2004). Thus the same doctrine of killing the other in order to purify them occurs in both Aum Shinrikyo and in early Mormonism—the quintessential American apocalyptic religion.[4]

THE RELIGIOUS NATURE OF
RELIGIOUS TERRORISM

The foregoing discussion illustrates the sacrificial (that is to say religious) nature of these actions. And it is that sacrificial, religious nature of these acts of violence that gives them meaning in the eyes of their proponents.

That Muslim martyrdom operations are understood by their participants as religious acts is made clear by the rituals that surround them: "Sometimes the terrorists' purpose and means seemed so fixed that scholars describe their acts as a form of religious ritual," writes Rapoport (1998: 118). Of the most frightening documents to emerge in our twenty-first-century encounter with terrorism is the letter that Mohammed Atta left for posterity. The major themes of the letter are obedience, prayer, union with God, and sacrifice. Atta calls on his comrades to engage in devotions as preparation for their mission:

> Remember the words of Almighty God. . . . Remind yourself of the supplications. . . . Bless your body with some verses from the Qur'an. . . . Pray the morning prayer in a group and ponder the great rewards of that prayer. Make supplications afterward, and do not leave your apartment unless you have performed ablution before leaving. . . . Read the words of God. (Atta, n.d.)

Such religious ritualizing was not unique to the 9/11 cell; it is normal and a crucial part of the Muslim human bomber's mission:

> Just before the bomber sets out on his final journey, he performs a ritual ablution, puts on clean clothes, and tries to attend at least one communal prayer at a mosque. He says the traditional Islamic prayer that is customary before battle, and asks Allah to forgive his sins and bless his mission. He puts a Koran in his left breast pocket, above the heart, and he straps the explosives around his waist or picks up briefcase or a bag containing the bomb. The planner bids him farewell with the words, "May Allah be with you, may Allah give you success so that you achieve Paradise." The would-be martyr responds, "*Inshallah*, we will meet in Paradise." Hours later, as he presses the detonator, he says, "Allahu akbar"—"Allah is great. All praise to Him." (Hassan, 2001: 41)

Atta's letter stresses the need for continual supplication throughout the 9/11 hijacking and the assurance of divine protection, favor, and reward. "Everywhere you go, say that prayer and smile and be calm, for God is with the believers. And the angels will protect you without you feeling anything," Atta writes to his comrades. There are few references in his letter to anger or revenge; rather, the driving motivation is union with God. The letter makes it clear that the terrorists were not seeking political or social goals but rather that they "are heading toward eternal paradise." A leader of Hamas said, "Love of martyrdom is something deep inside the heart. But these rewards are not in themselves the goal of the martyr. The only aim is to win Allah's satisfaction. That can be done in the simplest and speediest manner by dying in the cause of Allah" (Hassan, 2001: 36).

The same attitude emerges from an interview with a Palestinian suicide bomber who survived a failed attempt and a gun battle with Israeli troops. Like Atta he describes his preparation for his martyrdom operation as a spiritual discipline:

> We were in a constant state of worship. We told each other that if the Israelis only knew how joyful we were they would whip us to death. Those were the happiest days of my life. . . . We were floating, swimming, in the feeling that we were about to enter eternity. We had no doubts. We had made on oath on the Koran, in the presence of Allah. . . . I know there are other ways to do jihad. But this one is sweet, the sweetest. All martyrdom operations, if done for Allah's sake, hurt less than a gnat's bite. (Hassan, 2001: 36–37)

Hafez summarizes the ritual and therefore sacred nature of martyrdom operations thus:

> Ritual and ceremony permeate all aspects of suicidal violence. The videotape to record the last will and testament of the bomber and solidify his or her commitment to martyrdom; the head band and banners emblazoned with Qur'anic verses to decorate the "living martyrs" quarters before they declare their intention to go on a "martyrdom" mission; the guns and bombs that serve as props for their last photos to symbolize empowered individuals making a free choice to self-sacrifice for the cause; the mass procession to commemorate the death of the "martyr"; the mourning ceremony where the women ululate and distribute candy to celebrate the martyr's entry into heaven, and men receive congratulatory handshakes because their sons or daughters achieved eternal salvation; the posters on the wall and electronic links on a website to immortalize the bombers; all these actions are undertaken repeatedly, routinely, and with procedural rigor. Martyrdom rituals elevate jihad and self-sacrifice into something higher

than core beliefs of the faith; they turn them into *performative* traditions and *redemptive* actions through which the faithful express their devotion. (Hafez, 2006a: 177, emphasis in original)

Such ritualizing of bloody deeds is far from unique to Islam. For example, a similar use of religious worship in the service of murder was carried out by the Reverend Paul Hill, who shot to death a physician and his bodyguard in front of a women's health clinic in Florida in 1994 and was later tried and convicted of capital murder and then executed in Florida in 2003 (for a discussion of possible psychological factors behind Hill's action, see Beier, 2006). After deciding to kill a doctor, Hill reports feeling sadness at the thought of separation from his family as the result of probably going to prison (he expresses no sadness for the families of the physician and the bodyguard whom he had vowed to kill and who would be permanently separated from their family member). In the face of this sadness, Hill turns to worship and prayer to steel his resolve to carry through his deadly vow. Writing to his co-religionists, Hill says that whenever he had doubts about his decision to kill, "As I lifted my heart and eyes upward, I was reminded of God's promise to bless Abraham and grant him descendents as numerous as the stars in the sky. I claimed that promise as my own and rejoiced with all my might, lest my eyes become clouded with tears and they betray me" (Hill, 1997: 3). The morning of the killing, Hill wrote, "I forced myself to rise about 4 A.M. to spend time in prayer and Bible reading. The strength I needed for the day was found in Psalm 91 "Do not be afraid of the terror by night, or of the arrow that flies by day. . . . For you have made the Lord, my [*sic*] refuge, even the Most High, your dwelling place" (4).

Shortly thereafter a physician and his guard lay dead on the Florida sidewalk. From prison, Hill wrote his fellow believers in a style that emulates the letters of Saint Paul. Hill begins with a salutation that follows the New Testament form, writing, "To my friends and all the saints . . . Greetings in the name of our savior. I trust the Lord is blessing and ministering to each of you. To know Him is to know the way, the truth, and the life. The Lord has been sustaining me in a wonderful way through your prayers" (Hill, 1997: 1). And Eric Rudolph, Hill's co-religionist serving a life term for killing an abortion provider, ends his statement with "And as I go to a prison cell for a lifetime, I know that I have fought a good fight, I have finished my course. I have kept the faith" (Rudolph, 2005: 6). Anyone familiar with the New Testament will see the obvious similarities here. Hill and Rudolph are using a traditional

Christian epistolary form. Perhaps they feel they are writing sacred texts when explaining why they killed the doctors and others.

The use of all these traditional religious and ritual forms underscores the religious nature of these acts of terror. One of the perpetrators of the first bombing of the World Trade Center is reported to have told a journalist that secular Americans will never understand why he did what he did because they miss "The soul of religion" (quoted in Juergensmeyer, 2000: 69). The 9/11 attacks were not a political act; they were a religious act. So the psychology involved here is the psychology of religion. While humiliation and relative deprivation clearly play a part in much of the terrorism in the Middle East, the usual sociological variables—poverty, lack of education, and so on—often appear to play little role and have little predictive value. One of the best predictors is religiosity. The Singapore Parliamentary report on captured members of terrorist cells in Southeast Asia emphasizes this: "These men were not ignorant, destitute, or disenfranchised. All 31 men had received secular education . . . they held normal, respectable jobs. . . . As a group, most of the detainees regarded religion as their most important personal value" (quoted in Atran, 2003a:1537).

This linkage of holiness and purification with death is found in many examples of religiously sponsored violence beyond Islam. Purification was central to Asahara's message virtually from the beginning; his techniques were supposed to enable a person to rid themselves of bad karma and other impurities. Themes of purity and purification are central in Japanese Shinto, and thus were surely present in Asahara's consciousness and that of his disciples. But such themes are present in some form in virtually every religion. They are not in the least unique to Shinto, Aum, or violent religious groups. Religious language that is saturated with violence is central in American apocalyptic Christianity and the sermons of the jihadists. Psychologically it is not the themes of sanctification or purification that are at issue. Rather, it is their linkage with violence and death that is at issue in the psychology of religiously motivated terrorism.

Because the human bombers (and the members of Aum Shinrikyo) are offering a religious sacrifice, Strenski (2003) argues, their actions are not primarily motivated by "a utilitarian or pragmatic calculus" (26). This point was recently made in a lecture by Scott Atran (2006c) as well. Likewise, Juergensmeyer (2000) concludes that most religiously motivated terrorist acts are "not done to achieve a strategic goal but to make a symbolic statement" (123). One important and perhaps unhappy practical conclusion of this, I suggest, is that it is a mistake to seek to understand religiously motivated terrorists using the game theoretic or rational choice models so prominent in the social sciences these days (for relevant reviews, see Moghaddam & Marsella, 2004; Victoroff, 2005). Rational choice models cannot really comprehend sacred values that are deeply held for noninstrumental reasons (Atran, 2006b, 2006c). Such values are not open to the instrumental calculus of statistically based social sciences. Social scientists trained only in these methodologies, and the policymakers they advise, may have only a limited understanding of religiously motivated terrorism.

In addition, given the sacred nature of these acts, counter-terrorism policies based on either appealing to the religiously motivated terrorists' self-interest or frightening them into surrendering by an overwhelming show of force will probably have little success. The religious drive to sacrifice and make one's life and one's cause holy transcends and subsumes any pragmatic or purely self-interested motivations. Identifying themselves as engaged in religious acts of sacrifice and understanding the West's orientation away from the spiritual and toward the pragmatic are two of the reasons that militant Islamicists repeatedly insist that the secular West will never understand them.[5]

The ritualized nature of many of these violent actions points to another element in religiously motivated terrorism—what Juergensmeyer calls their "symbolic nature" and Stern (2006) calls "terrorism as theater." Again, this ritualism underscores the sense in which these are symbolic, not primarily strategic, actions. Not only do religious rituals (purifications, prayers, scripture readings, etc.) surround these deeds, the deeds of terror themselves are ritualized. The targets chosen are not random or simply targets of convenience, nor are they necessarily of high strategic or military value. But they are highly symbolic both in terms of what they represent and in terms of the numbers who can be killed. The World Trade Towers and the Pentagon were clearly symbolic of American economic and military hegemony. Wounding or even destroying them would have little lasting impact of the actual conduct of the global economy or the American military, both of which are highly dispersed and have many organizational redundancies. But wounding or destroying them has tremendous symbolic value. Likewise with the federal building in Oakalhoma City, the London and Tokyo public transportation systems, international airline flights, and the mosque at the Dome of the Rock in Jerusalem. Bombing such targets does not bring the federal government to its knees, does not halt commerce and community in London or Tokyo, does not end the practice of Islam. But these acts have tremendous symbolic significance that creates profound emotional distress and dislocation in the people affected. The symbolic and ritualized nature of many of these deeds also connects them to their foundation in religion.

What sort of God is it that demands sacrifice as the means of purification? Most often it is an angry, punitive God. Here the psychologist of religion can contribute to the discussion by pointing to some of the correlates of such an image of God. There is research that suggests, at least for religiously committed populations, that punitive and wrathful images of God are associated with external locus of control, anxiety and depression, lack of empathy, and less mature interpersonal relations (Brokaw & Edwards, 1994; Spear, 1994; Tisdale, 1997). The reverse has also been found to be true: a more benevolent internal representation of God is associated with more mature psychological development and the capacity for more mature relationships. Thus it makes theoretical as well as empirical sense that a person who envisions God as wrathful and punitive would also be more inclined toward a rigid dichotomizing of the world and less capacity for empathy—traits that appear to characterize many religiously motivated terrorists.

THE DESIRE FOR UNION

Virtually every report on militant Muslims stresses the reward of entering paradise as a major motivator for their actions (Davis, 2005; Hassan, 2001, Post et al., 2003). Hafez (2000) emphasizes "religious redemption" as one of the primary enticements to undertake suicide bombing (6). In western accounts, often this is accompanied by descriptions of scores of beautiful virgins waiting to welcome the adolescent male martyr home, even though most traditional Islamic scholars insist that the delights of paradise are not erotic. But clearly the desire to be with God is a powerful motivation at work here. Hafez (2006a) underscores this when he points out the importance of reward in the afterlife:

> Kamal Abdelnasser Rajab, an Islamic Jihad suicide bomber, cites the following Prophetic tradition in his last will and testament: "In heaven, God has prepared 100 ranks for those holy fighters that fight in His path. The difference between one level and another is akin to the difference between heaven and earth." He goes on to declare: "O' father and mother, dearest

to my heart; O' brothers, sisters, and friends, life near God is the best of lives and better than life itself." (176)

Another human bomber wrote to his mother and father in his last will and testament: "I wanted to beat you to heaven so I can intercede with my God on your behalf" (Hafez, 2006a: 176).

A Palestinian militant, when asked about his motivation, replied, "the power of the spirit pulls us upward" (Hassan, 2001: 37). Atta told his fellow hijackers: "You should feel complete tranquility, because the time between you and your marriage [in heaven] is very short. Afterward begins the happy life, where God is satisfied with you and eternal bliss" (Atta, n.d.). A Palestinian recruiter said of his methods of recruitment, "we focus his attention on Paradise, on being in the presence of Allah, on meeting the Prophet Muhammad, on interceding for his loved ones so that they too can be saved from the agonies of Hell" (Hassan, 2001: 40). A Palestinian arrested by the Palestinian Authority before he could carry out his mission said of paradise, "It is very, very near—right in front of our eyes. It lies beneath the thumb. On the other side of the detonator" (Hassan, 2001: 40).

Clearly this is not unique to fanatical religions. Quite the reverse. The desire for an experience of union with a transcendental or divine reality appears foundational in virtually every religion: it may be union with the universal, nameless primal source of the Upanishads, Neo-Platonic Christian mysticism, and much Mahayana Buddhism; or with the personally beloved Other of devotional Hinduism, pietistic Christianity, and Tibetan guru yoga; or with the divine Creator of traditional Judaism, Christianity, and Islam. This desire for spiritual union may well be the beating heart of every living religion.

What is unique to fanatical religions is the linkage of this desire for spiritual union with violence, especially the violence of sacrificial killing or apocalyptic purification. It may be this linkage of an almost universal and powerful spiritual desire with the themes of blood sacrifice and purification through violence that turns spiritual longing into terrorist action.

How does this happen? As suggested earlier, the process appears to be connected to the image of God that is at work here—the image of a vengeful and punitive and overpowering patriarchal divine being. The believer must find a way to relate to an omnipotent being who appears to will the world's destruction. The believer must humiliate himself before this demanding figure, feeling himself profoundly worthless and deeply guilty. And the punitive, omnipotent being must be appeased, placated. A blood sacrifice must be offered. So we return again to the combination of a wrathful, punitive image of God, the insistence on purification at any cost, and the theme of blood sacrifice. In chapter 5, I examine some of the psychological dynamics involved in such a religious vision. The wish for a bloody, apocalyptic day of reckoning and acts of religiously motivated terrorism are not simply reactions against modernity (as stressed by Armstrong, 2001; Lawrence, 1989). While that antimodern sentiment may play a role, these groups are a potent force in their own right (and not just a reaction to modernity), driven by their need to purify the world.

SANCTIFYING VIOLENCE

Another way in which religion promotes terrorism and genocide is by directly sanctioning violence and killing and by providing a moral justification for terrorists' actions done in the name of God. Hafez (2006b) emphasizes this role for religion in his studies of the Palestinian human bombs, pointing out that they

> are religiously devout and their communiqués are replete with religious references to motivate self-sacrifice. Suicide bombers are often videotaped before an operation imploring their brothers to abandon their commitment to this ephemeral world and seek the eternal afterlife through self-sacrifice. Religious rituals and ceremonies also amplify the rewards of martyrdom to entice the faithful to take the leap toward a violent death. (5)

A team of psychologists who interviewed incarcerated Palestinian militants reported that "their acts were in defense of their faith and commanded by their faith, and they received religious absolution for the acts" (Post et al., 2003: 175). One said, "a martyrdom operation is the highest level of jihad, and highlights the depth of our faith. The bombers are holy fighters who carry out one of the most important articles of faith" (179). Another reported that "major [martyrdom] actions became the subject of sermons in the mosque, glorifying the attack and the attackers" (178). And another said simply, "those who carry out the attacks are doing Allah's work" (179). A graffito in Gaza reads "Death in the way of Allah is life" (photo in Atran, 2003a: 1536). This, too, is not unique to Islam. A Christian clergyman in the United States uses biblical and theological arguments to justify killing physicians at reproductive health clinics in a book titled *A Time to Kill*—a title that says it all (Bray, 1994). And as noted previously, one of the killers influenced by this book reports that, on the way to commit the murder, he opened his Bible and found a verse in the Psalms that he interpreted as justifying his actions (Hill, 1997; see also Juergensmeyer, 2000: 23).

Religions, however, do not simply justify violence the way other ideologies do. For religiously motivated terrorists, violence takes on a sacred purpose. Violence and genocide can become religious imperatives, carrying a cosmic or spiritual meaning beyond that provided by any political or legal authority. This inevitably leads to a significant reduction in the usual restrictions on the deployment of violence, opening up the possibility of full-scale, unrestricted genocidal campaigns with weapons of mass destruction. While all religions also have teachings and moral strictures designed precisely to restrain, if not eliminate, violent behavior (e.g., the "just war" traditions in Judaism and Christianity), such moral reasoning finds no place in the writings and theologies of religiously motivated terrorists. Hoffman (2006) writes,

> The reason that terrorist incidents perpetuated for religious motives result in so many more deaths may be found in the radically different value system, mechanisms of legitimation and justification, concepts of morality, and worldviews embraced by the religious terrorist and his secular counterpart. For the religious terrorist, violence is first and foremost a sacramental act or divine duty executed in direct response to some theological demand or imperative. Terrorism thus assumes a transcendental dimension, and its perpetrators therefore often disregard the political, moral, or practical constraints that may affect other terrorists . . . Religious terrorists often seek the elimination of broadly defined categories of enemies and accordingly regard such large-scale violence not only as morally justified but as necessary expedients for the attainment of their goals. (88)

Along this line, Abu Musab al-Zarqawi, al-Qaeda's chief of operations in Iraq, proclaims one of al-Qaeda's basic doctrines:

> Allah commanded us to strike the Kuffar (unbelievers), kill them, and fight them by any means necessary to achieve the goal. The servants of Allah who perform jihad to elevate the word (laws) of Allah, are permitted to use any and all means necessary to strike the active unbeliever combatants for the purpose of killing them, snatch their souls from their body, cleanse

the earth from their abomination, and lift their trial and persecution of the servants of Allah. The goal must be pursued even if the means to accomplish it affect both the intended active fighters and unintended passive ones such as women, children. . . . This permissibility extends to situations in which Muslims may get killed if they happen to be with or near the intended enemy. . . . Although spilling Muslim blood is a grave offense, it is not only permissible but it is mandated in order to prevent more serious adversity from happening, stalling or abandoning jihad. (quoted in Hoffman, 2006: 240)

Continuing jihad takes precedence over any other moral or theological imperative, including the traditional prohibitions against killing fellow Muslims and innocent noncombatants. For al-Qaeda, jihad means total, all-out, unrestricted warfare. We find exactly the same position modeled in the writings of American apocalyptic Christians and the *Left Behind* (LaHaye & Jenkins, 1995, 2004) series of novels. This mixing of religion and violence in combination with the increasing sophistication and lethality of modern technologies of killing result in contemporary terrorism's increasingly deadly results. This transcendental legitimation of killing is another way in which religions create and maintain a culture of violence out of which terrorism and genocide can easily emerge.

PROMOTING PREJUDICE AND AUTHORITARIANISM

Empirical research has found strong correlations between certain types of religion and measures of authoritarianism, which involve such traits such as submission to authority, aggressiveness and hostility, conventionality, and closed-mindedness (a good review is found in Wulff, 1991). Social psychologists have used four kinds of measures to investigate possible connections between religion, authoritarianism, and prejudice: measures of orthodox belief; measures of prejudices like racism, homophobia, and anti-Semitism; measures of the strength of the belief that one's religion is the only true religion; and what researchers call "right-wing authoritarianism," which consists of (1) authoritarian submission—the submission to external authorities and the demand for submission from others; (2) aggressiveness—support for very punitive measures in law enforcement and child rearing; and (3) conventionalism—a rigid adherence to conventional norms and expectations and hostility toward those who deviate from them (Altemeyer & Hunsberger, 2005).

All these measures tend to be very highly intercorrelated. Religious people in general tend to be more prejudiced, for example (Wulff, 1991: 219–221). But, if one looks more closely, one finds that three of these measures—right-wing authoritarianism, belief that one's religion is the only true religion, and various prejudices—tend to be tightly connected, whereas a fourth, orthodox belief and practice, is much less so. Orthodox belief and practice by itself is not particularly correlated with prejudice. This suggests two things. First, orthodoxy is not the same as fundamentalism or fanaticism. Nonfanatical religions, no matter how traditional they are in their beliefs and practices, do not demand authoritarian submission, are open to dialogue with other points of view, and are less prejudiced than North American society as a whole. Second, this research suggests that the association between religion and prejudice is mediated by right-wing authoritarianism. Authoritarian tendencies connect religion and prejudice. Religion by itself does not necessarily promote authoritarianism and prejudice. Only when combined with an authoritarian outlook on life does religion result in the kind of fanaticism that gives rise to terrorism and genocide (Altemeyer & Hunsberger, 1992).

People prone to authoritarianism tend to grow up in homes that were prejudiced against others and that were authoritarian in child-rearing practices and were self-righteous in attitude. According to one report,

> Certain types of religious training appear to promote right-wing authoritarianism. [Such people report] that their religious training taught them to submit to authority more, led them to be more hostile toward "outsiders" and "sinners," and imposed stricter rules about "proper behavior," than do less authoritarian persons. . . . So authoritarianism and certain types of religiosity appear to promote and sustain one another. (Altemeyer & Hunsberger, 1992: 115)

Summing up these studies of religious attitudes, Wulff writes in reference to certain rigid and controlling forms of religion that "researchers have consistently found positive correlations with ethnocentrism, authoritarianism, dogmatism, social distance, rigidity, intolerance of ambiguity, and specific forms of prejudice, especially against Jews and blacks" (Wulff, 1991: 219–220).

A BORN AGAIN MOVEMENT

Recent research suggests that most current jihadists are living in the Muslim diaspora and were not raised in strongly traditional Islamic families but rather are converts to this militant brand of Islam—"born again" in Scott Atran's words (2005b; see also Khosrokhavar, 2005). Members of Aum Shinrikyo and many of the extreme right-wing Christians interviewed by Stern were converts to those movements also. Since William James, the study of conversion has been a central theme in the psychology of religion (for reviews, see Hood, Spilka, Hunsberger & Gorsuch, 1996; Rambo, 1993). Like religion and terrorism, conversion is a complex, multidimensional phenomenon so "no one process of conversion applies to all conversion motifs" (Hood et al.,1996: 268)—once again we are in the realm of the multidetermined and the multidisciplinary.

Research confirms that conversion experiences can be powerfully transformative and produce lasting results in the lives of individuals (Paloutzian, 2005; Rambo, 1993). The question is, what kind of change is it? Not a total personality change. Basic personality traits, characters, and personality styles (as measured by standard personality inventories) do not change that much even in the most dramatic of conversion experiences—St. Paul remained a Pharisee in outlook even after he became a Christian. What does change, according to current research, is a person's goals, values, attitudes, long-range plans, and behaviors (Paloutzian, 2005). The content of these changes and how extensive or radical they are depends on the interaction of several factors: the person's cognitive style, especially whether it is more open or more closed (Batson, Schoenrade & Ventis, 1993; Paloutzian, 2005); the group context (Galanter, 1989); and the larger social context (Rambo, 1993). Research has found that while conversions can happen at any point in the life cycle, conversions in adolescence and early adulthood are most frequent (Hood et al., 1996). Current studies show that conversions need not necessarily be sudden, spontaneous, or dramatic in order to produce major changes in a person's life (Hood et al., 1996; Rambo, 1993).

All research on conversion, regardless of methodology, finds that there is virtually always some antecedent or precipitating stress, crisis, social influence, or other event. Paloutzian (2005) summarizes this common research finding: "A key element in any conversion or transformation process must be some element of doubt, pressure, or motivation to change: there is no reason to change one's belief system or worldview if one has no doubts whatsoever about them or if circumstances have not confronted the person's religious beliefs or practices sufficient for them to be called into question" (336). Certainly this has been my experience as a clinician dealing with religious patients. Even those conversions that on the surface appear most spontaneous, when they are examined in a careful interview, always have some antecedent event or process leading up to them. Often an encounter with another person or persons (whom Rambo [1993] refers to as "the advocate") is a significant factor in that process. "Much of the literature has documented the importance of social networks in facilitating conversions, especially among non-communal religions . . . the vast majority (from 59% to 82%) of Pentecostals, evangelicals, and Nichiren Shoshu Buddhists . . . were recruited through social networks" (Hood et al., 1996: 289). This is striking in light of the current research into contemporary jihadists that also emphasizes the centrality of social networks in the growth of the jihadist movement.

Most studies find that converts are better off psychologically for having undergone a conversion experience. In the words of one review of the literature, "conversion and intense religious experiences can be therapeutic with respect to a variety of symptoms" (Bergin, 1991: 401; see also Galanter, 1989). Also, most conversions are self-initiated and the end result of a spiritual search or struggle that the individual voluntarily undertakes (Hood et al., 1996; Rambo, 1993). Most conversions are not the result of brainwashing or coercion, even if they lead the individual to join an authoritarian group. The same appears true of those Muslims living in the diaspora who find their way to radical mosques or to jihadist websites on the Internet.

A new identity is one of the most universal results of the conversion process. Conversion experiences often serve as the solution to an identity crisis (Rambo, 1993). That is one of the reasons they most commonly occur during adolescence and early adulthood when issues of identity predominate. In the anomie of our postmodern, global society with its smorgasbord of options and lifestyles (Giddens, 2000), a religious conversion provides clear norms, a prefabricated answer to the postmodern dilemma of "who am I," and a sense of rootedness in a timeless tradition that transcends and feels more substantial than the ever-shifting kaleidoscope of contemporary communities of reference. Thus it has particular appeal to the young Muslim men in the immigrant communities of Europe (Khosrokhavar, 2005).

Based on interviews with jihadists around the world, Atran (2006b) speaks of them as "yearning for a sense of community and a deeper meaning in life" (135). These are the same desires that motivated young Japanese to join Aum Shinrikyo and that motivate religious converts around the world, whether it is contemporary American intellectuals embracing Buddhism or a New Age spirituality, suburbanites joining far-right mega-churches (Hedges, 2006), or students in the 1960s flocking to cults (Galanter, 1998). Interviews with and statements by jihadists make it clear that the lure of jihad is not simply the lure of revenge or rage but rather the lure of spiritual renewal, moral seriousness, and a meaningful life (Atran, 2006b; Stern, 2003). Of course, this is not an either-or situation: both religious motivations and social–political grievances can, and often do, coexist (e.g., see the interviews in Juergensmeyer, 2000; Stern, 2003). If we do not understand the spirituality that motivates the jihadists and the power of religious conversions to reorient and give meaning to people's lives, we will never counter them effectively. If part of the attraction of jihad is the attraction of personal transformation and spiritual renewal, then a crucial part of our response must be the articulation of an equally powerful alternative religious and moral vision (a point I return to in the last chapter).[6]

SUMMARY

The examples of Muslim jihadists and terrorists in other traditions as well show us that religions give rise to terrorist actions when they emphasize shame and humiliation, when they dichotomize the world into warring camps of the all-good against the all-evil, when they demonize those with whom they disagree and foment crusades against them, when they advocate violence and blood sacrifice as the primary means of purification, when their devotees seek to placate or be unified with a punitive and humiliating idealized figure or institution, when they offer theological justifications for violent acts, and when they promote prejudice and authoritarian behavior. These are some of the means by which religion makes people violent.

For the clinical psychologist of religion, then, the question is, what psychological processes are involved when religion leads to violence? My answer is that universal religious themes such as purification or the search for reunion with the source of life or the longing for personal meaning and transformation—the classic instigators of spiritual search and religious conversion—become subsumed into destructive psychological motivations such as a Manichean dichotomizing of the world into all-good, all-evil camps, or the drive to connect with and appease a humiliating or persecuting idealized patriarchal Other. The result is the psychological preconditions for religiously sponsored terrorism and violence. There are thus some general factors that might serve as warning signs that a religious group has a high potential for violence: (1) profound experiences of shame and humiliation either generated by social conditions outside the group and potentiated by it or generated from within the group, (2) splitting humanity into all-good and all-evil camps and the demonizing of the other, (3) a wrathful, punitive idealized deity or leader, (4) a conviction that purification requires the shedding of blood, and often (5) a fascination with violence.

Next I want to examine in depth two more examples of this linkage of religion and violence, coming out of two very different religious traditions: Aum Shinrikyo with its roots in Buddhism and apocalyptic Christianity in the United States as portrayed in the wildly popular *Left Behind* series of Christian novels. Then I will turn to a more detailed discussion of the psychological processes by which religion gives rise to violence, terrorism, and genocide.

CHAPTER 3

AUM SHINRIKYO

Violence and Terrorism in Japanese Buddhism

IN THE EARLY SPRING OF 1995, WITHOUT ANY WARNING, deadly sarin nerve gas was released into the Tokyo subway system. Twelve people died and 3,796 were injured. The perpetrators were all leaders of Aum Shinrikyo, one of Japan's many new religious movements. Led by a partially blind guru named Shoko Asahara, in the 1990s the group had members of all ages and from all strata of Japanese society and had opened centers in Europe and the United States as well as throughout Japan. The group's roots were in Japanese and Tibetan Buddhism, and most of its main teachings and spiritual practices were derived from Asahara's interpretation of Buddhism. During the early 1990s the teachings of Asahara and the leadership circle grew increasingly violent. But it was not always so.[1]

Aum began as a yoga center in 1984. The focus at that time appears to have been on spiritual discipline and training to develop psychic powers. Aum seems to have primarily attracted Japanese youth looking for spiritual renewal. That primary motive comes through virtually all the interviews recorded by Lifton (2000) and Reader (2000), as from an interview conducted by Juergensmeyer (2000: chapter 6). Even after the sarin gas attack, there were many members whose primary focus and motivation was spiritual discipline and not guru worship (Maekawa, 2001; Reader, 2000), a point often overlooked by those who make guru worship a primary interpretative category (e.g., Lifton and Kimball). Such devotees often remained in Aum even after the sarin gas attack because of the transforming spiritual experiences they had there (Maekawa, 2001). A young man who remained with Aum after the group's criminal activity came to light said, "I experienced things myself and knew that Aum was the real thing. Many others had also such experiences, so it had to be the truth. So now I continue to practice Aum with peace of mind" (Maekawa, 2001: 207). Another member in similar circumstances said, "What one can most depend on is one's own experience. . . . It is only what one has personally experienced that one can never deny no matter what" (Maekawa, 2001: 207). This central focus on personal, transforming experience was hardly unique to Aum; it was the major emphasis in virtually every new religious movement and New Age group in Japan and North America started at that time.

Another early Aum theme was holistic medicine. A statement called "Toward Future Medicine," from an Aum publication, reads:

> In addition to utilizing techniques culled from the frontiers of Western medicine, they [Aum's researchers] are researching the essence of various practices, such as Oriental medicine (acupuncture, herbs) Tibetan medicine, Ayruveda (ancient Indian medicine), and yoga. We have been placing particular emphasis on preventive care and improvement of one's constitution, which modern medicine has tended to neglect. In combination with the above, methods like astral medicine (derived from the astral world, a higher dimension) and holy empowerment by spiritual achievers (energy transfer) have yielded splendid results in curing fatal and rare diseases, imparting superhealth, and bettering mind and body. (Lifton, 2000: 139)

With hardly any changes in wording, this same statement can be found in the brochures and advertisements of countless New Age, holistic health, and yoga centers in operation across North America today.

Another often remarked upon characteristic of Aum is its religious syncretism, with a particular interest in the more esoteric religious traditions and practices. Like many New Age movements and teachers, Asahara felt free to roam through the religions of the world, mining them for any terms or practices that suited his personal vision. The sociological changes in communication, travel, and education that have uprooted the sacred texts of formerly unknown religions and brought them into corner bookstores throughout North America and Japan are beyond the scope of this book. But such changes meant that Asahara was hardly unique in this regard. Here too he can be paralleled with countless New

Age instructors and workshop leaders who currently fill what I call the "glossy brochure circuit" in North America and (I assume) Japan.

With its religious syncretism, concern with holistic healing and yoga, focus on immediate experience, psychospiritual discipline and the transformation of consciousness, at its beginning Aum was little if any different from any other new religious movement or New Age group at the time in Japan or North America. Most likely, the same things that attracted hordes of people to these groups also attracted people to Aum. This calls into question any attempt to pathologize the members of Aum. Reader (2000: chapter 4) emphasizes a sense of spiritual alienation or dissatisfaction on the part of converts; but I would refuse to call that a psychopathology. It is hard to maintain that all the people, of all social classes and educational levels, who were attracted to the New Age and new religious movements in North America and Japan were suffering from some diagnosable mental disorder. Psychopathology on the part of the members cannot be a convincing explanation of Aum's turn to violence (psychopathology on Asahara's part is a different story). This is in line with the research cited in earlier chapters that suggests that those who take part in terrorism and genocide are rarely mentally ill in any usual medical sense. Likewise, the members of Aum were probably no different psychologically from the members of other contemporary spiritual renewal groups. This also means that it would have been impossible to predict Aum's later turn toward violence from most of its history. Reader (2000) underscores this when he concludes,

> When Asahara Shoko first set up his yoga group in 1984, the group he established had not set its aims on causing mayhem or mass murder, and its interests appear to have been primarily located in yoga, spiritual development and the attainment of psychic powers. Even when, from around 1985, its leader began to have visions of a sacred mission, Aum's orientation remained optimistic and its incipient message of salvation affirmed spiritual transformation rather than the destruction and violence that became paramount in later Aum teachings and actions. (231)

Aum seems to have been relatively harmless until it came under suspicion. The humiliating loss of an election campaign, the increasing government surveillance, and the attacks in the media coincide with the increasing turn toward the apocalyptic (Kisala & Mullins, 2001). It's not at all clear how many in the lower ranks of membership actually shared Asahara's and the leadership's apocalyptic visions. Interviews with members after the subway attacks suggest that not all of the Aum members considered Asahara divine or enlightened. Most appear to have joined primarily for the spiritual training (Kisala & Mullins, 2001). Asahara appears to have become increasingly paranoid and grandiose and drew others in leadership into the circle of his vision. And, in some cases, members of the inner circle who would not be drawn in were either expelled or killed. While some commentators focus on psychopathology or alienation (Lifton, 2000), in response to these theories Professor Manabu Watanabe once asked me, "Would you consider all the young people interested in meditation, spiritual development, and holistic medicine to be pathological or alienated?"

For our purposes, it is most important to understand why a typical and relatively benign spiritual renewal group, indistinguishable from dozens of other such groups in Japan and the United States at the time, turned murderous. Shimazono (2001) traces several stages in Aum's religious history. At first, the goal was individual development and spiritual transformation. Later this was broadened to include the salvation of humanity through the establishment of the utopian kingdom of Shambhala. Here Aum displays a kind of religio-nationalistic syncretism by claiming that the traditional Tibetan kingdom of Shambhala is to come to earth in Japan. Aum claims that Japan therefore possess a cosmic mission to "bring happiness to the world" (331). This is another example of the religiously sponsored idealization and divinization of a nation or ethnic group found in many examples of religiously motivated terrorism. A 1988 Aum pamphlet states:

> There [in Shambhala] the world's saviors, whose goal it is to save all souls and lead them to *gedatsu* [release], progress in their own training. . . . This is why Aum Shinrikyo has developed a plan to transform Japan into Shambhala. This plan, unequaled in scope, will extend Aum's sacred sphere throughout the nation and foster the development of multitudes of holy people, making Japan the base for saving the entire world. . . . The plan to transform Japan into Shambhala is the first step toward transforming the entire world into Shambhala. (Shimazono, 2001: 33)

This plan was to begin with the construction of utopian communes called "Lotus Villages"—a kind of spiritual demonstration project.

> This means the construction of an Aum Village, so that everyone can live a life founded on truth. We will build a completely independent society, pro-

viding everything from food, clothing, and housing to places for religious practice, education, employment, medical treatment, weddings, and funerals. We will also establish facilities for creative research in medicine, science, and agriculture. (Shimazono, 2001: 33)

It is quite a jump from this idyllic utopian community bringing peace and happiness to the world to releasing nerve gas in towns and subways and murdering people. As Shimazono notes, "the desire to create a warm, tranquil community of believers formed part of Aum's plan for salvation, less than two years before the sect's turn toward apocalyptic thought" (Shimazono, 2001: 34). What changed?

Asahara's apocalyptic stream was already starting to flow slowly, in parallel to the optimistic vision of universal spiritual transformation and happiness. The same pamphlet that envisioned the creation of Shambhala also described Japan as a country in moral and spiritual decline (Shimazono, 2001: 33). And the legend of Shambhala itself is not all sweetness and light, for it too contains images of a climactic battle between good and evil. In 1985 Asahara had encountered prophecies of Armageddon centered in Japan (Shimazono, 2001: 32). And as early as 1987 Asahara was teaching his disciples his interpretations of Tibetan tantric teachings that allowed for and justified killing others, and even sacrificing oneself, for the sake of enlightenment (Watanabe, 1998: 84). But these teachings remained in the background. What brought them to the foreground?

Watanabe (1998) argues convincingly that "the year 1989 was a fateful one for Aum Shinrikyo, with major turning points" (87; Reader, 2000, supports such a conclusion). Watanabe lists several crucial events. Asahara published a commentary on the book of Revelation in the New Testament, which obviously contains apocalyptic themes. A disciple had died while engaged in one of the group's extreme spiritual practices. A friend of the dead man, Taguchi Shuji, upset at his death, spoke of leaving the group. When attempts to convince him to stay failed, Taguchi was strangled (so that the earlier death would not become known) and his body burned to cover up the murder. When the group found out that a television station was going to broadcast an interview with an attorney critical of the group who was threatening to sue them, they killed the attorney and his family. All these killings were motivated by the need to protect the reputation of the group, which is not a motivation unique to Aum or religious groups but one that can be found throughout the history of criminal organizations and politically revolutionary cells. Ironically, the same year Aum was recognized as a legitimate religious organization and entered politics. The next year Asahara and 24 members ran for election and all were roundly and embarrassingly defeated. More in the public eye, attacks on Aum in the media increased dramatically (Watanabe, 1998; see also Shimazono, 2001; Watanabe, n.d.: 35–40).

Needing to justify the murders brought to the fore Asahara's tantric doctrine of killing for the sake of enlightenment. Feeling increasingly threatened by hostile attacks from outside probably intensified the appeal of apocalyptic thinking. It is a common observation that apocalyptic visions of upcoming destruction increase when groups feel threatened. This combination made Aum withdraw more into itself, begin the production of mechanical and chemical weapons, and become more apocalyptic in its theology. At the same time, Shimazono reports, Aum was seeking to improve its public image and reach out to the media, which on one hand often brought the group a favorable response (Shimazono, 2001: 38–39). On the other hand, when the group tried to open offices in various locations, local residents vigorously opposed their presence. Apparently both trends—reaching out to the public and encountering opposition—continued in parallel until March 1995. Then, as Watanabe (1998) reports, "When he learned that the police were preparing to raid Aum facilities, Asahara decided to confuse the police by attacking the Tokyo subway system with sarin gas. In other words, this sarin attack was meant just to distract the police. On March 20, sarin was released on several Tokyo subway trains" (Watanabe, 1998: 92).

So what can we say psychologically about this complicated story? The argument that there was some obvious psychopathology in those attracted to Aum does not hold because there is no reason to think these people were any different from the thousands attracted to other New Age and new religious movements in Japan and America. Nor is it clear that the extreme devotion to the guru is really to blame. While the exaltation of the teacher to divine or semidivine status is virtually unheard of in indigenous North American religious groups (something like that might have happened in the case of David Koresh and the Branch Davidians, but it is rare in North American groups), it has a long history in Japan. Nichiren (1222–1292), founder of Nichiren Shoshu Buddhism of which Soka Gakkai is an offshoot, is described in *The Soka Gakkai News* as having "revealed the ultimate Buddhist teachings, to which his two predecessors Sakyamuni, or Gautama, and the Tendai sect in which Nichiren studied had aspired yet never realized in practice. . . . [He possesses] the secret, ultimate wisdom that all outstanding Buddhists since the time of Sakyamuni had acquired as part of final enlightenment, yet had never been able to expound" (quoted in Shupe, 1993: 232). Thus, Nichiren is described as being greater than Sakyamuni Buddha. And this parallels exactly what Aum writings said about Asahara. There is even an apocalyptic element in Nichiren's teaching that was taken over in Soka Gokkai. Shupe (1993) writes,

> This Nichiren came to be regarded as a Buddha. And not merely a Buddha, but instead the Buddha for our doomed age . . . when all other religions have become misguided or downright malevolent. It is clear that Nichiren the man believed that true faith was to vanish from the earth until the coming of the future (messianic) Maitreya Buddha. (232)

Despite these and other parallels to Aum and its intense militancy, Soka Gakkai never turned to violence or terrorism.

There are many other examples of the founders of new religious movements in Japan being divinized. The liturgy of one indigenous Japanese Christian movement addresses the deceased founder in prayer in the same breath as "Father, Son, and Holy Spirit" (Mullins, Shimazono & Swanson, 1993: 267). Many indigenous Japanese Christian groups read their founder's writings in their worship services alongside the New Testament, thus treating them as sacred texts. As many writers have pointed out, an extreme trust in a master or guru is an essential part of the spiritual practice of many sects of Buddhism. But none of these groups has turned to violence. And it seems that many people were attracted to Aum by the power of its spiritual practices, not the power of Asahara's personality. So guruism by itself, while clearly sometimes sponsoring various abuses, is not necessarily a cause of violence and terrorism.[2]

These explanations—members' psychopathology or extreme submission to a guru—although they may well be part of the picture, do not suffice to explain Aum's turn to violence. How well does Aum fit with the model I've proposed?

None of its original recruits came from politically or socially oppressed groups. They were not suffering the humiliation of occupation like the Palestinians or the Chechens. They may have felt socially marginal or humiliated in other ways, but there is no evidence of that. Reader's (2000: chapter 4) invocation of a spiritual alienation or dissatisfaction on the part of converts may point in that direction, but it is not clear. And I think Reader's description would fit most, if not all, spiritual seekers in Japan and North America. There are clearly reports of Asahara haranguing and humiliating his followers with extreme punishments and practices: hanging people upside down, immersing them in cold water, locking them in a small cell for days with speeches by the guru blaring at them, demanding thousands of prostrations and extremely long sitting meditation sessions, and exposing them to mind-altering drugs. Reader (2000: chapter 5) describes at length the culture of punishment and internally directed violence that developed in Aum in the late 1980s. Such potentially humiliating methods might well have stirred up intense aggressive feelings. However, it's not clear that extreme rage on the part of members was the cause of any of Aum's murders, including the sarin gas attack. Rather, it seems the murders were done to protect the sect from outside interference and that, likewise, the gas attack was supposed to divert police attention. It is possible that Asahara became an idealized and humiliating figure, in the way I described in chapter 2, in the minds of some of his disciples, but we cannot be sure.

Also, unlike the Palestinians and the Chechens, for example, whose humiliation is primarily the result of political occupation and repression, the members of Aum voluntarily chose to involve themselves in a group that practiced such harsh measures, believing that these methods would bring more profound spiritual transformations. Such a belief in the power of harsh disciplines to produce spiritual transformations is far from rare in the history of religions. It is not known whether the voluntary nature of these punishing and humiliating practices changes their psychological effect.

It is clear there was a strong and increasingly violent apocalyptic element in Asahara's later teaching. But it is not clear how important this element was at the beginning or what role it played in the founding of the group. Thus it may be not be right to compare Aum to apocalyptic Christian and Jewish groups, where the apocalyptic theme has been central to the meaning-system of the group from the beginning. Nor is it clear what is cause and what is effect in the case of Aum. Shimazono (2001) and Watanabe (1998) suggest that the apocalyptic element did not come strongly into play until after Aum felt threatened by the larger society, a conclusion Reader (2000) also endorses. It is common to argue that apocalypticism arises in groups that feel their existence is threatened. But then it is hard to argue that apocalypticism is a cause. Rather, it seems more like a symptom of the group's feeling threatened—a feeling that may be justified if the group has committed kidnapping and murder or is under the thumb of an occupying power. Reader (2000: 218) has reversed his earlier (1996: 93) conclusion, that the sarin attack was an attempt to enact an apocalyptic scenario. Earlier Reader (1996) wrote:

> Quite simply, once the prophecies had been made, and their truth proclaimed, once Armageddon had been seen coming *without fail*, and once Asahara had made it clear not just that the cataclysm could not be prevented, but that in fact it was a necessary event to rid the world of its ills and to allow a true and ideal new world to emerge, then it had to occur for Asahara's and Aum's sake. . . . The cataclysm prophesied thus had to occur, or if not, then at least some fairly dramatic events had to happen to show that what he had been saying was on target, to reinforce his authority as a spiritual leader, and to verify the attainment of his disciples. (93, emphasis in original)

Wessinger (2000) asserted that,

> According to his own teachings, the Buddha Asahara could not err in his prophecies. If Asahara's predictions proved false, then the whole Aum Shinrikyo edifice would crumble. The necessity for Armageddon to arrive as predicted led to the decision within Asahara's inner circle to develop weapons to create Armageddon. . . . The decision to create weapons of mass destruction to orchestrate Armageddon was to fulfill Asahara's prophecies and achieve the millennial goal of establishing Shambhala. (143, 148)

But Reader (2000) now concludes:

> Although Asahara willed some form of massive destruction, there is little evidence of a coordinated or coherent plan of such a sort. Nor were there any indications that the subway attack was part of a strategy to spread turmoil so as to make it appear that Asahara's prophecies were coming true, or in order to precipitate the final war and the millennial scenario that was, in his prophetic view, inevitable. (218)

So Reader, like Watanabe (1998), concludes that Aum's murderous actions were "all *ad hoc* and reactive outbursts . . . carried out in order to prevent something from happening, and were responses with punitive dimensions to specific situations" (Reader, 2000: 218). Reader's in-depth interviews clearly portray followers who were drawn to Aum because of its spiritual mission and who were disinterested in Asahara's apocalyptic message. So, contrary to Lifton's (2000) argument (and that of Wessinger [2000]), apocalypticism does not appear to be a major cause of Aum's crimes.[3]

There was clearly a demonizing of the larger society and a feeling that society was in decline and decay. But it is hard to maintain that these Japanese students were prejudiced against the larger society in the way described in the literature of authoritarianism. There is no evidence that Aum's terrorism was the result of the kind of demonizing hatred that motivated the killing of Theo van Gogh in the Netherlands by a Muslin fanatic, especially if the crimes were done primarily to protect the sect or divert the police. But Aum's official proclamations and the published interviews with Aum members reveal a very strong element of splitting the world into all-good and all-corrupt and evil camps. This rigid polarizing of experience is one area where Aum clearly fits my model of the psychological processes involved in violent religions. This aspect of the apocalyptic psychology may well be an important ingredient in religiously motivated violence. But the apocalyptic teaching may be less a cause in this regard than is the underlying psychological tendency to polarize the world and demonize the other.

Asahara's doctrine of killing the person to save them (called *poa*) clearly provides the kind of sanctification and justification of killing that we have seen in every case of religiously sponsored terrorism. In addition, this doctrine supports a failure of empathy and an inability to empathize with victims in a way that can easily promote their social death and, like the results of Milgram's experiments (chapter 1), increase the possibility of blind obedience. Many of Aum's remaining members do indeed express an astonishing lack of empathy for their victims. The most extreme is the Aum member who responded to Reader's mention of the subway attack with "Wonderful, wasn't it?" because of the attention it brought to Aum (Reader, 2000: 222; see Maekawa, 2001, for many more examples of this lack of empathy for the victims).

Shimazono (2001), to some extent, and Watanabe (1998), more strongly, lay much of the blame for Aum's crimes on Asahara's doctrine of *poa*. And we have seen that the idea of sacrifice (either of oneself or others), leading to sanctification, which is also found in the history of the Mormon religion in America, is central in much religiously sponsored terrorism.

This claim of Asahara's that there is a Buddhist tradition of compassionate killing, while universally condemned by those who write about Aum, is actually not far from the truth. While Buddhism is almost universally understood in the West to be a religion of pacifism and nonviolence, the actual history of Buddhism (as with every world religion) is much more complex. There is a common simile in Buddhism comparing the bodhisattva to a physician who amputates a finger bitten by a poisonous snake, suggesting that physical violence in the service of a greater good can be justified. There is the story in which Sakyamuni, in an earlier lifetime, kills several Brahmin priests who would have spoken against the Buddhadharma and so acquired worse karmic repercussions (Maher, 2006). Aryadeva, who together his master Nagarjuna, is credited with the founding of the Madhyamika or "Middle Way" tradition in the second or third century, which became the central tradition of Mahayana Buddhism (Williams, 1989: 55), affirms in no uncertain terms that intention makes an act meritorious or not: "because of their intention both the bad . . . and the good . . . become auspicious for the bodhisattva" (Jenkins, 2006).

Asanga, one of the founders of the "mind only" philosophy in Buddhism, said that "any act is possible including sex, killing and robbery with the aim of helping beings . . . and that should a bodhisattva take life in this way there is no fault, but a spread of much merit" (Jenkins, 2006). Asanga suggests that by killing him before he commits serious crimes, the bodhisattva is saving his victim from worse karma and producing merit for both of them. Jenkins cites other texts that say that "if one's motivation is pure, it is possible to kill someone who is persecuting Buddhists or deriding the Mahayana without incurring karmic retribution" and that "even if a bodhisattva in his superior wisdom and skillful means should commit ten sinful acts of murder . . . he would nevertheless remain unsullied and guiltless, gaining instead immeasurable merits" (Jenkins, 2006). The so-called sutra of skillful means tells the story (which exists in several forms in the Buddhist literature) of the Buddha in an earlier life killing a man to prevent that man from killing 500 others and so being reborn in the lowest of hells. This act of compassionate killing resulted in much merit for the Buddha and a rebirth in heaven for the potential murderer (Jenkins, 2006; Williams, 1989: 145). The same sutra also describes how the Buddha allows a female ascetic to be killed so that her killers might suffer the karmic consequences and be reborn in hell (Jenkins, 2006). The point here is the same as that made by Asahara, that killing done with a compassionate intention or to reduce negative karmic consequences can be sanctioned in Buddhist tradition. Jenkins (2006) quotes a sutra that says "A King, who is well prepared for battle, having used skillful means in this way, even if he kills or wounds opposing troops, has little moral fault or demerit and there will certainly be no bad karmic result. Why is that? It is because the action was conjoined with intentions of compassion."

As an example of the royal use of these "skillful means," the Indian ruler Asoka, "the archetype of a Buddhist king" (Gethin, 1998: 100), who spread Buddhism throughout India, was hardly a nonviolent leader. He waged a bloody war of conquest against a province in eastern India, and contemporary scholars are convinced that this murderous campaign of conquest was *after* he converted to Buddhism (Jenkins, 2006; Tambiah, 1976). When a Jain pictured the Buddha worshipping a Jain guru, Asoka retaliated by killing 18,000 Jains. Learning of another sacrilege, he burnt a Jain family alive and then offered a royal bounty for the head of any Jain killed and brought to him. Concerned about the behavior of the forest people, Asoka threatened them with a military campaign, and his edicts make clear that torture and capital punishment were accepted practices in his kingdom (Strong, 1983; Tambiah, 1976). Asoka was not alone. There are Buddhist inscriptions in India that "glorify the bloody swords of widow-making Buddhist kings" (Jenkins, 2006).

In Tibet in the seventeenth century, the fifth Dalai Lama (Losang Gyatso, memorialized in Tibetan history as "The Great Fifth") wrote a history of Buddhist warfare in Tibet entitled *Song of the Queen of Spring* (all the references to this text are from Maher, 2006). In the ninth century, after three kings had patronized Buddhism, an anti-Buddhist king began to work against Buddhism and seek to return Tibet to its traditional re-ligious roots. In response, a Buddhist monk shot the king dead with an arrow and used his tantric powers to escape unharmed (see also Powers, 1995: 135). The fifth Dalai Lama approved of this murder in the name of compassion.

The fifth Dalai Lama himself was involved in a bloody military cam-paign that eventually brought him to power. For several decades before "The Great Fifth" came to power, two major schools of Tibetan Buddhism had been engaged in a sometimes violent struggle for power in Tibet (Powers, 1995: 144). The older Kagyu school was said to be persecuting the Geluk school to which the Dalai Lama belonged. In the early seven-teenth century there was open fighting in Lhasa, and Geluk partisans killed numerous Kagyu supporters. In a counterattack, two major Geluk monasteries were looted, and others were compelled by threats of force to switch allegiance to Kagyu practices. In response, the fifth Dalai Lama called on the help of the Mongolian army—the Mongolians had been converted to Buddhism in the prior century by previous Dalai Lamas and so were loyal Geluk partisans—which responded by invading Tibet in a large military campaign in which many monks, soldiers, and civilians were killed, the opponents of the Dalai Lama defeated, the remaining proponents of Tibet's indigenous religion imprisoned, and the fifth Dalai Lama brought to power and his hegemony firmly established, becoming the first in a series of religious rulers of Tibet (Powers, 1995: 144). Non-Geluk monasteries were seized, forcefully converted, and forbidden to teach their traditions, bequests were redirected toward Geluk centers, and the basic narrative structure of Tibetan Buddhism was changed to make the institution of the Dalai Lama central (Maher, 2006). In writing the *Song of the Queen of Spring*, the fifth Dalai Lama extols the Buddhist virtues of the Mongolian general whose bloody campaign brought the Dalai Lama to power, likening the bloody general to a bodhisattva and maybe even another Buddha. The Dalai Lama's message is that a righteous warrior can use sanctified violence to further the Buddhist cause.

In a similar way an ancient and traditional Sri Lankan Buddhist text tells of a military campaign against a Tamil king to further the cause of the dharma (Gethin, 1998: 101). This tradition continues in Sri Lanka to this day, with the Sri Lankan monks preaching and encouraging war against the Tamils in the name of the Buddhist cause (Kent, 2006). Such sermons often cite the army's responsibility to "preserve the integrity of the land," which clearly refers to opposing the Tamils or converting them the Buddhism. A rally for peace in Sri Lanka in 2006 was broken up by Buddhist monks (Kent, 2006).

An in-depth discussion of Buddhist ethics is outside the scope of this book. Nor is my point that, despite the Buddha's clear teachings on compassion and refraining from killing, Buddhism is really a militaristic religion. The least one can say on this point is that Buddhism's history is as ambiguous and complex as that of any other world religion. My point is that when Asahara argued there is a traditional teaching of compassionate killing and using any means possible for the reduction of karma, he was not entirely wrong.

The examples of the fifth Dalai Lama, Asoka, and the Sri Lankan sangha, the teaching of sutras like the *Sutra of Skillful Means*, and the writings of Asanga and others make it clear that the Buddhist tradition is not univocally one of absolute pacifism and undercut the common assertion that (in contrast with the Abrahamic religions) Buddhist kings and monks never used violence or warfare in the service of Buddhist conversions or sectarian causes. While extreme, Asahara was far from unique in the history of Buddhism when he supported the use of violence in the name of Buddhist ideals of compassion and peace.

Psychologically, why does such an extreme doctrine as *poa* take root in some people's minds? Is it primarily, as Shimazono (2001) and Lifton (2000) seem to imply, because of their extreme devotion to guru Asahara? Or is there a deeper, psychological reason that inclines people to accept the idea of sanctifying oneself (and others, too, in the case of *poa* and nineteenth-century American Mormonism) through death?

Once again we return to the psychodynamic linking of holiness and purification with death that is found in many examples of religiously sponsored violence. The theme of purification was central in Asahara's message virtually from the beginning; his techniques were supposed to enable a person to rid him- or herself of "bad karma" and other impurities. Themes of purity and purification are central in Japanese Shinto and thus were surely present in Asahara's consciousness and that of his disciples long before Aum began. But such themes are present in some form in virtually every religion. They are not in the least unique to Shinto, Aum, or violent religious groups. Again, psychologically it is not the themes of sanctification or purification that are at issue. Rather, it is their linkage with violence and death that is central in the psychology of religiously motivated terrorism. How did this come about in the case of Aum?

I have suggested that one way sanctification and death become linked is when the deity to be appeased by sacrifice is humiliating and punitive. But there was no transcendental deity in Aum. As Watanabe (n.d.) astutely points out, when Asahara had his vision anointing him with a messianic vocation, the result was not a religion of devotion to that god (as is usually the result in the history of religions), but rather a cult based on devotion to Asahara himself. So did Asahara himself serve as a humiliating but sacred Other that had to be appeased by abject submission and sacrificing oneself and others?

There is evidence that Asahara subjected many of his disciples to severe and humiliating disciplines: people were confined in tiny cells, were subject to beatings, dunkings in hot and cold water, and were kept isolated (Lifton, 2000; Reader, 2000). Of course, Tantric Buddhism has a long history of extreme and unconventional disciplines. Such measures are virtually the mark of some traditional Hindu and Buddhist Tantric sects (Kakar, 1982; Powers, 1995). Buddhism has its pantheon of wrathful and violent deities, traditions of harsh and ascetic disciplines. In Japan, Zen and other sects have an extensive history of interconnection with Japanese militarism, from warrior monks and the Samurai to emperor worship in the modern area (Heisig & Maraldo, 1994; Victoria, 1997).

Watanabe (personal communication) reminded me that such extreme disciplines, often involving water, were a traditional part of Shinto initiations. So Asahara was drawing on tradition as much as he was deviating from it.

Psychologically harsh, punitive measures can inspire closer bonding. Fraternity initiations and boot camp create group loyalty and solidarity. Abused children often defend and protect their abusers. Freud called this "identification with the aggressor," whereby humiliation and abuse become reframed as love and acceptance. Something like that operated in Aum. At least one person reported that such extreme disciplines only bound the devotees tighter to Asahara: "Takahashi commented that the more Asahara made things difficult for his disciples, the more they felt drawn to him. They explained his demands on them, his creation of distance between himself and them, and his harshness towards them as examples of the guru's love" (Reader, 2000: 238).

In addition, identification with Asahara may have provided another link with humiliation. Asahara himself suffered much humiliation in his own life. Born partially blind, shunned by peers, he was a figure of humiliation. Identifying with him as guru and master (as well as a source of punishment) meant identifying with him in his humiliation. So any sense of shame and humiliation that devotees brought with them into Aum might easily have been potentiated by their experiences in the cult and their identification with Asahara. And by subjecting his devotees to such harsh treatment, Asahara himself became an abjecting and humiliating divine (or semi-divine) figure whom the disciples both idealized and to whom they submitted. This is exactly the religious and psychological constellation seen in other religious groups that gave rise to terrorism.[4]

The story of Aum Shinrikyo and the sarin gas attack illustrates the multidimensional and multidetermined nature of religiously sponsored terrorism. Aum has its roots in Tantric Buddhism with its history of "crazy wisdom," anticonventional and often harsh practices, and total commitment to the guru. While often portrayed in the West as a religion totally dedicated to love and peace, we have seen that Buddhism also has a history of warrior monks and bloody battles among differing sects. Japanese Shinto also has a total devotion to the emperor and a history of fierce physical initiations. So Aum's roots run deep in Buddhism and Japanese religion. Aum, the People's Temple, and even some Muslim jihadist groups, began in a search for a deeper spirituality; their violent actions were often the culmination of a spiritual journey.

While often mentioned in books on religiously motivated terrorism because of its roots in the syncretist Japanese religious milieu, Lifton's (2000) account makes clear that Aum Shinrikyo relies as much on science, science fiction, and the idealization of high technology as on religion (see also Reader, 2000: 185–187). In this sense Lifton links Aum Shinrikyo with the Heaven's Gate cult, a UFO cult in the United States whose members committed suicide in 1997. Both groups would have been impossible apart from a milieu saturated by popular science, science fiction, video game culture with its merger of science fiction and violence, and the idealization of technology. Yet in popular accounts of Aum Shinrikyo, religion is featured and science and technology are ignored. Apocalypticism is not limited to religion these days. It has moved out of its original theological context and taken root in popular culture, especially in the domains of science fiction and other popular portrayals of technology, which often ignore the original religious source of their apocalyptic imagery and themes. Charles Strozier (1996) argues that this is due, in part, to the presence of nuclear weapons and other weapons of mass destruction. Technology has given us the power to end life on planet earth, the power formerly reserved for God or the gods. After Hiroshima and Nagasaki, death, technology, and the apocalyptic end of all life have become inextricably linked (Strozier, 1996). Aum Shinrikyo's (and al-Qaeda's) quest for nuclear weapons perfectly illustrates this conjunction of nuclear technology and apocalyptic religion.

Asahara's teachings gradually became increasingly apocalyptic as the sect felt more and more threatened. But whether this was a cause or an effect is hard to disentangle. At the same time, Asahara was elaborating his doctrine of *poa* that clearly legitimated and encouraged violence. But these apocalyptic teachings and *poa* doctrine are only part of the story, I suggest. These teachings and practices gained their hold on the minds of Aum's adherents through their congruence and reciprocal interaction with the devotees' psychological character. Those members exposed to Aum's teachings and disciplines whose psychodynamics were not congruent with Asahara's developing doctrines either dropped out or remained focused on their own spiritual growth and not on the guru's schemes. To the extent that Aum demonized the larger society and split reality into the pure against the impure, sanctified violence and killing (*poa*), humiliated and shamed its devotees, and sought purification through bloodshed, it contains many of the salient themes found in other religiously motivated terrorist groups and appealed to similar psychological motivations. One route to the connection between religion and violence is through shame and humiliation and a connection between the wish for purification and the shedding of blood. The psychological connection between purification and the shedding of blood, which seems operative in so much religiously motivated violence, was probably present in some Aum members as well and was clearly expressed in Asahara's doctrine of *poa*—the most unique thing about Aum Shinrikyo.

The story of Aum Shinrikyo illustrates that desires and motivations for personal spiritual renewal and transformation are not necessarily benign—a point I return to in the final chapter. Such wishes can slowly and imperceptibly lead certain individuals and groups in destructive directions. Again, the psychological question is, what allows some individuals to follow their religious and spiritual inclinations into the pit of violence and terrorism and others with the same inclinations to take them in more benign and constructive directions?[5]

CHAPTER 4

THE DIVINE TERRORIST

Religion and Violence in American Apocalyptic Christianity

I NEED TO BEGIN WITH AN EXPLANATION FOR THE PROVOCATIVE title of this chapter. Ironically, I was reading *Left Behind* (the first volume in the *Left Behind* series; it describes the "rapture") on July 7, 2005, the day of the terrorist bombings in London. I could not help but notice the parallel between what I was hearing about happening in real time in London as the result of a terrorist attack and what I was reading about happening as the result of God's rapturing his chosen people from the earth. Many of the scenes described as the result of the rapture had an eerie and sickening resonance to terrorist attacks. As someone who lived through the 9/11 attacks up close and was personally touched by them, as well someone who closely followed the reports of the Madrid train bombing and who has friends in England and closely followed the reports of the London subway bombings, I could not help noticing the similarities. Planes crashed to the ground or smashed into buildings, trains wrecked and piled into each other, cars smashed up, first responders had trouble getting to the scene, chaos ruled, and in grief and panic people searched desperately for missing loved ones. Except this was supposed to be an act of God, not of a fanatical terrorist group.[1]

The idea of the rapture and the biblical literalism that is necessary to support it are the foundations of the *Left Behind* series. They are probably the two areas where American apocalyptic Christianity differs most significantly from the larger Christian tradition. They also arose about the same time in American Christianity: after the Civil War as America was modernizing and transitioning from a rural-based to an urban-centered society (Strozier, 1994). Only American apocalyptic Christianity takes Saint Paul's brief phrase in his New Testament letter to the Thessalonians that when Christ returns believers "who remain alive will be caught up in the clouds to meet Christ in the air" (I Thessalonians 4:17)—which clearly refers to something Paul thinks will happen in his own lifetime and at the same time as Christ returns and not in some far distant future time and years before Christ returns—and makes it into a discrete historical event called "the rapture."

While apocalyptic scenarios have existed from time to time throughout the history of Christianity (McGinn, 2005), only in certain strands of American evangelical Christianity can one find the doctrine of the rapture. Nor do all American evangelicals subscribe to this rapture theology. There are several evangelical websites and recent books designed to refute the basic ideas of the *Left Behind* series. Outside of a few American conservative evangelical schools, no biblical scholar finds any basis in scripture or tradition for this idea. The widely recognized biblical historian Marcus Borg writes, "The rapture is a relatively recent notion, and I know of no New Testament scholar who takes it seriously" (Borg & Wright, 1998: 274). Even the more conservative biblical scholar N. T. Wright says of the passage in Thessalonians, "through the literalistic reading of its apocalyptic imagery, [it] has spawned many a fanciful eschatological scheme among fundamentalists in particular" (Borg & Wright, 1998: 203). Nor does any Christian group other than the American apocalypticists think that the book of Revelation provides a literal blueprint for historical events at the end of the world. Eastern Orthodox churches do not even consider the book of Revelation as a regular part of the canon of scripture, and they do not include it in their lectionary readings. Christian groups who are not doctrinally committed to a literalistic interpretation of scriptures have a very different reading of Paul and Revelation.

These major innovations on the part of American apocalyptic Christianity are the result of the writings of John Nelson Darby, which were produced at about the same time that theologians at Princeton Theological Seminary were codifying a doctrinally literalistic method for interpreting scriptures (Sandeen, 1970; Strozier, 1994). Darby was the one who conceived of the rapture as a special event and fit it into the schema of the book of Revelation to make a compelling end-times narrative. An

Irishman born in London, Darby left the Church of England (in which he was ordained) for the Brethren Community. In the 1840s he left the Brethren to found a group called the Plymouth Brethren. Darby called his schema "premillennial dispensationalism." This schema divided history into a series of "dispensations." The time of the ancient Israelites and the Hebrew scriptures was one dispensation. It came to an end with the coming of Christ. The time of the apostles and the early church was another dispensation. It ended with the death of the apostles and the writing of the New Testament. We are now living "between the times"— between the time of the early church and the beginning of the "end times." Such a framework makes it possible to argue that the teachings of Jesus about love and forgiveness belonged to an earlier time, an earlier dispensation. Sayings about loving one's enemies are no longer relevant when the "end times" arrive and the "day of judgment" draws near. Timothy LaHaye (1999), one of the authors of the *Left Behind* series, has written that

> The book of Revelation is the only book in the New Testament that presents Jesus Christ as He really is today. The Gospels introduce Him as the "man of sorrows and familiar with suffering" during his incarnation. Revelation presents Him in His true glory and majesty after His resurrection and ascension into heaven, never again to be reviled, rebuked, and spat upon. No wonder John entitled it "The Revelation of Jesus Christ." (9–10)

Jesus the "Prince of Peace" is out of date; soon it will be time for Jesus "the man of war."

The rapture was the key to Darby's system. Its occurrence marks the beginning of the end. Believers are to be lifted up into heaven in order to escape a 7-year period of tribulation during which various plagues, battles, violence, and bloodshed take place as described in the vision of John of Patmos, the author of Revelation. After this 7-year period, during which most people left on earth die vicious and terrible deaths while the raptured saints look on, Jesus returns and brings in the millennium, 1,000 years of peace and joy before the final resurrection and last judgment when the true believers are at last ushered into heaven and the unbelievers are resurrected from the dead and cast forever into a lake of fire.

After the Civil War, Darby made several trips to the United States. "Biblical prophecy" conferences were held throughout the United States at the end of the nineteenth century. In 1909 Cyrus Scofield published a version of the King James Bible with a complete premillennial dispensationalist commentary in which all the books of the Bible are read as single unified text with only one theme—the end of the world will come, according to the schema articulated by Darby, beginning with the rapture and ending with the final judgment. In the course of his ethnography of fundamentalist churches in New York, Charles Strozier (1994) reports that "the Scofield Bible *is* the inerrant text of God in the minds of many unsophisticated fundamentalist believers" (188, emphasis in original). While there are disagreements within the fundamentalist community about details such as the exact timing of the rapture, the fate of the Jews, and the state of Israel in God's plan, and exactly what the seals, bowls, and plagues of the book of Revelation literally refer to, Darby's schema defines the way in which American apocalyptic Christianity foresees the future. It is this schema that is fictionalized in the *Left Behind* series.

The first volume in the *Left Behind* series, entitled *Left Behind*, was published in 1995 (throughout this chapter *Left Behind* refers only to this initial volume, while the group is a whole is referred to as the *Left Behind* series). Since then 12 volumes have been published and, as of 2006, two more are on the way (a sequel and a prequel), and more than 65 million copies have been sold (Ungar, 2005: 204). The series has made more than $650 million for Tyndale House, which has now become the largest privately owned religious publishing house in the United States (Ungar, 2005: 220). According to one set of figures, 84% of the readers of the series describe themselves as "born again," 72% attend church at least once a week, 14% are members of mainline churches, 8% are Roman Catholic, and 16% surprisingly say they are non-Christian (Pahl, 2005). Thus the majority of the readers identify themselves as born again and attend non-mainline or non-Catholic evangelical and nondenominational churches. A survey in 2005 found that 19% of Americans had read the *Left Behind* books (Grossman, 2006). A survey done in 2004 found that 38% of all Americans said they believe that the "Bible is the literal word of God and is to be taken literally word for word" (the conviction on which the *Left Behind* series is premised), and more than 70% of those considered evangelicals endorsed this belief (interestingly, 25% of all American college graduates, evangelical and nonevangelical, agreed with this statement) (*Religion and Ethics Newsweekly*, 2004). According to a survey by the Pew Forum on Religion and Public Life in 2004, recently published in the *New York Times* (Sunday Week in Review, 2006), white evangelical Protestants make up 26.3% of the American people. Of that group, a little more than 50% of them, or about 16% of the American people as a whole, say they believe that "the world will end in a battle at Armageddon between Jesus and the antichrist"—the belief that lies at the heart of the *Left Behind* series. The more traditional an evangelical claims to be, the more likely he or she is to believe in the literal end-times scenario presented in the *Left Behind* series: 77% of the traditionalists among the white evangelicals affirmed this belief, but only 29% of the more moderate evangelicals did.

The purpose of this chapter is to offer the beginnings of a psychological analysis of the *Left Behind* series, not to provide a history of American apocalyptic thought, a theological critique, or a literary evaluation. I will try to remain focused on the books' psychological themes and their connection to the question of the relationship of religion and violence. I will be treating them here from a very limited but important perspective: not as works of literature or as theological, exegetical, or devotional texts but rather as primary sources for some of the ways in which the connection between religion and violence is articulated in American apocalyptic Christianity.

An important point here concerns the process of scriptural interpretation. Throughout the *Left Behind* series, the protagonists continually justify their actions by reference to individual Bible verses, or sometimes even just bits of verses or phrases. Almost always these textual bits are cited without any reference to their context. The assumption here appears to be that the Bible is a repository of concepts and images that are independent and autonomous and can be taken out of their larger textual or narrative context and treated as isolated slogans or bits of wisdom. The same thing happens in other religiously motivated terrorist movements. For example, many commentators have pointed out that when jihadists quote the Koran to justify terrorist actions and the killing of civilians (acts that most Muslim scholars agree are against Koranic principles), they almost always take passages out of context, ignoring either the text's immediate context or the larger message of the Koran taken as a whole (Khosrokhavar, 2005; Kimball, 2002; Lawrence, 1989; Venkatraman, 2007). Scholars have said the same thing about Asahara's use of texts from the Tibetan Tantras: in order to justify his violent and apocalyptic teachings, Asahara either took texts out of context or interpreted passages literally that were meant to be interpreted symbolically (Kisala & Mullins, 2001). The same is true of the way the authors of the *Left Behind* series treat the New Testament. Such a style of interpretation and the concomitant assumption that a sacred text can be treated as

simply a collection of independent textual fragments seems to characterize the use of sacred texts on the part of violence-prone religionists.

The very words "left behind" have deep psychological resonances.
They clearly evoke some of our most primal fears. Fears of abandonment
and insecure attachments, which are some of our most basic fears, are
captured by the title. Nobody wants to be left behind, whether it is when
parents go out for the evening, when teams are chosen in the schoolyard,
or when the thread of time is finally rolled up. The title page alone presents us with issues of abandonment and disconnection.

This theme is stated right at the beginning. The series opens with a
vignette of an airline pilot fantasizing about an affair with a flight attendant. Then he discovers that many of his passengers have simply disappeared. From the flight radio he hears reports of chaos and destruction
everywhere. When he is finally able to land and return home, his worst
fears are realized. His wife, with whom his relationship was becoming
strained due to her increasingly militant evangelical Christianity, is gone.
He searches for her in vain, knowing all along that she must have been
right. The rapture, about which she had tried to warn him, has happened. And he has been left behind. Bereft, he sinks into despair until
he arouses himself and goes on a religious search that leads to his conversion. But the message is clear from the beginning: think about sex too
much and you will be left behind.[2]

Amy Johnson Frykholm, in her ethnographic study of readers of the
Left Behind series, concludes by emphasizing the ways in which the books
evoke and potentiate the fears of many readers:

> Many of the stories readers in this study tell indicate that *Left Behind*
> cultivates fear. . . . Each of these readers articulates personal fear, and
> an anxiety about self, nation, and world permeates the interaction that
> many have with *Left Behind*. While these fears most certainly have mul-
> tiple sources, they also have commonalities. In various ways . . . readers
> express a fear of themselves being left behind. Fear of being left behind
> is fear of separation and isolation; it is fear of failure and loss. (Frykholm,
> 2004: 180)

Pahl (2005) concurs, saying that the series plays upon the fears of readers.

The opening volume is pervaded by a constant background feeling of
fear, panic, and confusion. Where are my children? What has happened to
my spouse? Are my parents all right? What will happen next? Is it already
too late? If not, will it be too late soon? These questions and the anxieties

associated with them run throughout the first novel. From working with many religious patients over many years, my impression is that many of the accounts of people's conversions in the novel *Left Behind* have the ring of authenticity about them. However, in the background of the novel there is always a sense that here the motivation for conversion is fear rather than an experience of love or a simple recognition of the truth. So evoking and playing upon powerful emotions such as fear, abandonment, and loss must account for some of the books' effect on people. But what sort of religion is built on fear, anxiety, and loss?

For Christian readers, this anxiety is heightened in *Left Behind*, not only through these accounts of the catastrophes poured out upon those who fail to be carried away to heaven, but also through the figure of Pastor Barnes. He was the associate pastor of an evangelical church. The chief pastor and virtually all the congregation were raptured away. Pastor Barnes was left behind. Why? He was devout, active, an inspiring preacher, a knowledgeable teacher, and a caring pastor. He certainly confessed his faith in Jesus publicly over and over. But apparently he was enamored of the role of pastor; he enjoyed the adulation of those he served. Such mixed motivations apparently compromised his salvation. Frykholm (2004) says about this character,

> The inauthenticity of Pastor Barnes' salvation is intriguing. Presumably, his public display of faith was flawless, his actions impeccable. Even his own wife did not suspect. He said and did "the right things." . . . Pastor Barnes was not an evil deceiver. . . . He was entirely sincere and yet completely inauthentic at the same time. . . . Stories like Pastor Barnes' work to confirm the insecurities that readers already face about their own salvation. Are they a "Pastor Barnes'" for whom faith is merely a show? (147)

In other words, will they, too, be left behind?

Such fear may run deep in the evangelical psyche. While (in my experience) evangelical families can be close, warm, and supportive, there may often be another side to them as well. From talking with evangelicals and working with patients from that tradition, I have often sensed that such warmth and support feels very conditional to the child growing up in this milieu. Evangelical parents often say that they have a primary responsibility to make sure their child is "saved." This can be out of a genuine concern for the child's spiritual and moral well-being. It can also be out of anxiety on the parents' part that they will be forever separated from their child at the rapture or the last judgment if their child is not saved.

And the child may very well pick up this anxiety and become anxious himself. In addition, evangelical parents often appear to feel that the way to ensure their children are saved is to make sure the children "toe the line" (as one person put it). But this often gives the growing child the sense that love and acceptance are conditional on "toeing the line." If they don't, they fear that warmth and acceptance will disappear.

This is exactly the fear that *Left Behind* plays upon. The anxiety growing out of a conditional view of love and acceptance—which the clinician often encounters in work with patients—is a major subtext in the *Left Behind* series. Those who don't follow the prescribed path are those who are left behind in the rapture. This breeds exactly the fears of separation, isolation, failure, and loss that Frykholm found in many of the readers of the series. The theology here is clearly a theology of conditional acceptance. The psychology is a psychology of fear and anxiety about the loss of that love and acceptance. This is part of the reason the scene of the last judgment in the novel *Glorious Appearing* (which is so horrific in one way with its screams and cries and burning bodies) is such a relief to the evangelical mind. Now, at last, we know who is saved and who is damned. The anxiety born of conditional love can finally cease.

In addition to the theme of fear and anxiety, another theme of the series from the beginning is that of violence, blood, and gore. Here are three quotations that describe the results of the rapture.

> Even the newscasters' voices were terror filled, as much as they tried to mask it. . . . Thousands were dead in plane crashes and car pileups. Emergency crews were trying to clear expressways and runways, all the while grieving over loved ones and coworkers who had disappeared. . . . Cars driven by people who spontaneously disappeared had careened out of control, of course. (LaHaye & Jenkins, 1995: 29)

> Some of the worst disasters in the city were the result of disappearing motormen and dispatchers. Six trains were involved in head-ons with lots of deaths. Several trains ran up the back of other ones. (LaHaye & Jenkins, 1995: 126)

> The news was full of crime, looting, people taking advantage of chaos. People being shot, maimed, raped, killed. The roadways were more dangerous than ever. Emergency units were understaffed, fewer air- and ground-traffic controllers manned the airports, fewer qualified pilots and crews flew the planes. (LaHaye & Jenkins, 1995: 207)

Remember that all this disaster, death, loss and grief are presented as the action of God. What sort of God is that would do this to his creation? And, presumably, the truly pious are watching all of this from their front-row seats in heaven. In the last volume, *Glorious Appearing*, when all the holy people are reunited, it is, in fact, suggested that the raptured saints watched while their loved ones died in plane crashes, were incapacitated in train wrecks, were crushed by colliding cars and collapsing buildings. How is that psychologically possible? What were they thinking as they watched from the safety of paradise this divine carnage heaped on those they cared about?

As the world sinks into chaos after the rapture, a few left-behind souls (including the pilot protagonist, his daughter, a journalist she falls in love with, and the newly recommitted Pastor Barnes) see the error of their ways, make the "transaction" (the term for conversion in *Left Behind*) of giving their lives to Jesus, and begin the formation of the "Tribula-tion Force," an underground battalion of Christian fighters opposing the antichrist. Here LaHaye and Jenkins make a major innovation of their own in dispensationalist theology. The traditional model insisted that, as Paul clearly states in Thessalonians, the "rapture" coincided with the re-turn of Christ. This marks the end of human history as we know it. After that no more conversions are possible. This is the doctrine that Strozier (1994) encountered in the early 1990s in his interviews: after the rap-ture and during the tribulation, no one can choose Jesus or be saved; by then everyone's fate is sealed.

What does this scenario really mean? That a horrifying and brutal life continues on earth for 7 more years after the rapture before the final judgment? That the doomed suffer through 7 more years of hell on earth, only then to be sent forever into the eternal hell of the lake of fire? Strozier did find at least one church member who tried to modify the doc-trine and hint that maybe some conversions during the tribulation might be possible. Strozier commented to me that that this church member "revised the theory to make it more humane and allow for redemption not only during tribulation but during the entire millennium. She is 'wrong' about the theory but right in human terms" (Strozier, 2005). La-Haye and Jenkins make that same modification the center of their novels. This is done not to make the doctrine more humane but so the tribula-tion force can "fight it out with the beast with their Uzis," in the words of Chuck Strozier (personal communication). This possibility, unknown in traditional premillennial dispensationalism, makes LaHaye and Jenkins' narrative possible: during the tribulation a few heroic warriors convert to Christianity and, for volume after volume, fight an increasingly high-tech and bloody war against the antichrist.

This theme of blood and gore intensifies throughout the series. In his wrath, Jesus, the Lamb of God, causes an earthquake that wipes out a third of the world's population (*Soul Harvest*, published in 1998). Hail, fire, and blood rain down on the earth—one third of the planet is burned up. All catastrophes are described in excruciating detail. In the next volume a plague of scorpions is "so horrifying that men try to kill themselves but are not allowed to die" (from the book jacket for *Apollyon*, published in 1999).

All of this reaches its climax in the final novel, *Glorious Appearing*, which describes the final return of Christ and the climatic battle of Arma-geddon against the forces of the antichrist. The antichrist is the secretary general of the United Nations. He has established a stronger world gov-ernment with the promise of world peace and collected an army of mil-lions to fight for world unity. The idea of world government as an agent of Satan has a history in American apocalyptic Christianity. And this has often focused on the United Nations. For example, the American tel-evangelist Pat Robertson "has often denounced the United Nations as the first step towards a dangerous 'one world' government" (Goodstein, 2005). In his study of evangelical Christianity done in New York City in the 1990s, long before the *Left Behind* series dramatized and popular-ized this idea, Strozier found it pervasive in evangelical circles. He writes, "In the scheme of things, Antichrist makes world peace, including peace with Israel, before revealing himself in all his horror. . . . The greater the world leader, and the more he speaks to global issues of peace . . . the more he is ultimately to be feared as the probable Antichrist" (Strozier, 1994: 147–148). As Strozier comments tersely, "The subtextual message is beware the peacemaker" (147).[3]

For volume after volume, the *Left Behind* series dramatizes the Satanic machinations of this world government as it rises to power. Parallel to this, the blood and gore increase, climaxing in the battle of Armaged-don described in *Glorious Appearing*. The previous volumes detailed the many ways in which the few Christians remaining on earth took arms and fought against the antichrist, becoming, in the words of many commenta-tors, God's green berets. In *Glorious Appearing*, God's green berets watch from the sidelines while Jesus himself viciously and mercilessly slaughters his opponents. (Here I am including many quotations from that novel so that you do not think I am just selecting one or two particularly violent passages out of context simply to make a point.)

> And with those very first words [from Jesus], tens of thousands of Unity Army soldiers fell dead, simply dropping where they stood, their bodies ripped open, blood pooling in great masses. (LaHaye & Jenkins, 2004: 204)

What appears most glorious to the authors and their chief protagonists appears to be scenes of slaughter and bloodshed.

> As Rayford slowly made his way down to the desert plains, though he had to concentrate on missing craters and keeping from hitting splayed and filleted bodies of men and women and horses, Jesus still appeared before his eyes—shining, magnificent, powerful, and victorious. (LaHaye & Jenkins, 2004: 208)

> Rayford watched through his binocs as men and women soldiers and horses seemed to explode where they stood. It was as if the very words of the Lord had superheated their blood, causing it to burst through their veins and skin. (LaHaye & Jenkins, 2004: 225)

> Tens of thousands of foot soldiers dropped their weapons, grabbed their heads and their chests, fell to their knees, and writhed as they were invisibly sliced asunder. Their innards and entrails gushed to the desert floor, and as those around them turned to run, they too were slain, their blood pooling and rising in the unforgiving brightness of the glory of Christ. (LaHaye & Jenkins, 2004: 226)

Animals, too, were not spared the most cruel and hideous of fates:

> The riders not thrown leaped from their horses and tried to control them with reins, but even as they struggled, their own flesh dissolved and their eyes melted, and their tongues disintegrated. . . . Seconds later the same plague affected the horses, their flesh and eyes and tongues melting away, leaving grotesque skeletons standing, before they too rattled to the pavement. . . . First blindness and madness on the part of the horses, then the bodies of the soldiers melting and dissolving. Then the falling and piling of bones. (LaHaye & Jenkins, 2004: 273–274)

Throughout the battle narrative, special attention is lavished on its bloodiness. For example, "The great army was in pandemonium, tens of thousands at a time screaming in terror and pain and dying in the open air. Their blood poured from them in great waves, combining to make a river that quickly became a swamp" (LaHaye & Jenkins, 2004: 249) So bloody is Jesus' victory that it results in a river of blood wider by far than the Mississippi. "Mile after mile after mile [they] drove next to a river of blood several miles wide and now some five feet deep" (LaHaye & Jenkins, 2004: 258).

The scene ends with the victorious Jesus walking across the battlefield sloshing around in the blood of his enemies. "Bodies were strewn for miles and the desert floor was red with blood. . . . Jesus dismounted. The army of heaven . . . following as He strode through the battlefield, the hem of His robe turning red in the blood of his enemies" (LaHaye & Jenkins, 2004: 228).[4]

On one hand, neither Frykholm nor any of her respondents appear to comment on the violent imagery in the novels or the impact of all this gratuitous violence on them. On the other hand, Strozier, in his study of evangelicals, even before the *Left Behind* series dramatized it so graphically, commented on the high level of violence in their discourse:

> There is also a potential for violence in fundamentalism that I found troubling. As we have seen, violence often defines their discourse. They talk of washing their robes in the blood of the lamb (Revelation 7: 14) and warm to the cascading images of destruction and death in Revelation as trumpets are blown, seals opened, and bowls emptied in the heavens. These waves of violence form a rising and interconnected spiral. . . . The churches themselves are awash in this imagery. (Strozier, 1994: 165)

This is certainly true. For example, a student of mine counted 28 songs in *The United Methodist Hymnal* having to do with "blood." Their titles include "The Blood Will Never Lose Its Power," "Nothing but the Blood," and "There is a Fountain Filled with Blood." More than one contemporary Christian rock group has songs with "blood" in the title or lyrics, including "The Blood Song" by Kirk Franklin.[5] We must ask psychologically in what ways and for what goals are devotees conditioned or desensitized by singing such blood-soaked lyrics week after week.

The idea of apocalyptic Christians "warming to cascading images of destruction and death" fits in with one of the ways the religious imagination operates in evangelical circles. A friend and colleague of mine who knows the evangelical ethos well commented to me:

> Evangelicals and Pentecostals seem to feel that the more detail they can get into their narratives, the more solid their faith is. If you listen to their testimonies and the stories they tell, it makes me think that they think there's a

connection between the amount of detail they can produce and the inten-sity of their experience. They spend a lot of time imagining and discussing what the rapture will be like, what the last judgment will look like, what heaven will look like, down to the last detail. (Mark Lewis Taylor, personal communication, October 2005)

For example, one reader of the series comments regarding the Jezreel Valley in Israel, "Can you imagine this entire valley filled with blood? That would be a 200-mile-long river of blood, four and a half feet deep. We've done the math. That's the blood of as many as two and a half bil-lion people" (Unger, 2005: 206).

The *Left Behind* series engages this process by elaborating in exqui-site detail the bloodiest and most gruesome events imaginable in the book of Revelation. The novels also colonize the evangelical imagination by providing readers with these powerful images and leaving nothing to the reader's imagination. In the past, readers of the Bible were free to imagine the scenes in their own way, according to their psychological and spiritual state at the time. From the Middle Ages onward there were spiritual disciplines (e.g., the *Spiritual Exercises* of Ignatius Loyola) that called upon readers to personalize the biblical narrative by visualizing important scenes in their mind's eye. The violent imagery of the *Left Behind* series as well as that of a string of Christian movies and violent video games (one Christian video game is entitled *Eternal Warfare*) short-circuits this personalizing imagination. Instead, like many contemporary secular films and popular electronic games, they fill the heads of read-ers with scenes of barely imaginable blood and gore (Jones, 2007). The question of the effects of all this violent imagery on those who consume it is quite controversial in the psychological literature. But there is certainly a large body of research that suggests that exposure to violent imagery can lead to increased violent fantasies and even actions in a person's life and can desensitize people to the effects of violence.[6] At least the exis-tence of such books and video games means that part of a generation of Christian adolescents in America are being taught to imagine and even practice killing nonbelievers in the name of Jesus.

Strozier returns to this theme of violence at the end of his study:

> The most troubling dimension of endism is its relationship to violence. In the endist imagination, transformation out of our current misery . . . occupies a central place. . . . Fundamentalists generally believe that this transformation can only be accomplished violently, and that the move from

our time into the next requires mass death and destruction. . . . The more passionate forms of endism I encountered in this study seem to require violence to produce the transformation that will end what is experienced as the tormenting ambiguity and pain of human existence, indeed of time itself, and re-make history. That is the point of the biblical genocide described in the book of Revelation. (Strozier, 1994: 251)

Pahl (2005) also emphasizes a direct connection between the *Left Behind* series and violence. And we have seen in earlier chapters, there is a link between religion and violence and the connection between purification and the shedding of blood in the history of American religion.

This conviction that spiritual transformation requires violence and that purification is linked to bloodshed is amply illustrated in the *Left Behind* series and in ways that directly parallel the connection of violence and purification found in the discourse of religiously motivated terrorists. At the end of this chapter I consider the possible connections between this violence-soaked discourse in preaching, hymnology, and most graphically in the *Left Behind* series and the potential for violent, terrorist actions in the name of apocalyptic Christianity and its vengeful Jesus.

After the battle of Armageddon and the garroting and ripping open of the unbelievers, the bloodshed continues in *Glorious Appearing*. Now the dead are resurrected and Jesus sits in judgment. With no expression of feeling, an impassive Jesus sends some to eternal bliss and others to never-ending torture. Those condemned

> beat their breasts and fell wailing to the desert floor, gnashing their teeth and pulling their hair. Jesus merely raised one hand a few inches and a yawning chasm opened in the earth, stretching far and wide enough to swallow all of them. They tumbled in, howling and screeching all of them but their wailing was soon quashed and all was silent when the earth closed itself again. (LaHaye & Jenkins, 2004: 380)

Concretized in this scene of the last judgment—a staple of Christian art for centuries—is a clear and final demarcation of the saved and the damned, of good and evil. We have seen this splitting in other religious texts of terror, and many have commented on its salience in American apocalyptic Christianity. Many writers have noted that this splitting is central to any violent apocalyptic vision (Strozier, 1994). Frykholm (2004) cites one classic scholarly text.

In his classic study of apocalytpicism, *Disaster and the Millennium,* Michael Barkun argues that the distinction between a righteous microcosm and an evil macrocosm is crucial to the formation of the apocalyptic. Apocalyptic movements create a microcosm, "an insular social world with distinctive norms and goals." The microcosm simultaneously creates a macrocosm "perceived as evil, decaying, and doomed." A macrocosm provides reason for the microcosm's existence and contributes to a sense of group identity and cohesion. (14)

We have seen over and over how splitting of the world into all-good, all-evil camps and abjecting the evil other is one of the ways in which the apocalyptic imagination facilitates the move to religiously sponsored terrorism.

In the *Left Behind* series this process of splitting, separation, and demarcation goes on at a very concrete, literal level. First there is the rapture that separates the true believers from everyone else. As the series progresses and the antichrist tightens his control, the unsaved receive the mark of the beast and the saved receive a mark of Christ on their foreheads. Yet these "tribulation saints" remain immersed in a life dominated by technology and violence. At the end is the last judgment, where the redeemed join Christ in the millennial kingdom and the unbelievers are separated out and condemned to eternal suffering (Frykholm, 2004). Many of Frykholm's respondents express this very polarized view of the world, which she argues is encouraged by reading these books. For example:

> Sarah's boundaries remain very black and white. She is rigidly certain in her own life about who is saved and who is unsaved, about right thinking and wrong thinking, right belief and wrong belief. The apocalypticism of *Left Behind* feeds Sarah's sense of self-assurance and self-righteousness. She has no doubt that she will go in the rapture and is fairly certain she can identify those who will go with her. (Frykholm, 2004: 49–50)

Frykholm describes an experience that she had when visiting a church where the minister asked those who were "saved" to raise their hands. This created a no-win situation for the author that she got temporarily caught in (Frykholm 2004: 160–161). She comments afterwards, "The minister has created a universe in which there are only two answers— either you have accepted Jesus and are saved. . . . Or you are damned" (Frykholm, 2004: 160). This radically split universe is the universe of

the *Left Behind* series and American apocalyptic Christianity. It is also the
universe of religiously sponsored terrorism.

Strozier also observed this dichotomized worldview in many of those
he interviewed:

> The difference between self and others is sacralized, which provides a total-
> istic framework for dismissing all those who do not fit into the holy world
> in which the fundamentalist is blessed. The fundamentalist's chosenness
> defines the nonbeliever's abandonment, the one's salvation the other's
> ultimate punishment. Nonbelievers are rejected by God and thus in some
> inexplicable way are only tentatively human. (Strozier, 1994: 90)

This view comes perilously close to what we see in other religiously
motivated texts of terror: the way in which religion contributes to the
social death of the other and so makes the other available as a legitimate
object of violence. After saying that apocalyptic Christians feel that "nonbelievers are rejected by God and thus in some inexplicable way are only
tentatively human," Strozier adds that "as such, nonbelievers are dispens-
able. If they intrude in the believer's world, the psychological conditions
exist to make it possible for believers to accommodate violence toward
nonbelievers" (Strozier, 1994: 90). In light of what we've learned about
the social–psychological conditions that facilitate the move to violence,
at the end of this chapter I will consider what might bring the potential
within American apocalyptic Christianity for religiously sponsored violence closer to realization.

Both Frykholm and Strozier comment on a dissonance between the
warmth, friendliness, and genuine compassion of those they interviewed
and the violence and callousness of their theology. Strozier (1994) writes,
"I must stress that for most fundamentalists, and certainly for all I met,
such violence was nowhere near being realized" (90). Throughout her
book, Frykholm (2004) reiterates how much she came to like most of the
people she met. Strozier often refers to them as "good people with a bad
theory." But their coldness toward those deemed unbelievers remains
startling. For example, Strozier describes one of his respondents (called
"Otto" in the text):

> Otto's embrace of end time violence, as it was with most fundamentalists
> I met, had an oddly dissociated quality. He was personally a gentle man, yet
> he nourished in his mind a stirring cauldron of images of end time destruc-
> tion. After my first interview with him in which he laid out the violence of

the end time justified by human sin and disbelief, he told me a touching story of the crib death of one of his children. . . . This same man can have God wipe out 2.5 billion people without blinking an eye because they are not saved. (Strozier, 1994: 70)

We are left to wonder about the psychology behind such dissonance and dissociation. What does it cost the adherents to maintain it? And under what conditions might it break down and result in actual violence toward the abjected other? We have seen this same ferocious lack of empathy for potential victims in every instance of religiously motivated violent and terrorist groups. In this way the ideology of American apocalyptic Christianity, and especially the *Left Behind* series, furthers the social death of the other that is a major ingredient in genocide and terrorism.

Such an apocalyptic vision provides its adherents a way of making sense of their experience. Events that others might consider random or unconnected form a pattern for those with eyes to see it.

Political events, diplomatic missions, wars, earthquakes, floods, and other natural disasters are not random, but woven into a complex narrative about the world's approaching end. This method of interpretation highly structures readers' understanding of the world they live in. It offers coherence to what otherwise appear random and secures for them a very specific and special place in world history. (Frykholm, 2004: 106)

Many commentators refer to the *Left Behind* series as gnostic (e.g., Pahl, 2005). I am not inclined to use that term because there are such basic differences with classical, early Christian gnosticism. But premillennial dispensationalism probably does provide a Christian version of the same motivation that draws New Agers to the writings of Nostradamus. In his private lectures to Aum members, Asahara also claimed to have secret knowledge of the end times. In the *Left Behind* series there is also the lure of secret, occult knowledge, and a sense of belonging to an in-group that really knows the truth. Psychologically, besides the common human need to make sense of experience, there certainly are elements of grandiosity and narcissism here.

What sort of God is it that presides over all this torture and bloodletting as described in *Glorious Appearing*? Clearly a God of wrath and vengeance. The authors leave no doubt that all these lakes and rivers of blood, this spilling of entrails, these hideous ways of dying, these melting eyes and bursting bodies were God's doing. "God had, in the meantime, hardened many hearts. And when these unbelievers changed their minds—or tried to—they were not even capable of repenting and turning to God. . . . God knew that eventually sinners would grow weary of their poverty, but His patience had a limit. There came a time when enough was enough" (LaHaye & Jenkins, 2004: 179). A Jesus who rips open the stomachs of his opponents and a God who mercilessly deprives men and women of the ability to repent and change certainly fit the image of the wrathful, controlling, and abjecting deities that research has associated with diminished empathy, authoritarian tendencies, hostility and that, not surprisingly, we have found in virtually all the texts and discourses of religiously motivated terrorists. A 2005 survey found that 31% of Americans believe in this "authoritarian God" as portrayed in *The Left Behind* series, while only 23% believe in a more benevolent God, and less than 9% decline any belief in God (Grossman, 2006).

In the next chapter, I describe in more detail some probable psychodynamic aspects of such a theology, including Fairbairn's (1952) model of the "moral defense against bad objects," whereby the child preserves his idealized view of his abusive or neglectful parents by blaming himself for the pain he is suffering. The idealization of the other is preserved by taking the experience of badness on himself. If the burden of that badness gets too great, he may discharge it by projecting it onto a despised other. Thus a tradeoff ensues: he feels better and better the more he can despise and hate the other instead of himself. Strozier notices precisely this dynamic in many of the American apocalyptic Christians he interviewed.

> A striking aspect of the fundamentalist system is that just as individual guilt and shame diminish, collective evil increases. The badness, one might say, shifts its venue. Fundamentalists believe that the number of true Christians will decrease as we approach the end of time, for evil will increase everywhere else. The world implodes on itself from the weight of all its evil. End time violence is the indirect expression of all that accumulated sin, and it helps maintain individual purity as it unloads destruction. Such is the effect in fundamentalist theology of transforming guilt. The purer Christians are, the more sinful nonbelievers become. (Strozier, 1994: 107)

The *Left Behind* series models and sanctions unleashing the most extreme and brutalizing forms of anger and hatred on the despised others in the name of purifying the self and the world. The person weighed down with a burden of self-condemnation and guilt and desperate for a sense of purity can engage in this tradeoff and purify himself at the cost of torturing and destroying the others, at least in fantasy. In *Glorious Appearing* even Jesus himself appears to engage in this tradeoff and purifies his world through the hideous killing and torturing of the abjected ones.

We have noted many thematic parallels between the *Left Behind* series and the language of many religiously motivated terrorists: the wrathful, controlling, abjecting image of God, the drive for purity and the connection between purification and bloodshed, the splitting of the world into a battle between the completely pure and the totally evil, and the concomitant social death of the outsider. Given these parallels, the question about the possibility of American apocalyptic Christianity giving rise to terrorist violence must be raised.

In some cases that question has already been answered positively. Spurred on by a Christian theology of terror like that portrayed in the *Left Behind* series and contained in the book *A Time to Kill* (Bray, 1994) with its apocalyptic vision of Christians at war with a secular America, physicians and other health care providers have already been murdered and women's health centers bombed. This murdering of the providers of reproductive health services brings us back to a theme with which I began this chapter—sex. It is probably not coincidence that the *Left Behind* series begins with a man's sexual fantasies and the move to violence on the part of some American apocalyptic Christians begins with violence against women's reproductive health centers. The dangers and sinfulness of sexuality and the necessity of its repression and the repression of women, even violently if necessary, are also themes that American apocalyptic Christianity shares with religiously motivated terrorist groups.

For example, the violent antiabortion movement has a much broader agenda than simply ending abortions. Much of it centers on sex. Their vision for America goes far beyond shutting down reproductive health clinics. The Army of God website contains more than bloody images of aborted fetuses. There are pages condemning birth control (since God said "be fruitful and multiply"); there are pages that contain long lists of gays and lesbians convicted of molesting children (called "The Homo News"); there are instructions on how to send bloody postcards to pro-choice judges, politicians, and neighbors; and there is a link called "Dead Abortionists and the Nuremberg Files." A corresponding site (www.saltshaker.us) contains not only antiabortion essays, bloody fetal pictures, and antigay arguments but also instructions on how to repeal divorce laws and undermine divorce proceedings. The Army of God is fighting not only to ban abortions and execute abortion providers, it would ban all forms of contraception, criminalize all forms of homosexuality, and end the possibility of divorce. This is a war to rid the world of any form of sexual expression other than intercourse in the confines of heterosexual marriage for the purpose of producing children.

The Christian Reconstructionists' (and Timothy LaHaye is an ardent Reconstructionist) long-term plan to regulate sexuality and turn America into a theocracy was clearly revealed in their activities during the early days of the administration of George W. Bush. For example, they used their new-found political power to make sure that false, misleading, unscientific (and potential lethal) information about sex and women's health was provided to physicians and laypersons from government sources. Statements that condoms were ineffective against sexually transmitted diseases regularly appeared in United States government-produced pamphlets and websites, whereas all researchers (except those directly connected to the religious right) agreed then and still agree that the opposite is clearly true (the information in this and the following two paragraphs is from Alexander, 2006). The only exception was that, some years ago, there was no research demonstrating that condoms were effective against a virus occasionally associated with cervical cancer (the human papilloma virus). This lack of evidence, at the time, that there was such protection was turned upside down into a campaign against condoms by arguing there was evidence that condoms were ineffective. And in this campaign the chance of developing cervical cancer in this way was exaggerated out of all real proportion. Later research has shown that condoms are at least somewhat effective against this virus and all research shows that condoms are effective against all other sexually transmitted diseases, including HIV. Yet in 2002 a fact sheet providing information on condoms was removed from the website of the Centers for Disease Control. And this is not the only example. *Glamour* magazine (Alexander, 2006) reported that in 2006 "*Glamour* has also discovered that blatantly false anticondom information has been incorporated into several federal and state health websites" (7). And when a vaccine against the human papilloma virus was being developed by Merck, the religious right used its influence to keep that vaccine off the market! As one researcher from Columbia medical school commented at the time, "We have a vaccine that could prevent cancer . . . yet people are actually opposing it (Alexander, 2006: 9). The opposition of the religious right was eventually overcome, and this vaccine is now available.

In the early years of the George W. Bush administration, government programs routinely contained claims that abortions cause later pregnancies to result in birth defects (no evidence), or sterility (no evidence), or breast cancer (false). On the later point an editor of the *New England Journal of Medicine* wrote, "The government allowed people to believe—and encouraged people to believe—that abortions were a risk factor for breast cancer, even when the government knew that this research had been discredited and better research showed no connection" (Alexander, 2006: 11). Several states, where the religious right is especially strong, have passed laws mandating that physicians tell patients there is a link between abortion and cancer, thereby legally forcing them to provide false information to their patients. The federal government gave more than half a million dollars to a research foundation known to produce false and misleading studies regarding women's sexuality and has interfered in numerous ways with legitimate researchers seeking to understand more about the transmission of sexually transmitted diseases and other aspects of human sexuality.

In addition, as has been widely reported, the government delayed approving the so-called morning-after pill ("plan B") despite the fact that all 28 members of the scientific advisory committee recommended it. Why? A former National Institutes of Health scientist said that her colleagues "believe that religiously based social conservatives have direct lines to the powers that be within the U.S. government, the administration, Congress, and are influencing public-health policy, practice and research in ways that are unprecedented and very dangerous" (Alexander, 2006: 1). This is certainly supported by the fact that many conservative denominations and groups lobbied the congress and administration against the morning-after pill and later took credit for influencing the Food and Drug Administration (FDA) when it announced that it was postponing a decision on the drug. As a former head of the Women's Health Office in the FDA said, "This decision was not based on science and clinical evidence. This threatens the FDA's credibility and it threatens the faith the public has in the FDA for making sure products are safe and effective" (Alexander, 2006: 4). It took until 2006 for the morning-after pill to become available over the counter. However, this availability is limited to women over the age of 18, and pharmacists are allowed to refuse to dispense it if they have religious objections.

In addition, in 2002 emergency contraception was removed from the list of approved interventions for women serving in the military or getting their medical treatment on military bases. And the Justice Department refused to make the offer of emergency contraception part of their protocol for the handling of rape victims. An attempt to change this in Congress was defeated in 2005. As a result, studies done in 2006 found that rape victims were denied access to emergency contraception or even information about it when they went to emergency rooms after an assault. As a result, a physician and head of a large West coast medical research facility said at the time, "I no longer trust FDA decisions or materials generated [by the government] . . . I do not feel comfortable giving it to my patients" (Alexander, 2006: 1). Dr. Richard Carmona, who served as George W. Bush's surgeon general from 2002–2006, recently (July 2007) testified to Congress that the Bush administration censored his speeches and restrained him from speaking in public about stem-cell research, contraception, and misgivings about "abstinence only" sex education. "Anything that doesn't fit [their] ideological, theological, or political agenda is ignored, marginalized or simply buried," Carmona is reported to have told Congress (Durham, 2007: 1). "Political interference with the work of the surgeon general appears to have reached a new level," one congressman is reported to have said (Durham, 2007: 1).

An important dimension of this discussion is the way in which Christian Reconstructionists such as LaHaye and their antiabortion allies have moved from seeking the criminalization of abortion to seeking the outlawing of contraception. Contraception has been legal for more than 40 years (10 years more than abortion after *Roe v. Wade*), and most Americans surely take it as a natural right and, often, as a matter of good public and private health. Some members of the religious right do not see it that way. "We see a direct connection between the practice of abortion and the practice of contraception," says the leader of an antiabortion group that "now has a larger mission." "The mind-set that invites couples to use contraception is an antichild mind-set. . . . We oppose all forms of contraception" (Shorto, 2006). While formerly the opposition to contraception was almost entirely associated with the Roman Catholic Church, it has spread to larger segments of the religious right. For example, President Bush's appointment to the Reproductive Health Drugs Advisory Committee of the FDA was a vigorous opponent of medical contraception. While cast in scientific-like terms of conflicting research reports, it is clear that the primary issue is the regulation of sexual behavior. An article in the *New York Times* put it this way, "Many Christians who are active in the evolving anti-birth-control arena state frankly that what links their efforts is a religious commitment to altering the moral landscape of the country. In particular, and not to put too fine a point on it, they want to change the way Americans have sex" (Shorto, 2006).

In 2006 the *New York Times* reported that the drive to legally impose a conservative Christian understanding of sexual morality on the entire American people was well underway: "The linking of abortion and contraception is indicative of a larger agenda, which is putting sex back in the box, as something that only happens within marriage," said an expert on American sexual practices (Shorto, 2006). For Christian Reconstructionsts, even within marriage contraception is not acceptable and should not be available. And this drive focusing on sexual issues is part of a larger Reconstructionist agenda to make the United States a theocracy where all aspects of life are subject to their interpretation of biblical morality. Such a program is shared by the authors of the *Left Behind* series and the Reconstructionist movement. This agenda of denying medical information, especially about women's health, criminalizing sexual behavior, and repressing women is also shared with religiously motivated terrorist groups around the world.

The dangers of sexuality, the repression of women, and the conjoining of sex and violence are the salient themes of patriarchal religion, and terroristic religions are almost always patriarchal (Juergensmeyer, 2001; Lawrence, 1989). The *Left Behind* series also illustrates this conjunction of patriarchy, sex, and violence. Besides being awash in blood and gore, the novels consistently place women in subordinate roles (see Frykholm, 2004, for many examples of this portrayal of women as subordinate). And it is probably not coincidence that Mormonism is historically one of the most violent and also one of the most patriarchal of American religions, with its tradition of polygamy and absence of any female leadership in the church (see Krakauer, 2004, for a history of violence in Mormonism). The next chapter explores some of the psychological dynamics involved in these patriarchal religions. Although Strozier says "I must stress that for most fundamentalists, and certainly for all I met, such violence was nowhere near being realized" (Strozier, 1994: 90), he is clearly aware of the possibility of active violence latent in this theology:

With most fundamentalists, however, this violent undertow remains an unforeseen counterforce beneath a relatively calm demeanor because of the shift in agency to God. The violence is ultimate rather than proximate. It comes from the heavens rather than from within us. Believers alone will be saved and all others killed. Believers are pure in faith. And in that faith they can overcome death and the sins of everyday life. Such a shift in agency allows individual fundamentalists to separate themselves from the violence that suffuses their ideology and present themselves as decent, law-abiding citizens with enduring family commitments. But I found that at important psychological levels they move toward the violence that distinguishes their elaborate system of belief. Under individual or social duress that violence can turn from latent to overt forms. (Strozier, 1994: 165)

Juergensmeyer (2000) argues that one of the signs that an apocalyptic group is moving toward violent actions is the shift in thinking from divine to human agency. Even the most militantly apocalyptic passages in the New Testament insist that it is God, not man, who will bring the millennium. So that shift to an ideology of human activity to bring the end times has been almost universally eschewed in the history of Christianity.

Strozier notes two other reasons that he thinks will prevent American apocalyptic Christianity from turning violent.

Two important factors . . . mitigate the dangers of fundamentalists acting on or realizing the potential for violence that exists within their belief system or within themselves. . . . One has an obligation to reach and convert others, to help them, to recognize their weakness, to bring them to Christ. Such an impulse within Christianity tends to expand fundamentalist empathy out of necessity. . . . Equally significant, the fundamentalist shares a specific psychological connection with the nonbeliever. . . . The nonbeliever symbolizes the believer's pre-Christian, earlier self. (Strozier, 1994: 91)

So these factors—especially an insistence on divine and not human agency and an imperative to reach out and convert the nonbeliever—should keep the violence latent within American apocalyptic Christianity in check.[7]

However, in the *Left Behind* series that latent violence breaks out in the most gruesome and bloody ways. For volume after volume, God's green berets fight a bloody, high-tech, brutal war against the world government. While this is going on, God himself is slaughtering millions in earthquakes, plagues, hailstorms, and rampages of grotesque insects especially created to inflict suffering on the human race. How is this possible?

As we have seen, within their prevailing theology, the authors of the *Left Behind* series have made a brilliant rhetorical move. They set their narrative in the period of tribulation, when the antichrist himself is in power. The antichrist and his minions are either agents of the devil or possessed by the devil. By definition, in this schema they are beyond redemption. So there is no imperative to convert them. Just the reverse. In the *Left Behind* series, God models the destruction of almost all of the human race. And the "tribulation force" is forever finding scripture passages to support the taking up of arms, the slaughtering of enemies, the use of deception and torture. The message seems to be, in the apocalyptic world, when it is a battle against the antichrist, no rules apply and taking matters in one's own hands is justified. Thus the *Left Behind* series implicitly provides the kind of sanctification of total violence and the literal demonizing of the other that we have seen in the writings of the leadership of al-Qaeda and other religious terrorists.

In this sense the *Left Behind* series can be read as a Christianized version of the *Turner Diaries*—the novel that contains explicit instructions for would-be Christian Identity Believers and other survivalists on how to make bombs and carry on a guerrilla war against the federal government; it was said that Timothy McVeigh slept with the *Turner Diaries* under his pillow. The idea that in a Christian war against the antichrist anything goes has already taken root in certain Christian circles in the United States. Paul Hill said in reference to chemical and biological weapons, "I wouldn't want to rule those out" (Stern, 2003: 170). Hill also told Jessica Stern that "killing Supreme Court justices, considering the majority of them favor mass murder. . . . It's hard for me to escape the conclusion it would be just for someone to kill them" (Stern, 2003: 169–170).

The belief that it is God's timing and God's action that must initiate the apocalypse and judge and destroy the nonbelievers has so far kept American apocalyptic Christianity from becoming overtly violent. But the *Left Behind* series, by setting the tribulation as a time ruled by the antichrist and his minions, who are beyond the possibility of redemption, makes it possible, even required, that true Christians fight violently against the government of the antichrist. Thus the stage is set for a series of war stories in which true Christians become military heroes. For those who like that sort of thing (and can tolerate the wooden and stereotypical characters) this makes for average reading. But there is another subtext. If Christians become convinced that the government is really the antichrist, or if a world unity government were to come into being, then Christians would

THE DIVINE TERRORIST • 113

be called upon to prove their devotion by becoming Christian versions of the Muslim jihadists.

For some American Christians that time is now. Any doubt that there is a segment of the Christian population of the United States that is at war with the rest of society can be laid to rest by examining the Army of God website. Clearly the Army of God feels that they are in a religious war right now; their site (www.armyofgod.com) is festooned with Bible verses such as "cursed be he that keepeth back his sword from blood" (Jeremiah, 48: 10), "surely thou wilt slay the wicked, O God" (Psalm, 139: 19), and "the righteous shall rejoice when he seeth the vengeance done: he shall wash his feet in the blood of the wicked" (Psalm, 58: 10).

This site also contains a statement by Eric Rudolph, who was responsible for several clinic bombings, the bombing of a gay club, and the bomb that exploded at the Atlanta's Centennial Olympic Park. He was captured in 2003 after 6 years of eluding federal and state law enforcement agents. His statement is captioned "Psalm 144: 1: Blessed be the LORD my strength which teacheth my hands to war, and my fingers to fight." In his statement Rudolph defends his bombing of several clinics including one where an employee was killed and another wounded ("the abortionist is the attendant who helps bloated partiers disgorge themselves so they can return to the rotten feast of materialism and self-indulgence," [Rudolph, n.d.: 6]); his bombing of a gay nightclub ("To pronounce it [homosexuality] to be just as legitimate a lifestyle choice is a direct assault upon the long term health of civilization and a vital threat to the very foundation of society. . . . Every effort should be made, including force if necessary, to halt this effort. . . . [It] should be ruthlessly opposed" [4, 30]; and his setting off a bomb during the 1996 Atlanta summer Olympics where one person was killed and more than 100 wounded ("The purpose of the so-called Olympic movement is the [sic] promote the values of global socialism as perfectly expressed in the song 'Imagine' by John Lennon, which was the theme of the 1966 Games" [4]). Rudolph also says that he planned to bomb an FBI headquarters building (7). Before his execution, Paul Hill wrote from prison that "The crying need is for people with the courage to affirm that it would be just to go to war against, or otherwise overthrow, any government that legalizes abortion" (Hill, 2003: 34). At the time of the anthrax scare in the east, in November 2001, letters appearing to contain anthrax (actually they contained a harmless white powder) were sent to two private abortion-providing clinics in New Jersey and to more than 150 Planned

Parenthood clinics around the United States. The letters were signed "The Army of God" (Stern, 2003: 330n5). For the Army of God, the Christian jihad against America has already begun.

My point is that the *Left Behind* series contains many of the same themes that we have found in all terrorist and fanatically violent religious movements: the punitive and abjecting image of God, the splitting of the world into all-good and all-evil camps, which accompanies the loss of empathy for others and their social death, the sanctification of violence, and the connection of purification with bloodshed. I am not suggesting that all the devotees of this series are about to become violent terrorists. But, to repeat what I said earlier, if social and psychological conditions were to change— for example, if these devotees came to feel there was no hope of converting the unconverted, or that God was calling them from a stance of waiting for him to act to a stance of taking matters into their own hands and acting to bring about the apocalypse, or that the government was under the control of the antichrist, or that a "world unity government" was coming into being, or if American apocalyptic Christians came to feel humiliated and shamed by a larger, secular culture—then all the religious and psychological conditions would be in place for a turn toward violent actions in the name of apocalyptic American Christianity. Along this line Anatol Lieven in his book *America Right or Wrong* has written of the sense of humiliation already felt on the part of large segments of religiously traditional, often rural, white populations—one of the main sources of readers of the *Left Behind* series. And Chris Hedges (2005) in *American Fascists* describes the sense of humiliation felt by many supporters of the religious right.

So while it was true in the early 1990s that for those whom Strozier met "violence was nowhere near being realized," he also realized that "under individual or social duress that violence can turn from latent to overt forms." The *Left Behind* series spells out, within the American apocalyptic Christian worldview, what those conditions are for the move from covert to overt violence: when it appears the end times are near, when it is the apocalyptic battle of good against evil, or, most important, when the enemy is demonic. It may be that for most readers, the *Left Behind* series portrays what will happen at the end of time. But it may also be that it portrays the way some apocalyptic American Christians see the world right now. On Jerry Falwell's talk show *Listen America*, Timothy LaHaye said, "We're in a religious war and we need to aggressively oppose secular humanism; these people are as religiously motivated as we are and they are filled with the devil" (quoted in Frykholm, 2004: 175).

CHAPTER 5

THE ROLE OF THE INDIVIDUAL

Toward a Clinical Psychology of Religious Terrorism

CARLA (NOT HER REAL NAME) HAD BARELY AVOIDED GOING TO prison for a very long time. At first she sat up stiffly in my office chair, short black hair sticking out at all angles, pale face flat and expressionless, dark eyes staring blankly straight ahead. Thin and tense, she looked considerably younger than her 20 years. At the beginning of the year she had been a student in my religious studies class at the midwestern liberal arts college at which I was teaching that year. In the middle of the first term she had disappeared. Now it was April, still chilly in Minnesota, and she had reappeared, knocking on my office door, not to study but just to talk and try to make sense of what had happened to her.

She had been raised in an upper-middle-class suburb of Chicago. Her father was a successful attorney; her mother was a research scientist at a university there. Her family attended the Unitarian church in their town. Her parents liked to sing and were avid members of the church choral society, and they liked to discuss ideas and so looked forward to the discussion group that followed the service each week. There was also a high school discussion group where Carla and her younger brother spent Sunday mornings. She remembered very little talk of God at these meetings. The "golden rule" and the acceptance of diverse opinions were emphasized. If God was mentioned, she said, it was usually as the force of love and good will.

In her freshman year of college she had taken a required course in world religions. To her surprise she had found herself fascinated. She took another religious studies course the next term and was known around campus, I found out, as the young woman always looking to get into a discussion with everyone about their personal beliefs. Various students who lived in Minneapolis or St. Paul often took her with them on Sundays to their home churches. One of these featured a particularly flamboyant and dynamic preacher who combined Pentecostal enthusiasm with a fierce commitment to social change. From the south and of mixed race himself, some years before he had led a group from his church to join the civil rights marches there. The group had been arrested and spent several nights in jail. His church ran a soup kitchen and homeless shelter. Carla decided not to go home for the summer after her freshman year but to stay and work there. She also signed up for a summer school course and so was able to stay in the dorm that summer. Her parents encouraged this as an indication of her commitment to social causes.

That summer, she told me, the pastor's preaching was taken entirely from the Hebrew prophets and their excoriation of their society for its injustices. This was a God of wrath and thunder whose fury was poured out on those who abused the poor and the unfortunate; a far cry from the mild God of love Carla had grown up with. Something inside her thrilled to this message. She said it just felt true to her. More and more anger against injustice rang from the pulpit. Carla was there every Sunday and at the Wednesday night service as well.

That October the paper reported that a local chemical company was the recipient of a government contract to study and develop possible biological warfare agents for the U.S. government. On the last day of October at night, a bomb went off in the lobby of that company's building. No one was injured, and a letter was found quoting the prophet Jeremiah. Only a couple days had to pass before people noticed that almost everyone associated with Carla's church, including Carla, had disappeared. It took the FBI about 2 months to find them in a small town just across the Canadian border and to bring them back and charge them with the bombing. The pastor and the principals were given prison time. Carla had been in the car that carried the bomb but her high-priced lawyer, provided by her parents, convinced the jury she did not know what their mission was that night. So she was given probation.

As we talked over several weeks, she became more animated and angry. She was convinced that God's judgment would fall upon the twin cities of Minnesota and the U.S. government for ignoring her pastor's prophetic denunciations and instead putting him in jail. She hoped that she could return to school the next fall and eventually study social work. She wanted to work with the poor for a church-related charity. She did not seem psychotic or dangerous; her aspirations for her life were realistic. The church she had joined was now closed and so she no longer attended any church regularly, for she said she could not find any church that preached the true gospel of God's judgment on an unjust world. As a young adult she had exchanged the benign God of her family and adolescence for the vengeful God of social justice.

A ROLE FOR INDIVIDUAL PSYCHOLOGY IN UNDERSTANDING RELIGION

Although quite dramatic, Carla's story is not unique. I've seen patients from terrifyingly judgmental and punitive religious groups who still retain a very benign view of their God and of human nature. And I have seen patients like Carla, raised in the most liberal, humanistic, tolerant congregations who still feel that their God is a cosmic score-keeper judging their every fault and everybody else as well. As both a clinician and a student of religious traditions, I have spent more than two decades trying to understand this phenomenon. Contemporary relational psychoanalysis is the framework that I have found most helpful in figuring out how this happens as well as for grasping more generally some of the motivational processes involved in religion and for working with patients around their religious issues. In cases like Carla's and others who find themselves drawn to religious beliefs and practices quite at variance with those of their family or social group, something more is going on than cultural influence alone (Jones, 2002).

In this chapter I want to pull together the most important characteristics of religiously motivated terrorism that emerge from our discussion so far and offer some analysis of these characteristics based on contemporary relational psychoanalytic theory (Jones, 1991, 2002). Past psychodynamic writing has tended to remove the person from history and culture.

I do not think we will get very far in understanding religiously motivated terrorism by concentrating on individual dynamics alone, but focusing only on social processes will leave out half the story. In this chapter I attend not only to individual dynamics but also to the interaction between the individual's psychology and their cultural, historical context and to the psychological processes evoked by this historical, cultural moment, what Erik Erikson called the meeting of "life history and the historical moment."

I certainly agree with Horgan (2006) that "explanations of terrorism in terms of personality traits are insufficient alone in trying to understand why some people become terrorists and others do not" (76). No one explanation is sufficient alone to explain terrorist behavior. But this does not mean that individual factors play no role. There remains the fact that some people have "a greater openness to increased engagement than others" with terrorist groups (Horgan, 2006: 101). Hafez (2006a) raises precisely this issue when he asks, "Why do some religious frames resonate with people whereas others fail to gain adherents?" (169).

It is understandable that an uprooted Muslim student might be attracted to a strident mosque that provides them community and identity and social support, or that a searching Japanese adolescent might be attracted to an Aum meditation center. But it seems that if the teachings and ethos of a religion don't mesh with the psychological dynamics and structures of the seekers, they will walk away or only follow the religion so far.

Individual factors cannot be totally ruled out. While intense religious devotion is clearly a salient factor in much contemporary terrorism, only a very small minority of devout Muslims take up the cause of jihad against the West. Not every displaced Arab student in Germany joins a fanatical mosque; not every member of the fanatical mosques pledge a loyalty to bin Laden, many walk away when offered the chance. Likewise, not every spiritual seeker in Japan joined Aum, and not every Aum member followed Asahara in his descent into apocalyptic violence. Not every committed evangelical Christian in America looks forward with relish to the ripping open and flaying of their non-Christian neighbors, just as not every subject of Milgram's experiments inflicted torture on the experimental victim. Likewise, not everyone from an oppressed or occupied community joins a suicide campaign. There is no question that, as the research reviewed in chapter 1 demonstrates, group processes can transform normal individuals into agents of terror. But not everyone is equally susceptible to those pressures or is equally motivated to engage in those acts.

In addition, social psychologists tell us that certain traits that are central to religiously sponsored terrorism go together—an authoritarian view of society, the belief that my religion is the only one, and prejudices against outsiders. But there is an additional question about why these traits are often found together. To more fully understand this, we need an account of the individual, private religious processes that serve as a template and filter for later experience. Relational psychoanalytic theory provides such a template, which is clinically useful in understanding how such an internal template arises and gains motivational power (Jones, 1991).

A RELATIONAL
PSYCHOANALYTIC APPROACH

Relational theory maintains that our personality, character, thoughts, and feelings are shaped by our early childhood experiences. Although relational theorists differ on exactly how these experiences influence our development, they agree that these experiences affect our developing sense of ourselves and our motivations, goals, and ways of thinking. And all agree that a crucial aspect of this early influence is the emotional tenor of those early interactions. This process of being shaped by our relational experiences does not end with childhood. It continues throughout our lives.

The early and influential parent–child dyad does not exist in a vacuum. The social organization and milieu surrounding that dyad impacts those early interpersonal experiences and the emotional world of the infant and child. A child growing up in a Palestinian refugee camp seething with frustration and anger or one coming of age in an American inner-city neighborhood plagued by fear and violence or attending school in Tel Aviv fearful of boarding a bus lest a human bomber be on board will have a very different early environment with very different affective experiences from a child growing up in a close-knit rural village in Scandinavia or a family with two children living in a suburban mansion in the United States saturated with video games and television programs. So relational psychoanalytic theories can be sensitive to the role the cultural surroundings play in the development of personality.

In addition, relational theories recognize that cultural and group influences play a major role in religious violence and terrorism and are part of the relational context and history that shape a terrorist's experience. Everyone agrees that there would have been no 9/11 without al-Qaeda. All the leaders of the 9/11 attacks were Muslim students slightly adrift in Germany and recruited into a fanatical mosque in Hamburg. Without that network of fanatical mosques in Europe, 9/11 would not have happened. The same appears, at this time, to be true of the July 7, 2005, London bombers and their link to a mosque in Leeds. Likewise, the sarin attack in Tokyo would never have happened without the subculture of Aum Shinrikyo, and it would also not have happened without the state of the larger Japanese society that produced a certain kind of spiritual alienation in many of its youth and provided few psychological or spiritual ways of addressing it. Understanding these cultures of violence is clearly a crucial part of understanding religious terrorism. This is where so much current psychological writing on the topic begins and ends. A fuller psychological understanding might begin there but cannot end there. In addition, we must also ask about the psychological functions within the individual of these cultures of violence, not only about their recruitment methods or group processes. Particularly we might inquire about the ways they manipulate, play upon, and potentiate an individual's personal history and about what makes an individual susceptible to them.

Psychological studies of terrorists—especially from a psychodynamic standpoint—have tended to engage in simple pathologizing and psychological name-calling. Simply giving a diagnostic label to an individual terrorist or to a terrorist group adds little to our understanding of religiously motivated violence. And, more perniciously, labels can be used to dismiss any legitimate grievances on the part of the communities from which the terrorists came. Partly in reaction against these tendencies on the part of clinicians writing about terrorism, most of the recent psychological articles dealing with this topic are written from a social rather than a clinical standpoint. These studies emphasize group processes and social conditioning as the most salient psychological factors in terrorist behavior (e.g., Moghaddam, 2005; Moghaddam, & Marsella, 2004; Waller, 2002; Zimbardo, 2004).

However, understanding the individual psychological dynamics and forces that motivate a person does not necessarily mean engaging in pathologizing and psychological name-calling. The same is true of clinical practice. The psychodynamic clinician seeks to fathom the idiosyncratic factors in the history and character that motivate a patient, not to attach some label to them, but to better understand them. The same is true here. I am not interested in pathologizing or labeling religiously motivated terrorists. I am interested in seeing if there are any possible commonalties of character and style that run through many of those who contemplate or commit violence in the name of their religion. Again, my main focus here is the psychology of religion and what such motivations might tell us about the nature of religion, first, and terrorism, second.

From a clinical psychodynamic standpoint, what appears most salient in this discussion are the themes of shame and humiliation, the apocalyptic splitting of the world into all-good/all-evil camps and with it the need for absolute purity, an overly idealized deity or leader who is wrathful and punitive and so functions as a source of shame and humiliation, a fascination with violence and the linkage of violence and purification, and the authoritarian concern with submission and prejudice against outsiders. How does a relational theory cast light on these themes?

THE PSYCHOLOGY OF RELIGIOUS HUMILIATION

Research suggests that shame and humiliation may be crucial elements in most religiously sponsored violence. Several different types of findings convince me of the connection between shame and humiliation and religiously sponsored violence. During my forensic work at a maximum security prison and in the juvenile justice system, I found that the research literature contains many studies connecting shame and humiliation with violent behavior, including revenge. Several writers describing the psychologically destructive effects of religion have emphasized the negative role of shaming, humiliating religious beliefs and practices, especially in the case of patriarchal or superego-driven forms of religion (the kinds of religion Freud knew and wrote about). Finally, many writing about the politics of terrorism stress the feelings of humiliation often shared by groups that produce terrorists. All of these pieces fit together to create a convincing connection between the psychological factors of shame and humiliation and the appeal of religiously motivated violent actions.

Religion can become involved with humiliation-driven violence in one or both of two ways. First, people may be humiliated by the circumstances of their lives (e.g., Palestinians under Israeli occupation, Chechens under Russian occupation, Iraqis under U.S. occupation), and their religion may play upon that humiliation and potentiate it and channel it for its own purposes. Remember the Palestinian recruiter who said, "Much of the work is already done by the suffering these people have been subject to. . . . Only 10 percent comes from me" (Davis, 2003: 154).

We should also note that religion may mute and transform that humiliation rather than reinforce it, as the Dalai Lama is trying to do with the Tibetans under Chinese occupation and as Martin Luther King attempted to do with the humiliation of African Americans in the face of American racism. Clearly a different psychology—a different view of the divine, a rejection of splitting and dichotomizing, a conscious muting or transformation of aggression—is at work in those who seek to transform humiliation rather than magnify it. Beyond that, we have discussed the lack of empathy that characterizes terrorists and how research has shown that the ability to empathize with a victim decreases the use of violence. So religions that seek to move those feeling humiliated away from violence work to encourage compassion and empathy for the other, even the other who is a source of social or economic humiliation.

Second, along with playing upon any social humiliation, religions may directly evoke and exacerbate feelings of shame and humiliation. Images of a wrathful punitive deity, or a revered master or leader who harangues and humiliates his disciples, or a sacred text read in a way to aggravate shame and condemnation are all vehicles for intensifying feelings of humiliation. Here we can begin to see some of the connections among these themes often found in religiously motivated terrorists, such as their punitive image of God or some other religious figure and their humiliation-driven turn toward violence. My suggestion is that when the divine, the revered master, or the sacred text is experienced as a source of humiliation and shame, the possibility of violence increases. Previously I argued that idealization was central to religion and to religious violence (and also to religious transformation) (Jones, 2002). Here I am revising that thesis to say that it is not idealization alone that is central to the psychology of religious violence but an idealized figure that is also a source of shame and humiliation. The psychodynamic connection to something sacred that results in religious violence is not just a tie to an idealized figure but, in addition, to an idealized humiliating or overpowering one. For example, in the Buddhist and Hindu religions devotees have ties to idealized figures—pantheons of divine beings or enlightened masters—which, when they turn punitive and humiliating (as perhaps in the case Aum Shinrikyo or the devotees of Kali), these devotees turn violent too.

In addition to the connections between religions of shame and humiliation and violence, research done with religious believers in North America suggests that punitive images of God tend to be associated with an external locus of control, a lack of empathy for others, a tendency toward psychological splitting, and less self-esteem. This research suggests that people who hold punitive, wrathful images of God (the kind associated with religions that are shaming and guilt producing) often show authoritarian personality traits and a lack of empathy, among other traits. These empirical studies also find that psychological maturity—that is, the capacity for empathy, a sense of basic trust, a feeling of secure attachment, self-esteem, low levels or anxiety and depression, and little suspicion of others—is associated with images of God as loving and benevolent (Brokaw & Edwards, 1994; Spear, 1994; Tisdale, 1997). Images of God as wrathful and controlling are associated with themes of the kind found among many religiously motivated terrorists: the splitting of the world, lack of empathy, and suspicion of outsiders. So there appear to be demonstrable connections between the punitive experience of the divine, authoritarian personality traits, and the appeal of an apocalyptic polarization of the world.

By pushing for submission to a humiliating but idealized god or leader, religion makes terror possible. This drive to connect to an idealized and humiliating divine figure sublates all other human desires. The desire for this God overwhelms all connections between human beings. The result is a detachment from empathic connections between human beings (one of the traits of many religious terrorists) and their replacement by a totalizing connection with God alone. Love of this demanding God replaces love for other human beings. By identifying with God and what is supposed to be God's perspective, other human beings appear small and insignificant. As opposed to those religions that see each human spirit as infinitely precious, created in God's image, terrorist forms of the religious imagination envision individual human beings as insignificant in the larger context of God's eternal plan. The tie to an idealized and overpowering or persecutory object results in a psychological state that Ruth Stein (2006) describes as "the libidinal and perverted relations between a certain kind of believer and his God, in which the libidinal and the violent come together" (205). Stein calls this "vertical desire," which is "the mystical longing for merger with the idealized other who requires abjection" (209).

This is a religion focused on obedience, submission, purification, and earning divine favor. One might call these the central themes of a patriarchal religion. Although there are women suicide bombers in Sri Lanka, Palestine, and Chechnya, the 9/11 action was an all-male rite. And most fanatical religious groups are clearly male dominated (Lawrence, 1989). So part of the psychology involved in terrorist religions is the psychology of patriarchal religion.

FREUD ON PATRIARCHY AND RELIGION

Sigmund Freud provides one of the most profound analyses of the patriarchal religion often found in terrorist groups in his book *Totem and Taboo* (a fuller discussion of *Totem and Taboo* can be found in Jones, 1996). The first social group was a patriarchal clan, according to Freud. The sons of the patriarch hated their father, who stood in the way of their boundless desire. But they loved and admired him too. So first they murdered him. Then their affection for him, which they had to deny in order to kill him, reappeared as guilt and remorse. This is how guilt, on which all religion depends according to Freud, originated (Freud, 1913/1950: 143).

The murderous sons of the primal father, the harbingers of culture and religion, had to make peace with their returning repressed guilt. A substitute father had to be found. Like Freud's phobic child patient named "little Hans," who projected his fear of his father onto an animal, the guilty sons projected their feelings onto an animal, and totemism, and with it religion, was born. If totemism is the beginning of religion (a claim found in many anthropological texts of Freud's time), patriarchal theism is the end. Freud remains convinced that the root of every religion is a "longing for the father" (Freud, 1913/1950: 148). The first religious object, the totem, could only be a surrogate father. As time went on and the primal murder faded into unconsciousness, an object entered consciousness that carried a more complete resemblance to the lost father—a god "in which the father has regained his human shape" (148).

This legacy of patriarchal religion becomes the lens through which Freud sees all religious history. "The god of each of them is formed in the likeness of the father, his personal relation to God depends on his relation to his father. . . . At bottom God is nothing other than an exalted father" (Freud, 1913/1950: 47). Freud was convinced that the murder of the father (the oedipal complex enacted in real time) and its continual replay in fantasy and culture is the hinge on which history turns. Thus he easily reads religious development forward or backward from that point.

In a letter to Freud responding to his antireligious tract *The Future of an Illusion*, Freud's friend Romain Rolland, a student of Hindu religion and biographer of Ramakrishna and Vivekenanda, proposed a pre-oedipal origin to religion in a "feeling of something limitless, unbounded—as it were, oceanic . . . a purely subjective fact, not an article of faith" (Freud, 1930/1962: 12; see also Parsons, 1999). Freud, having firmly committed himself to the centrality of the father, the father God, the oedipal struggle, and the masculine gender, denied Rolland's claim that religion arises from pre-oedipal, maternal dynamics. The only definition of religion Freud would consider is a patriarchal religion of law and guilt built around the father God.

Freud's analysis of religion depends on a very specific image of God. The patriarchal God of law and conscience is the only religion Freud's theory will countenance. If he had given up that paternal representation of God as normative, his argument would have lost much of its force. Freud reproduced the exclusive, patriarchal monotheism of Western religion in his theory of the exclusively oedipal and paternal origins of culture, religion, and morality. Freud had to insist that religion is essentially patriarchal, for that is the only religion that fit within the frame of his oedipal drama.

In tying morality tightly to the Oedipus complex so that "religion, morals, society converge in the Oedipus complex" (Freud, 1913/1950: 157), Freud insisted that morality consists mainly of rules and prohibitions. His tendency to limit morality to a set of prohibitions, like his restriction of religion to patriarchal theism, followed naturally from the centrality of the oedipal period in his theory. The importance of the pre-oedipal, maternal period was forgotten. Just as forms of religion may be rooted in pre-oedipal, maternal dynamics, so may morality have these roots. Along with a post-oedipal, paternal morality of law and authority, there may well be a pre-oedipal, maternal morality of connection and relationship. An appreciation of the integrity and centrality of pre-oedipal dynamics might point to an ethic of relatedness in which the maintenance of connections between people is more central than the imposition of rules (Jones, 1996).

While Freud's *Totem and Taboo* is clearly a work of fiction, his proposal points to the deep psychodynamic connections between patriarchal cultures, paternalistic deities, and guilt-engendering religions. Such connections, common in the history of religion, are not accidental but can be explored through the Oedipus complex read not as biological necessity but rather as cultural expression. Exploring oedipal dynamics clinically reveals the ways boys in a patriarchal culture identify with the father and internalize the motifs of dominance and submission, impersonal experiences of power, and the need for detachment. When something that is sacred is encountered in the context of these masculine identifications, religion is experienced in terms of dominance and submission and transcendental power and control. And when morality is worked out in that context, the result is an ethics of law backed up by sacred power and dominance. This produces a patriarchal religion of divine law and power in which submission to the law of the father is the primary moral imperative and guilt is the main religious emotion. The point here is not to defend Freud's theory, which I certainly do not accept as a full account of human life or as the way I treat patients. Rather, I use Freud's theory to point out connections among certain psychological themes that are present in patriarchal theologies and terroristic religions. From a psychodynamic standpoint the connections among these themes is not coincidental. Whether this is a complete account of the psychology of patriarchy is less important than the insistence never to lose sight of the role of patriarchal thinking and the connections between engendering guilt, legalistic ethics, and judgmental deities that form part of the psychological–theological preconditions for much religious terrorism.

The Problem of Submission

I have suggested that an important element common to religiously motivated terrorists is the insistence on submission to an overidealized and humiliating Other. Since all the major religions call for some submission to some higher authority or ultimate reality, we must ask whether religion inevitably leads to the kind of authoritarianism that is so central to religious terrorism. Emmanuel Ghent (1990) has perceptively nuanced the issue of submission in the contemporary psychoanalytic discussion. Ghent builds on D. W. Winnicott's (1971) suggestion that if the parents interfere with the infant's creative spontaneity by imposing their will on the infant's play, the child develops a compliant persona. If this parental impingement consistently overwhelms the child's spontaneity, the child may lose touch with her creative core (or "true self") and completely identify with the compliant façade. This results in what Winnicott calls a "false self" organization.

For new psychological growth to take place, this false self must be broken through. Ghent (1990) proposes that beneath the false exterior there is a wish to lay down the façade and or have it penetrated (the sexual connotations here are intentional) so that the true self can be known. This he calls a longing for surrender—that is, surrendering the false self for the sake of "the discovery of one's identity, one's sense of self, one's sense of wholeness, even one's sense of unity with other living beings" (111).

If the path of surrender is closed, then the longing for surrender may be perverted into what Ghent calls an act of submission in which one denies one's own desires and intentions and allows oneself to be overpowered by another. With submission, "one feels one's self as a puppet in the power of another; one's sense of identity atrophies" (Ghent, 1990: 111), exactly the feeling one often finds in the language of religious terrorists. In other words, one becomes masochistic, hence the subtitle of Ghent's paper: "masochism as a perversion of surrender." The stark submission of authoritarian religion or the sexual penetration of masochism becomes a poor substitute for the penetration of the false façade and the knowledge of the true self.

For the adult who has lost touch with the true self, one way to recover it is through surrender, the putting aside of the false self. Surrender opens a way to encounter again the true self. Ghent (1990) thus suggests that surrendering to experience (especially in a religious milieu) is transformative because the façade of false selfhood is (at least temporarily) put aside, and the true, free, spontaneous self is reawakened (for examples, see Jones, 2002). Awakening the true self is a powerfully transformative experience: defensiveness is replaced by spontaneity and depletion gives way to what Winnicott (1971) calls "feeling fully alive."

We saw earlier how Qutb and other fundamentalists made law and submission the central aspects of true piety. Fundamentalist religions, whether or not they turn violent, tend to be legalistic. For them devotion to God means submission to a divine law. For them such submissiveness is the main ingredient in true religion. But there are other possibilities. Ghent (1990) makes clear that devotion to an idealized figure does not necessarily imply the submissiveness indicative of the authoritarian personality or the religious terrorist. Religious conversion may also represent the transforming power of surrender through which addictions are overcome, creative abilities released, and neurotic traits transformed (Jones, 2002).

THE LURE OF POLARIZATION: FAIRBAIRN, KLEIN, AND KOHUT

The point of this chapter is that there may be something within certain individuals that predisposes them to be attracted to and to accept a religion built around a patriarchal theology and characterized by an apocalyptic view of the world and the splitting of humanity into all-good and all-bad camps, leading to prejudice and crusades against outsiders. How might we understand this factor?

The twentieth-century British analyst W.R.D. Fairbairn confronted precisely this issue in the clinical, rather than the political, setting. He proposed a dynamic he called "the moral defense against bad objects" (Fairbairn, 1952), which seems to fit the frame of mind found in many fundamentalist and terrorist religions. According to Fairbairn, the child begins absolutely dependent on his parents. If they are experienced as unavailable, untrustworthy, unable to care for the child, or otherwise "bad," the child's very existence feels endangered. He must do anything he can to make the world feel safe, even going so far as blaming himself for the experience of badness so that the external, parental world can appear good. Fairbairn (1952) writes, "the child would rather be bad himself than have bad objects . . . one of his motives in becoming bad is to make his objects good . . . he is rewarded by the sense of security which an environment of good objects confers" (66).

To maintain the experience of the parents as good, the child splits the sense of badness off from the parents and takes it on himself. Thus the child maintains an idealized view of the parents at his own expense, experiencing himself as bad and seeing the parents, on whose goodness he depends, as good. The child sanitizes the image of the parents at the cost of his own self-esteem and self-worth, protecting his idealization of them by taking the pain and pathology of their relationship into himself, bearing "the burden of badness" (Fairbairn, 1952: 65). Thus a dichotomy is created in the child's, and later the adult's, experience between an all-good, overly idealized, external parental object (such as God, a religious teacher, or a sacred text) and an entirely bad self.

What is the poor self to do with this "burden of badness" he has taken up in order to make the world seem good? He may turn it against himself in the kind of depressive symptomotology that led Fairbairn (1952) to his reflections on the "moral defense." Here religion may play a crucially facilitative role. In that psychological context, which Fairbairn called the "moral defense," encountering an overly idealized other (perhaps God, or a religious teacher, text, or institution that claims divinity and perfection) inevitably evokes both a splitting of experience into all-good and all-bad domains and also denigrating oneself and everything connected to oneself. We have seen how common this combination of splitting and self-denigration is in religious communities that give rise to terrorism. They often call upon their devotees to demean themselves and bemoan their unworthiness in the face of some ideal other. For example, one contemporary fundamentalist Protestant theologian insists that even church members "at their very core they are slaves to sin, perverse, self-aggrandizing, anti-God, rebellious, weak, fallen, possessed of a twisted heart" (quoted in Ritter & O'Neill, 1996: 49). Such self-abnegation and humiliation are central to the common life of fanatically violent religious traditions. It is not coincidence that Fairbairn (1952) uses theological language to describe this moral defense and the splitting that results from it when he writes, "it is better to be a sinner in a world ruled by God than to live in a world ruled by the Devil" (67).

Another possibility, besides turning the burden of badness against oneself, is to expel the feeling of badness from oneself by projecting it onto the outside world. Here again religion facilitates such a move. Weighed down by this sense of badness, a person may identify with an idealized tradition or group and then project that sense of badness onto some outside person or group, thereby seeing some other group, race, or religion as evil. The experience of badness that the individual has taken into himself is so painful that often it must be discharged by being projected onto a despised group. Religious groups that encourage this splitting of the world into all-good and all-bad camps inevitably find others to demonize and carry this sense of badness. As we have seen, the research on religious fanaticism and terrorism provides countless examples of this dynamic. It is not coincidence that this research has found that the more fanatical groups are also the most racist, homophobic, and anti-Semitic. Thus the psychological appeal of what Juergensmeyer (2000) calls satanization. Such a denigration of the other, an almost inevitable result of the moral defense with its overidealization of an object and the splitting of the world, makes the denigrated other a ready victim of terrorist violence.

Fairbairn (1952) describes a clinical constellation that appears to map readily onto fanatical religions and certain religiously motivated terrorist groups. There is the uncritical overidealization of an object. In the face of that overidealized object, religious devotees experience shame and a sense of badness which they both turn against themselves in rituals and assertions of self-deprecation and against others by demonizing them as impure and unrighteous. Such feelings of shame and humiliation may further provoke intense feelings of hostility that can then be discharged against the demonized others. People carrying this psychological tendency to demean themselves in the face of an idealized God, text, teacher, institution, or tradition may find their experience confirmed in fanatical religious groups with their demands for human self-abnegation.

But there is an additional factor that Fairbairn downplays—aggression. Melanie Klein (1975a, 1975b) postulates an innate aggressive drive rather than thinking of aggression as the result of shame and humiliation. Klein thereby provides an additional reason for the projection of this dichotomy of all good/all bad onto the external world, a projection that is so crucial to understanding fanatical and violent religions. Klein claims that the child is born with both aggressive and pleasure-seeking drives. The infant fears that her own innate aggressiveness will destroy her, and so she removes this aggressiveness from herself by projecting it onto her mother. But now, of course, the infant fears she will be destroyed from the outside by the mother who now embodies the aggression originating in the infant. Klein terms this situation the "paranoid position" because it is characterized by anxiety over being persecuted by the mother.

Of course the infant also receives positive, pleasurable experiences from the feeding, cuddling, and other interactions with his mother. These experiences evoke his pleasure-seeking drive and are carried by the sense of the mother as good, pleasurable, and nurturing. The infant's experience is thus split between an image of the bad mother who threatens to annihilate the child and the good mother who provides satisfaction and pleasure. According to Klein (1975a), the relative health of the child and his later development hinges on the presence of enough good-mother experiences to contain and modulate the anxiety created by the child's projection of his own aggression onto his mother.

Still the infant feels he must protect his image of his mother as good from the destructiveness the child feels is present in his inner and outer worlds. To protect the good mother experience, Klein (1975a) suggests that the child further segregates his image of his mother as good. Thus the child's experience of his mother is further split into distinct good-mother and bad-mother compartments. And since both the good-mother and bad-mother images are directly tied to pleasurable and fearful experiential states within the infant, the infant's experience of himself also becomes split into good-self and bad-self compartments. The rigidity of this splitting, which is designed to protect the good-mother and the good-self experiences from the destructive forces within and without, is directly proportional to the amount of positive care-taking the child has received. If the infant has received sufficient nurturance and care, he has built up enough positive experiences to contain his fear of his own destructiveness. Then he is not so anxious about it and doesn't need to so rigidly split off the good mother and the good self in order to protect them from his own aggression. If he has few positive emotional resources to draw on in dealing with his own aggressiveness, the infant is much more anxious about the power of aggression. Feeling his own aggressiveness will heap destruction on his world, he needs more drastically to split off and protect the good-mother/good-self experiences.

In the course of normal development, if the degree of splitting is not too severe, the child moves from the "paranoid position" to what Klein (1975b) calls the "depressive position." If the child's contact with reality is not weakened by too profound a splitting, the child can grow to tolerate ambivalence and to recognize that her mother as well as herself contains both good and bad aspects. The child then comes to accept that she can hate and love the same object and learns to deal with her destructiveness not by splitting but by making reparations and by reaching out in reciprocal care to the parent and to others. The child begins to take responsibility for her own destructive fantasies rather than projecting them onto the external world. In the best of all possible outcomes, the child learns to tolerate ambiguity, and that relational ties are strong enough to contain aggression, that splitting is not necessary, and that love is stronger than hate (Klein, 1975a, 1975b).

If the balance of negative and positive early experiences is weighted toward the negative and too severe an internal split developed, and if later experiences failed to redress that imbalance, the individual enters adolescence and early adulthood with the defense of splitting still in place. Unable to tolerate ambivalence and still burdened with anger and

anxiety, the individual needs to continue to split the world into opposing camps of good and evil, to unrealistically idealize some object and
protect that overly idealized object from contamination by segregating
it from forces of impurity, and to externalize the persecutory rage by
threatening others. These are exactly the traits that often characterize
religious terrorists.

While theorizing its etiology very differently, Fairbairn and Klein both
call attention to an often-seen clinical constellation that must divide the
world into completely opposed black and white camps in which things
are either all good or all bad. Such a configuration appears to characterize much religiously driven terrorism. In addition, Klein's theory
addresses the drive for purity and purification, often found in conjunction with such splitting. Rites of purification, including violent crusades
against those considered evil, feel necessary to protect an idealized figure from contamination. Klein (1975a, 1975b) proposes that this fear
of contamination arises from within the self, from anxiety about one's
own aggression that is projected onto demonized others outside. Thus
many fanatical religions experience those different from themselves as
threats to their faith, which needs to be protected from those threatening others. These others are not just threats to be warded off but are also
impurities in need of elimination.

We have already seen the different ways that Fairbairn and Klein theo-
rize the origin of the need to split the world into dichotomized camps
and the refusal to acknowledge ambiguity, traits central in the texts of
most religions of terror. Heinz Kohut has another approach to this same
problem. In the best of all worlds, according to Kohut (1971), the infant
lives in a state of bliss, which he calls "primary narcissism." To hold onto
this idyllic experience, Kohut suggests that the child creates two internal
realities that continue to carry that experience: a grandiose image of the
self; and an idealized image of the parent. There is nothing pathological
about this—quite the reverse. Every normal child makes these psychological moves, and these two internal states—a grandiose, omnipotent
sense of herself and of her primary caretakers—are the basis of an adult's
healthy sense of self.

To keep that early blissful experience alive, the developing child needs
these two idealizations of herself and her parents. But since this early
state cannot last, the child also needs these idealizations to fail. But these
idealizations need to fail in a special way. Ideally, the child will experience gradual, not sudden or traumatic, disappointments in the idealized

parents or her idealized view of herself. Thus over time the child's view of her parents and herself will gradually become more and more realistic, and less overidealized and perfectionistic. This graded process of disappointment and increasingly realistic assessment leads, Kohut (1971) argues, to the internalization of the psychological capacities that the parents previously provided. For example, the experience of being joined to an idealized parent gradually becomes internalized as the capacity to choose one's own values and goals and commit oneself to them. Feeling connected to a greater, ideal reality is no longer dependent on the presence of an idealized parental figure. Through this internalization, the developing person gains a measure of autonomy. She no longer needs to depend on an idealized, omnipotent and perfect parent (or parent figure) but can choose her own ideals to which to commit herself.

Thus the idealizations of the parents and one's self are gradually replaced by a more realistic assessment, and the child assumes responsibility for the psychological functions previously provided by the idealization of the parents and their reinforcing of the child's narcissism. In this developmental process, experiences with external objects become transmuted into certain psychological capacities and abilities. The child begins by idealizing the parent and creating a grandiose image of herself. But these idealized and grandiose images of parents and one's self, carriers of the early state of primary narcissism, are open to correction and modification through actual experience. The gradual awareness of the parent's shortcomings and the limits of one's own grandiosity transform the experience of idealizing the parents into the ability to choose values and make commitments and the need for constant admiration from others becomes transmuted into a healthy and realistic sense of self-esteem (Kohut, 1971: 40–41).

If, at an early age, the child experiences a severe or sudden loss of the idealized parent through his or her disappearance from the child's life or a shattering disappointment in the parent, then this gradual process of internalization cannot happen. The child does not develop his own internal capacity to choose and commit himself to values and goals. Instead of gradually relinquishing his early need for overly idealized, omnipotent, and perfect objects and replacing them with realistic ideals and ambitions, he remains (even as an adult) totally dependent on external objects that claim to be perfect and ideal in order to provide that necessary sense of connection to something of value and to buttress his self-esteem.

If development goes well, interpersonal experiences are transformed into the structures that give the personality a relative sense of coherence and independence. If development goes poorly and those self structures do not develop, the individual is left pathologically dependent on and desperately hungry for overly idealized and apparently perfect external figures to provide the ideals he needs and to buttress his fragile sense of self-esteem. Since the normal childhood need for those perfect and omnipotent figures has been kept from gradual modification in a more realistic direction, the need for them remains. And so the person continues to be vulnerable to those leaders, institutions, and ideologies that hold out the promise of an experience of, or identification with, omnipotence and perfection, claims found in many religions. Admitting to any ambivalence or ambiguity would destroy that hoped-for experience of perfection on which the person's sense of self still depends. It would be experienced as a threat to the sense of self. As such it would bring forth storms of rage directed at others, a characteristic of many religious fanatics.

Relational psychoanalytic theory provides an account—grounded in clinical experience—of the genesis of the dichotomizing tendency that many commentators find at the heart of religious fanaticism. In fundamentalist Christianity, this dichotomizing is personified in the figure of the devil. In their writings one constantly encounters exhortations to "spiritual warfare." One pastor has written that Satan "knows if he can get you to let down the defenses of your mind it won't be long before he wraps his red-hot fingers around your heart" (quoted in Ritter & O'Neill, 1996: 44). Frykholm (2004) described how American apocalyptic Christianity "has created a universe in which there are only two answers—either you have accepted Jesus and are saved. . . . Or you are damned" (160). Ironically Sayyid Qutb expresses exactly the same sentiment in words that, if a few phrases were changed from Arabic to English, could have been uttered by any apocalyptic Christian:

> The callers of Islam should not have any superficial doubts in their hearts concerning the nature of *Jahiliyyah* and the nature of Islam. . . . Indeed, there is no Islam in a land where Islam is not dominant and where *Shari'ah* is not established. . . . There is nothing beyond faith except unbelief, nothing beyond Islam except *Jahiliyyah*, nothing beyond truth except falsehood.
> (Qutb, 1996: 239)

This radically split universe is the universe of religiously sponsored terrorism. The relational psychoanalytic theories of Fairbairn, Klein, and

Kohut suggest that the need for such splitting derives from the child's early interpersonal experiences. Early experiences may predispose a person to be attracted to fanatical religions whose teachings and practices express feelings of self-denigration, the need for splitting, and the projection of aggression onto others. This account also implies that such dichotomizing is not inevitably a part of the religious consciousness but is rather a function of a certain psychodynamic constellation characterized by an inability to tolerate ambiguity and a tendency to see everything in polarized, black-and-white terms.

The Demand for Purification

This dichotomizing of the world requires a strict boundary between the group and the outside world and a drive for purity which Marty and Appleby (1981) take as a defining characteristic of the groups they studied: "fundamentalists set boundaries, protect the group from contamination, and preserve purity" (821). The pure must keep themselves aloof from the impure in order to preserve their purity and superiority. As we have seen, this need for purity and purification often plays an important role in the minds of religiously motivated terrorists. For example, Qutb (1996) wrote that there must be a total "break between the Muslim's present Islam and his past *Jahiliyyah,* and this after a well thought out decision, as a result of which all his relationships with *Jahiliyyah* would be cut off and he would be joined completely to Islam" (31).

Fairbairn's and Klein's theories imply that the more rigid the split between the good and the bad, the more powerful the drive to expel it by projection and the stronger the need to protect the ideal from contamination. When good and evil are totally dichotomized, doing good, doing God's will, becomes easily equated with eliminating the bad, eliminating it from oneself through ritual self-abnegation, eliminating it from the world through the ritual purification of terrorist warfare against the evil ones. Thus in terrorist religions, doing good is not enough. In addition to doing good, the devotee must make war on evil. Eventually doing good comes to mean primarily fighting evil.[1] The impulse to do good becomes transformed into a motivation for war and violence. What are sacrificed in the first instance are disowned parts of oneself that are experienced as impure or evil. Later these are projected outward onto the world, onto the evildoers around one. Soon they must be sacrificed too. In this vein, Stein proposes that

The terrorist feels that God is pleased when his sons/followers annihilate His enemies. *But this is precisely why the terrorist loves God: because God allows, wants, and sanctifies the killing of the "bad part"* and, in addition, allows, desires, and sanctifies the orgiastic pleasure of disinhibited murdering and destruction. God is loved for both His licensing the ecstatic killing and for His offering a solution to the conflict-torn psyche at war with itself. (Stein, 2002: 411, emphasis in original)

Thus the terrorist sacrifices both himself and the godless other, purifying himself and the world and earning his Father's acceptance. For Stein, the destruction carried out for the sake of a beloved Father-God to whom the devotee submits unconditionally is central to religious terrorism. Such violent acts are done out of love more than hate—love for a God who rewards unconditional submission with a sanctified outlet for rage and humiliation.

This rigid dichotomizing and inability to tolerate ambivalence and ambiguity can easily lead to a wish for absolute purity. Such dreams of total purity and perfection become part of the problem of religious violence. The demand for total purity and perfection can never be met in this finite world. Such demands are inherently impossible. Living with such an impossible demand can easily build up rage and frustration when it cannot be met. So the demand for purification becomes linked to rage, and the rage has to be discharged—first, perhaps, in fantasies of apocalyptic violence and destruction. But if the rage builds up more, it may seek discharge in action as well.

Alongside the specific theories of Fairbairn and Klein, psychoanalysis has traditionally offered two kinds of explanations for this pursuit of total perfection, the refusal to tolerate any imperfection, and the concomitant drive for purification—one focusing on guilt, the other on shame. Guilt is the feeling of having done something wrong. It is the result of a critical conscience. Here purification means expelling what is impure and making peace with an overbearing and tyrannical conscience. Often such a tyrannical conscience demands increasing suppression of desire, especially sexual desire. Thus the repression of sexuality, as we have seen, often characterizes patriarchal forms of religion and of religious terrorism. Such repression builds up frustration that must be projected onto others or acted out in holy wars against the immoral ones who embody the freedom that the terrorist has repressed. The history of religions is full of examples of this close conjunction of guilt and patriarchal religion, like that described by Freud in *Totem and Taboo.*

Shame, in contrast, involves a lack of self-worth and the erosion of sense of self; it touches on who a person is and not just on what a person has done. The issue here is not moral perfection and a tyrannical conscience but self-worth and the need to bolster self-worth by identifying with an idealized, perfect other. I can feel better about myself if I can feel joined to an omnipotent or idealized group, leader, or divinity like that found in most religious traditions. But this sense of self-worth depends on preserving the idealization of that person or group. When that is threatened, my sense of self is threatened too. And that feeling of threat may cause me to react violently.

WHY HUMILIATION LEADS TO VIOLENCE

Heinz Kohut (1973) underscores this connection between humiliation and rage. Humiliation is an injury to a person's sense of self and their self-esteem, a threat to the self. The psychologically threatened self responds with violence, just as the physically threatened self sometimes does, especially if the self is inclined toward violence and lacks empathy for others. This parallels a finding from forensic psychology: men who batter or kill their wives or girlfriends often say openly that they felt they were losing control over their partners (when the partners talked about leaving them, for example, or had other friendships). This need for control often covers a psychological vulnerability that leads to violence when the self feels threatened, in this case threatened by the loss of control. Feelings of humiliation appear common in many of the oppressed groups that produce terrorists. Terman (2007) writes of the central role that humiliation plays in the lives of fanatical and violent individuals and groups. In his book *America Right or Wrong*, Anatol Lieven (2004) speaks of the humiliation that the white Christian American nationalistic cohorts felt during the 1960s—the groups that form the backbone of the Christian religious right whose apocalypticism is suffused with violence as described in the last chapter. The same point is made by Chris Hedges (2006) in his account of the radical Christian right in America. Such feelings of humiliation may indicate a self that feels threatened, and a self that feels threatened may dream of violence and revenge. So a religion that emphasizes divine vengeance (which either the true believer carries out with divine sanction or the true believer fantasizes about God carrying out in the near future) appeals to those feeling humiliation. Again, we are back to revenge because many religious terrorists see themselves explicitly as agents of divine vengeance. The theme of divine vengeance is all throughout the writings of contemporary American Christian apocalyptic literature and the literature of other religious texts of terror. Part of the origin of this violence lies in either threats to the self or threats to cherished institutions, beliefs, and worldviews that the believer feels are necessary to maintain their self-esteem and identity. And the response to those threats is violence.

Kohut (1977) suggests that "destructive rage, in particular, is always motivated by an injury to the self" (117). The injury that evokes this destructive rage can be a direct threat, or, more commonly, it can be a threat to some ideal, ideology, or institution on which the individual depends for his identity and self-esteem. If my identity and sense of self-worth are inextricably bound to my identification with a religious, political, ethnic, or professional community, when they are threatened, Kohut says, I feel threatened at my most basic level as a human person. One of the most relevant aspects of Kohut's theory for the psychology of religion is the way that beliefs, institutions, and ideals can become a part of my sense of self. Then I become dependent on them to maintain that sense of self. A threat to a cherished belief, ideal, of institution can feel like as much (if not more) of a threat than a direct physical threat to myself. Then I respond with what he calls "narcissistic rage" (Kohut, 1973: 379). Such rage is to be expected if a person's entire sense of themselves is built on a single identity as a religious devotee, a patriot, the partisan of a cause, or a rational scientist. Under such conditions, individuals are set up for narcissistic rage when those foundations of selfhood appear threatened. The main characteristic of such rage is that "those who are in the grip of narcissistic rage show total lack of empathy toward the offender" (Kohut, 1973: 386). Such a total lack of empathy is one of the most striking traits frequently seen in those who bomb innocent noncombatants, assassinate reproductive health care providers, and imagine (and sometimes plot) apocalyptic genocidal violence in the name of their deity.

Kohut (1973) distinguishes such narcissistic rage from ordinary aggression by its totalistic qualities and complete lack of empathy. There is a limitless, insatiable quality to the desire for revenge, like that seen in the apocalyptic fanatics who want to purge the world of all evildoers, sinners, and nonbelievers. In contrast to normal aggression or even normal desire for revenge, narcissistic rage "in its typical forms is an utter disregard for reasonable limitations and a boundless wish to redress an injury and to obtain revenge" (Kohut, 1973: 382). While some religiously motivated terrorists may employ violence purely tactically in the pursuit of limited and achievable political goals, others dream of complete purification and the apocalyptic eradication of all unholy people. Such totalistic schemes of divine vengeance reek of narcissistic rage born of threats to cherished beliefs and institutions.

> Aggressions employed in the pursuit of maturely experienced causes are not limitless. However vigorously mobilized, their goal is definite: the defeat of the enemy who blocks the way to a cherished goal. The narcissistically injured, on the other hand, cannot rest until he has blotted out a vaguely experienced offender who dared to oppose him, to disagree with him, or to outshine him. (Kohut, 1973: 385)

As we have seen, the terroristic religious imagination can even conceive of a God of narcissistic rage who "cannot rest until he has blotted out a vaguely experienced offender who dared to oppose him, to disagree with him" (Kohut, 1973: 385).

Such totalistic dreams of vengeance on the unrighteous do not necessarily coincide with a loss of cognitive functioning. Rather, Kohut accurately observes, "the irrationality of the vengeful attitude becomes even more frightening in view of the fact that . . . the reasoning capacity, while totally under the domination and in the service of the overriding emotion, is often not only intact but even sharpened" (Kohut, 1973: 382). Devotees motivated by narcissistic rage can still fly planes, make sophisticated bombs, and author brilliantly rhetorical texts in the service of their visions of terror.

JUSTIFYING TERRORISM RELIGIOUSLY

Another element in terrorist actions is their justification. Committing mass violence requires some ideology to justify it and sustain it; the more total or absolute the violence, the more absolute must be the ideology that justifies it. Religion (or quasi-religious movements such as Maoism or Nazism) evokes the most horrible violence because it deals in absolutes. Terrorist religions are "totalizing" religions; they make absolute claims upon their devotees. Here, too, there is a psychology—the psychology of the need for something absolute, certain, infallible. This is also the psychology of the the overly idealized. To say that terrorist religions are "totalizing" (Lifton, 1979; Piven, Boyd & Lawton, 2004; Strozier, 1996) means that they deal uncritically in absolutes and in overidealizations. A devotee may demonstrate his devotion to an overly idealized object by committing extreme acts of violence and murder.

Our question here concerns the psychology of those to whom such totalistic visions have an appeal. Totalistic visions erase all doubt and ambiguity and provide a claim of absolute certainty. So the theme of splitting the world into completely pure and totally evil groups and the inability to tolerate ambivalence and ambiguity reappear. Totalistic visions promise the eradication of all ambivalence and ambiguity.

One solution to overpowering guilt or shame appears in the pursuit of perfection and absolute purity that pacifies a demanding conscience and/or rids the self of self-hatred and self-loathing. In both cases the pure cannot tolerate the impure; the holy cannot tolerate the unholy. Thus the apocalyptic scenarios of Asahara and the *Left Behind* series, as well as bin Laden's pronouncements, conclude with a vision of the future in which all the impure and unrighteous have been eliminated, and the pure and holy can return to a paradise without complication or ambiguity or any sign remaining of the unrighteous and impure ones. The *Left Behind* series ends with all who are not apocalyptic Christians swallowed up by the earth and gone forever; Zarqawi advocates jihad to cleanse the earth from nonbelievers' abominations. Purification of oneself and the world comes to mean destroying impurity rather than transforming it, creating a perfectly clean, antiseptic, sterilized existence.

CONCLUSION

This chapter suggests that terrorist religion is characterized by certain psychological themes that, for developmental reasons, often occur together. As such, psychodynamic theories complement those of social psychology by examining possible individual factors at work in religious devotees who commit terrorist actions. The argument in favor of such an approach is as follows. Certain themes seem common to most religiously sponsored terrorists—teachings and texts that evoke shame and humiliation; the demand for submission to an overly idealized but humiliating institution, text, leader, or deity; a patriarchal religious milieu; an impatience with ambiguity and an inability to tolerate ambivalence that lead to a splitting of the world into polarized all-good and all-evil camps and the demonizing of the other; a drive for total purification and perfection; narcissistic rage and a fascination with violence and violent imagery; doctrines that link violence and purification; and the repression of sexuality. Such themes express certain wishes, fears, desires, and patterns of interaction. Relational psychoanalysis claims that such motivations have their roots in our early experience.[2] We do not have any information on the childrearing practices and early experiences of those who become religiously motivated terrorists, so this is clearly conjecture based on clinical experience.

This is not to suggest that terrorism can be eliminated by a change in childrearing practices. It does suggest that if family, social, and cultural practices produce people who are less inclined toward humiliation, shame, splitting, and a fascination with violence, religious groups inclined toward terrorism will be less attractive.

This chapter underscores, even for those who do not agree with its psychodynamic framework, that certain psychological themes almost always occur together in the texts of religiously motivated terrorists. Any complete account of the psychology of religious terrorism must address why this is so. Clinical psychodynamic theory is one way to address this issue.

CHAPTER 6

WHAT DOES THIS TELL US
ABOUT RELIGION?

MOST POST-WORLD WAR II PHILOSOPHERS AND SCHOLARS of religion described the primary function of religion as the search for meaning or as a means of addressing such existential concerns as finitude, suffering, and death. This may be in part because most academic scholars of religion have primarily had contact with the more mainstream forms of religion. A psychoanalytic interrogation of religious terrorism points in a less benign direction and reveals that religion is not only about the search for meaning and value but that religion is also a container for aggression, self-hatred, sacrifice, and various anxieties. If religion serves to contain some of humanity's most destructive impulses, including what Waller (2002) calls our "ancestral shadow," this raises the question of the extent of a direct link between religion and terrorism. All religions have sponsored terrorist acts somewhere in their history. Some still do. Is this inevitable? Some have argued that because all the major religions call for some submission to a higher authority or reality and promote some dialectic of death and rebirth, religions inevitably lead to the kind of authoritarian submission that is so central to religious terrorism. Is this argument correct?

Psychological research fails to find any necessary correlations between religion and an external locus of control or, as we have seen, between religion and authoritarianism. While certain religious people clearly display an authoritarian tendency, no research has found this to be universal among religious devotees. Nor has any research into terrorist movements and religion found them to be necessarily associated. Juergensmeyer writes,

> Religion is not innocent. But it does not ordinarily lead to violence. That happens only with the coalescence of a peculiar set of circumstances—political, social, and ideological—when religion becomes fused with violent expressions of social aspirations, personal pride, and movements for political change. (Juergensmeyer, 2000: 10)

And, of course, I would add when religion becomes fused with a certain psychological constellation of authoritarian personality traits and underlying psychodynamics. So there is no evidence of a necessary or inevitable connection between religion and terrorism.

This does not mean that there is no connection at all between religion and violence and terrorism. Quite the reverse. All the religions of the world contain storehouses of symbols and metaphors of war and violence. Near the beginning of the history of the Bible—the fountainhead of Judaism, Christianity and Islam, God hardens pharaoh's heart to set the Egyptians up for the slaughter that is to come. The first-born child of every Egyptian family from the pharaoh down to the poorest servant is slain, until there was not a house left that had not known death. There are bloody stories of warfare, pillage, rape, and conquest in the Torah: women and children are hacked to death on God's command, unborn infants torn from their mother's wombs by the sword, virgins taken on God's orders for the pleasure of his holy warriors. For example, in Deuteronomy Moses describes how God will "send a pestilence" against the people who are in the way of the ancient Israelites "until even the survivors and those who tried to flee are destroyed" (7:20). In Numbers God opens the earth and it swallows up several whole families and households who disobeyed him, and then he sends a fire that destroys another 250 men in one blaze (16:32–34). The next day God destroys another 14,000 by a plague (Numbers 16:49). The Hebrew God even commands his warriors to go back and slay the 50,000 captives whose lives Moses had spared and orders the conquest and virtual genocide of the peoples in the lands into which they moved—"you must utterly destroy them . . . show them no mercy . . . show no pity on them" (Deut. 7:12–16; also Deut. 20:16–17, Numbers 31:17, Joshua 11:20). So begins the sacred history of three world religions. Such texts lay the basis for the holy war tradition in Judaism, Christianity, and Islam. (These stories are found mainly in the books of Numbers, chapters 21, 25, 31, 33 and Joshua, chapters 1–11.)

Then there are the bloody portrayals of Jesus' suffering on the cross, Paul's metaphors of continual spiritual warfare, and the horrific images in the book of Revelation so dear to the readers of the *Left Behind* series. And there is the history of the Crusades, the Inquisition, and the European wars of religion following the Reformation. Islam tells and retells the stories of the Prophet's battles and conquests, and there is the history of Islam's bloody sweep across the Middle East and North Africa. The Pali chronicles contain many tales of the wars and conquests by Buddhist kings, tales that are told and retold among the Buddhists of Sri Lanka in their campaign to subdue the Tamil population there. In 1959 a Sri Lankan prime minister was assassinated by a Buddhist monk. Tibetan Buddhism also has many stories of warfare, and its divine pantheon contains countless images of bloodthirsty deities and semidivine beings. There is a long lineage of warrior Buddhist monks in China and Japan. The Hindu epics like the Ramayana and the Marabharata are full of epic battles and warrior heroes. As we have seen throughout this book, no world religion is without a storehouse of ample texts and tales to justify any acts of brutality, bloodshed, and terrorism. Historically and textually there are many connections between religion and violence and warfare. In my seminars on religious terrorism, after reading statements by religiously motivated killers, my students often protest, saying, "but religion teaches us to be non-violent." I'm not so sure.

VIOLENCE AND THE SACRED: RENE GIRARD

The French literary critic Rene Girard has thought deeply about the connections between religion and violence. In his book *Violence and the Sacred*, Girard (1977) offers an account of how religion (and the entire social order) arises out of acts of violence (the following discussion is based on Girard, 1977, 1987). In tribal societies, which lack a full-blown system of laws and jurisprudence, when violence breaks out, it threatens to destroy the social order. There are no encompassing checks on the tendency of violence to escalate in small groups, as we have seen so often in the modern world as crowds, mass meetings, and gangs turn violent and genocidal. The solution arrived at by our ancestors, Girard suggests, is the whole society coming together and channeling the urge for violence onto an object, person, or animal—the scapegoat—who is then rejected, exiled, and killed. With the scapegoat sacrificed, the community is again reconciled; peace and harmony reign, at least temporarily. The sacrificed victim, bringer of a new order of peace and harmony, comes to be regarded as a hero, a savior, or a god. Because of the scapegoat we are reconciled. Thus the scapegoat comes to be worshiped after the fact. So religious ritual develops. For Girard, religious ritual comes *after* the sacrificial deed, not before it. Religion develops out of the sacrificial action rather than sacrificial rituals being an expression of some religious impulse.

In all societies, but especially tribal ones, violence is immensely powerful. It must be channeled and controlled; ways must be found to limit its destructive power. In a tribal society, conflict between two people can draw in their families and soon spread to engulf the whole society. Violence is contagious in this way. Scapegoating and sacrifice serve to contain and mute the devastating possibilities of violence. They acquire the penumbra of the sacred by their power to do this. Because of "the scapegoating mechanism" (Girard's term), religious rituals of sacrifice thus succeed in containing violence and restoring and maintaining social solidarity.

Then repetition sets in. Every time violence threatens, we seek to do again what worked in the past. We seek out another victim, another scapegoat, to sacrifice. So sacrificial acts repeat themselves; thus ritual arises and becomes established. The sacrificers, now bound together by this bloody act, vow not to repeat the violent crime that led to the escalation of violence that only a sacrifice could stop. Thus prohibitions, such as "thou shall not kill" (unless it is a ritual sacrifice), arise and become established. Eventually this process must be explicated; it must enter into language and so a narrative grows up to explain the ritual. Myth thus arises and is established. Here then are the core processes of religion—ritual, prohibition, and myth—all arising out of the scapegoating mechanism. Religion becomes the major way of containing violence; that is its first and most basic function. So religion and violence are inextricably linked. Religions, like societies, soon develop an amnesia concerning the violence that gave them birth, but the necessary connection is there for those with the eyes to see it.

The idea that a bloody deed is the foundation of civilization is not new. It goes back at least to the Hebrew scriptures and the story of the first brothers, Cain and Abel, one of whom slays the other. In *Totem and Taboo,* Freud tells a similar story and reaches a similar conclusion. The brothers of the primal horde kill their father and then, to stop them from all killing each other in the attempt to replace him, band together in a social compact and deify the dead patriarch. The implication of all these accounts, including Girard's, is that religion and with it social solidarity come at the price of bloodshed; a bloody sacrifice lies at the basis of the social order. The necessity to shed blood in order to create a new social order is recapitulated in the revolutionary violence of America, France, Russia, and China and the Holocaust at the foundation of the Third Reich in Germany. But for Girard these myths of revolutionary transformation never solve the problem of violence; they simply recapitulate it. For Girard, scapegoating and sacrifice are never long-term solutions to the problem of violence. They wear out after a while. They demand more and more victims.

How does violence get started in the first place? Envy is a cousin to desire. We desire an object, a thing, a person, a trait, a position. Desire, for Girard, is always acquisitive. But we do not simply and directly desire an object, we also envy the other who possesses that desired object. Thus desire is not simply a dyadic relationship between me and the object I desire. Rather desire has a triadic structure—myself, the object I desire, and the other who already posses it, whom Girard calls the "model." I do not simply attend to what I desire, I also attend to the other(s) who have what I desire. Thus for Girard envy is always a concomitant of desire. To desire something is to envy those who possess it, those who possess what I want and do not have. Thus desire inevitably generates rivalry in its wake. I feel insufficient in the face of those who possess what I lack. This feeling of insufficiency is obviously very aversive, humiliating, and shameful. I have presented ample evidence of the ways that shame and humiliation lead to violence, and thus there is support for Girard's hypothesis that violence has its roots in an acquisitive desire that breeds envy and rivalry. Desire inevitably gives rise to rivalry, and rivalry inevitably gives rise to violence. This is the originating event at the core of civilization and religion—desire leading to rivalry, leading to violence leading to scapegoating. The biblical the story of Cain and Abel carries, for Girard, the memory of this fact. At the beginning of civilization lies a murder inspired by rivalry. Cain murders Abel because he is envious of God's favor, then he fears others will kill him out of vengeance—that is, make him a scapegoat, a sacrifice.

Desire, for Girard, does not originate in the subject. Rather desire is always evoked. Desire is not a drive or an instinct in Freud's sense, a motivation hard wired into the subject. Rather, from outside desire is induced in the subject by the model. Desire makes me want to become like my rival, to have what he has. I want my life to be like his life. I want my life to imitate his life. Girard calls this mimetic desire, the desire to imitate, to *be*, the other who has what I want.

Mimetic desire is, for Girard, the core of human being and doing. We are all caught up in a web of mimetic desire from which we cannot extricate ourselves. The dangers of rivalry, envy, and thus violence always lurk just below the surface. And as soon as violence breaks out, the scapegoat mechanism—the search for someone to blame and to violently sacrifice—will come into play. There will many who insist that "good violence" is the only solution to "bad violence." Thus sacrificers always claim their killing is virtuous. Girard's insistence on the unalterable reality of mimetic desire and the concomitant inevitability of rivalry, violence, and scapegoating functions as a kind of psychosocial original sin, a statement of the human condition as being problematic in a way that is "inevitable but not necessary" (as Reinhold Neibuhr said of original sin itself).

Take a clichéd story line. Two adolescent male friends are as close as brothers. One buys a new shirt, the other has to have the same brand. One buys an iPod, the other must have one, too. Friendship based on imitation. But then one falls in love with a girl. Soon, in imitation, the other finds himself falling in love with the same girl. Now there is rivalry. The friends fight. There is misunderstanding. The friends grow apart. Gradually one, then the other, loses interest in the girl. The boys get back together as friends, and they blame the girl for almost destroying their friendship. She gets scapegoated. The boys could, hypothetically, recognize the situation for what it was. They could understand the way their friendship and rivalry arose from their imitation of each other. They could acknowledge their rivalry and scapegoating from a position of humility and insight. They probably won't, however. It is easier to scapegoat the girl, call her names, blame her, and reconnect around triangulating her. Here is the deep structure of mimetic theory in this story: desire, imitation, rivalry, and the threat of violence (perhaps the boys get into a fistfight) and then scapegoating and harmony restored. Maybe this restoration even gets ritualized in rituals of male bonding: the boys go out for a beer together and complain about women.

On the interpersonal and social levels, Girard's insight is that scapegoating and triangulating actually lead to renewed peace and harmony. By ganging up on a scapegoat, intragroup conflict really is reduced. So the scapegoating practice is experienced as effective and so gets ritualized in rituals of sacrifice, of expelling or killing the supposed cause of conflict. Worship, ritual, and narrative arise from conflict and violence. They have violence at their core.

MIMESIS AND THE GLOBALIZATION
OF RELIGIOUS TERROR

Our desires are evoked in imitation of the desires of others. Advertising, obviously, is premised on this. We want to be like that famous athlete, rock star, or celebrity. We can be like them if we imitate them—drive the car they drive, wear the clothes they wear, drink what they drink. The message is, if you buy this, if you imitate them, then you will be like them. Thus advertising must generate a world of celebrities, a storehouse of people to imitate. Terrorist religious groups, too, by turning their devotees into martyrs and heroes, recruit members by mimesis. Others in their cohort want to be like the hero or the martyr. So they imitate them and blow up a train or assassinate a doctor or a nurse. The Internet and other means of mass communication make this recruiting by mimesis easier by continually showing pictures of the martyrs on their websites. A potential jihadist in Spain can be inspired by a picture of a martyr in Iraq; a potential bomber in California can be inspired by a Christian fanatic in Maryland, all thanks to TV coverage and the Internet. Thus technology extends the range of mimesis, and terrorism becomes a globalized phenomena. For example, William Pierce's *Turner Diaries*—the bible of the Christian Identity movement and the one book that Timothy McVeigh always had with him—ends with the hero crashing his jet into the Pentagon on a suicide mission. The book was written decades before 9/11, and right before his death Pierce is reported to have described the 9/11 attacks as the right thing done by the wrong people (Atran, 2005b).

The role of the media in terrorism is a very important element in understanding contemporary terrorist movements. It is beyond the scope of this book, but virtually all commentators agree that analyzing the role of the media is a crucial part of any understanding of modern terrorism (Atran, 2005b, 2006b; Atran & Stern, 2005; Hoffman, 2006; Kirby, 2007; Moghadam, 2006; Weimann, 2006). Often terrorists are very sophisticated in their use of the media and in knowing how to manipulate it. If terrorism is partly a theater performed for an audience (Juergensmeyer, 2000), the perpetrators must know how to use technology to reach that audience. The Internet has enabled jihadist movements, like al-Qaeda, to morph from more centralized, top-down paramilitary organizations to self-organizing and self-directed cells. Disaffected Muslims anywhere in the world, Christian Identity soldiers in remote parts of America, or nationalistic Sikhs in Europe can easily download jihadist materials or Christian Identity Tracts or the inflammatory sermons of the Sikh saint Bhindranwale. They can also download bomb-making instructions and tactical advice from each other's websites. For example, "information for the do-it-yourself explosives used in the Madrid and London bombings is available on the Internet" (Atran, 2006b: 135). Even technical plans for a nuclear device can be found there (Atran, 2005c). No state sponsorship or contact with bin Laden or any Christian Identity leadership is necessary to carry out a "sacred mission." The Aryan Nation website calls for the decentralizing of Aryan militancy and the self-conscious development of leaderless groups, virtually impossible for outsiders to penetrate, initiating violent actions on their own. And in a striking example of terrorist mimesis, it now refers to itself as the "Aryan jihad" (www.aryan-nations.org).

Such Internet linkages raise the probability that violent antisecular groups (who totally abhor each other's theologies) can communicate and cooperate in terrorist attacks against what are perceived as common enemies: for example, fundamentalist Jews and apocalyptic Christians working together to blow up the mosque on the Dome of the Rock or Christian Identity soldiers working with Islamic terrorists within the United States to blow up government buildings or symbols of immorality like women's reproductive health clinics or bars and churches frequented by gays. Given the ease of Internet communication, it is not out of the question for groups that agree on the evils of secularization to temporarily join forces against secular, liberal democratic institutions and more tolerant branches of their respective religions. Neal Horsely, advocate of killing physicians who perform abortions and creator of the Nuremburg Files, on his present website calls for an alliance of the "People of the Book"—Christians, Muslims, and Jews—to work together to violently put an end to abortion and to the tolerance for homosexuality, and the same anti-abortion website reports that they have used the servers in a Muslim country to host their Internet anti-abortion campaign (Christian Gallery, 2007).

Likewise, contemporary terrorism's global reach is tangential to our concerns here except in one particular aspect. Many commentators emphasize the way in which contemporary globalization weakens the modern nation-state (e.g., Giddens, 2000). This is usually discussed in economic terms. The power of national governments to influence their economies weakens as economic power shifts decisively to multinational corporations with little or no political loyalty beyond their own self-interest.

So the hegemony of national governments is increasingly replaced by the hegemony of multinational economic entities. What is less often noticed is that besides multinational corporations and international economic agencies, many religions are multinational and international in scope. So as the nation-state weakens, religious commitments become another form of multinational loyalty. So, for example, a Muslim in an Arabian kingdom may feel greater loyalty to the worldwide Muslim community than to the country he lives in. Or a Muslim from Egypt who moves to England and becomes a British citizen may still feel more loyalty to the international Muslim community than to either Egypt or England. Many of the most fanatical jihadists, including the leaders of the 9/11 attacks, the Madrid train bombers, and the London subway bombers were recruited from the Muslim diaspora (Khosrokhavar, 2005). Similarly, an American Jew who grew up on heroic stories of the founding of the state of Israel and spent his junior year of college living there may be feel more emotional investment in the future of Israel than of the United States, may view American foreign policy through an Israeli lens, and may even be moved to join a settlement in the occupied territories and take up the settler cause. Several such people are portrayed in Juergensmeyer's book (2000, chapter 3), and many of the most fanatical Jewish partisans in Israel originally came from the United States (e.g., Yoel Lerner, Baruch Goldstein, Meir Kahane). As national governments weaken under the impact of globalization, international religious loyalties, especially to fanatical groups who are so very sophisticated in their use of the Internet and mass-media, may increase (Khosrokhavar [2005] makes a similar point). And the sources of terrorist violence move from local groups with local grievances to groups with a global agenda and a global reach. It is no exaggeration to say that contemporary religious terrorism is a media driven, multinational movement, in which technology drives the mimesis of terror (Weimann, 2006).

SCAPEGOATS, SACRIFICE, AND THE PSYCHOLOGY OF RELIGIOUS TERROR

The sacrificial system and the scapegoat mechanism assume that the victim is really guilty, is really the cause of the conflict, is really the source of the problem of violence. Only in that context does it make any sense to think that doing away with the scapegoat will solve the problem. So the scapegoat process depends on an amnesia about what is really going on. It depends on blindness about the actual cause of violence—desire and rivalry. For sacrifice to work, the sacrificial victim must truly be thought to be guilty, to be to blame. Thus culture, religion, ritual, and sacrifice are based on a falsehood—that bloody sacrifice will actually solve the problem of violence because the victim really is to blame, really is responsible and guilty. This is a lie.

A further and deeper level of false consciousness is created when the idea is introduced that a god demands the sacrifice. Originally, for Girard, sacrifice had nothing to do with god. Rather it was the way a community protects "the entire community from its own violence" (Girard, 1996: 77). The idea of a bloodthirsty god demanding a sacrifice further mystifies the real function of sacrifice—that it is the way a community creates solidarity and cohesion by projecting and channeling its aggression onto another and scapegoating them. The sacralizing of ritual violence and sacrifice is part of the false consciousness generated by religion. Thus the violent images of blood sacrifice and holy war take up their home in the heart of sacred texts and rituals. Religions perpetuate the illusion that violence can be a lasting solution to violence.

What, then, does ritual sacrifice and purification achieve? By expelling the guilty and unclean, the community is kept pure. Hitler created ghettos and later extermination camps for the Jews because he saw them as a virus that would contaminate the purity of the Aryan nation (Koenigsburg, 1975). The Ayatollah Khomeini issued a fatwa against Salman Rushdie as a blasphemer whom it was every good Muslim's duty to try to kill and so eliminate from the community. In the midst of all the discussions about homosexuality in American society, I heard a preacher on the radio say that homosexuals should be rounded up and segregated in special enclaves so they didn't spread their lifestyle to others. In all these examples, purification means removing some supposed source of contamination by expelling it from the community. As we have seen, this sense of purification as the elimination of the supposed source of the problem—the core of the scapegoating mechanism—is at the heart of much religiously motivated terrorism because it is central to many theologies of purification found in the world's religions. Such theologies of purification easily slide into justifications for genocide and terrorism and are a major way religion contributes to terrorism.

I have suggested that this connection of purification, scapegoating, and bloody sacrifice has deep psychological roots—something like what Fairbairn (1952) describes as the "moral defense" and Klein (1975a) refers to as "splitting" seems to be at work here. A person or community, weighed down by guilt, shame, or humiliation, can come to feel pure and purposeful by scapegoating another, expelling those feelings by projecting them onto another, and finally being rid of the feelings by getting rid of the scapegoats in acts of terror and genocide.

The idea that purification requires a bloody sacrifice is central to much religiously motivated terrorism. This illustrates one of the central arguments of this book: that religiously motivated terrorism results when common religious themes—in this case the desire for purity—are directed in certain ways. The desire for purification or transformation is a normal part of the religious life; it may well be the heart of every living religion (Jones, 2002). When this natural desire for transformation becomes entangled in the scapegoating mechanism, religiously sponsored terrorism is close at hand.

If we are trapped in the cycle of violence and scapegoating, is there no way out? For Girard there is no way out from within the cycle of rivalry and violence. The only way out must come from outside that cycle. Bound up as it is with violence and rituals of sacrifice, religion is thus inevitably part of the problem. But it is also necessarily part of the solution as well. By religion here Girard means revealed religion, primarily Judaism and Christianity. Revelation provides precisely the input from outside the cycle of violence that is necessary to break it. For Judaism Girard references the prophet tradition. While the Torah contains long sections devoted to ritual sacrifices, the later books—especially the prophets— explicitly repudiate the sacrificial system.[1]

> What to me is the multitude of your sacrifices?
> Says the Lord.
> I have had enough of burnt offerings of rams
> And the fat of fed beasts;
> I do not delight in the blood of bulls, or of lambs or of goats. . . .
> Wash yourselves, make yourselves clean
> Remove the evil of your doings from my eyes;
> Cease to do evil, learn to do good;
> See justice, rescue the oppressed
> Defend the orphan, plead for the widow. (Isaiah 1:11, 16–17)

I desire steadfast love and not sacrifice
The knowledge of God rather than burnt offerings. (Hosea 6:6)

Even though you offer me your burnt offerings and your grain offerings,
I will not accept them;
And the offerings of well-being of your fatted animals
I will not look upon. . . .
But let justice roll down like waters,
And righteousness like an everflowing stream. (Amos 5:22, 24)

With what shall I come before the Lord,
And bow myself before the God on high?
Shall I come before him with burnt offerings, with calves a year old?
Will the Lord be pleased with thousands of rams,
With ten thousand rivers of oil?
Shall I give my firstborn for my transgression
The fruit of my body for the sin of my soul?
He has told you mortal one what is good;
And what does the Lord require of you, but to do justice, love kindness,
And walk humbly with your God? (Micah 6: 6–8)

I will not accept a bull from your house, or goats from your folds.
For every wild animal of the forest is mine, the cattle on a thousand hills. . . .
If I were hungry, I would not tell you
For the world and all that is in it is mine.
Do I eat the flesh of bulls or drink the blood of goats?
Offer to God a sacrifice of thanksgiving and make your vows to the Most
High. (Psalm 50: 9–10, 12–14).

Thus the Jewish prophetic tradition displays a fierce critique of the theology of the blood sacrifice.

The Christian example is more complicated. At the time of Jesus, animal sacrifices were still being offered at the Jewish temple in Jerusalem. The Jews of the diaspora, on the other hand, worshiped in the synagogue. Their religious life centered on the study of texts and holiness of life. Scholarship and morality, not sacrifice, were the heart of their religion. So by the time of Jesus there was a living stream of Judaism disconnected from the Levitical sacrificial system; it was centered in the synagogue and could build on the prophetic critique of that system.

The story of Jesus driving the sellers of the animals necessary for the ritual sacrifices out of the temple and demanding it be a "house of prayer for all people" (Mark 11:17) and not a place for offering sacrifices stands in the lineage of that prophetic critique. Like the prophet's message, this action implies that Jesus advocates the life of prayer instead of ritual sacrifice. And the Greek word in the New Testament (*thusia*) that is often translated into English as "sacrifice" also means just an "offering" or a "self-giving" and has no necessary connections to a bloody sacrifice (e.g., in Romans 12:1 "present yourselves as a living sacrifice [*thusian* in Greek] to God"). For Paul and the rest of the New Testament, the Christian life is referred to as a "sacrifice" in the sense of an offering to God, not a bloody slaughter (Klauck, 1992; Mitton, 1962).

In contrast, the death of Jesus on the cross has often been seen as a sacrificial offering. Girard explicitly repudiates this interpretation of Jesus' death. After several long and careful exegetical discussions throughout *Things Hidden From the Foundation of the World,* Girard concludes:

> There is nothing in the Gospels to suggest that the death of Jesus is a sacrifice, whatever definition (expiation, substitution, etc.) we give for that sacrifice. At no point in the Gospels is the death of Jesus defined as a sacrifice. The passages that are invoked to justify a sacrificial conception of the Passion both can and should be interpreted with no reference to sacrifice in any of the accepted meanings. Certainly the Passion is presented in the Gospels as an act that brings salvation to humanity. But it is no way presented as a sacrifice. (Girard, 1996: 178)

Rather, Girard argues that in his life and teaching Jesus repudiates the sacrificial system. Jesus, quoting Hosea, tells the Pharisees, "Go learn what this means, I desire mercy, not sacrifice" (Matthew 8: 13). This is a favorite text of Girard's. To say that Jesus' life and death accomplish what the ancient Hebrew temple sacrificial system sought to accomplish—a claim made in several places in the New Testament—does not logically entail that it must be a blood sacrifice, too. Such a conclusion assumes that God requires blood sacrifice and so the argument for the equation of Jesus' death with the temple sacrifice is purely circular. Rather, the New Testament claim is only that Jesus' death and the temple sacrifices have the same function—reunion of the human and the divine. Also, in the Jewish milieu at the time of Jesus, the main language for that divine–human reconciliation was sacrificial language. That is the only terminology the first Christians (who were Jews) had on hand. Again, Girard insists, use of that language does not necessarily entail that Jesus' death was, literally, a sacrifice.

Also, the kingdom of God, as Jesus presents it, is characterized by brotherly-sisterly love and nonviolence. For Girard, the coming of the kingdom of God marks the end of the sacrificial system and inaugurates a radically new social order based on mutual service and *agape* love, rather than on revenge and reprisal. By being innocent and nonviolent, Jesus' violent death exposes for all to see the deep structure of the scapegoating mechanism—that "It is better that one man should die for the people than to have the whole nation destroyed" (John 11:50)—and that it can bring no closure to the cycle of violence. The Christian community that grows up in his wake shows that a social order can be founded on something other than killing; its solidarity is based on an identification with the violence-victim (Christ) rather than an identification with the executioners. This transvaluation of values by which social solidarity is grounded on an identification with a victim rather than with the victimizers is, for Gerard, one of the most radical outcomes of the crucifixion.

Of course, the sacrificial mentality did not come to an end with the appropriation of the Hebrew prophetic tradition or the birth of Christianity. Far from it. World wars, mass killings, executions, calls for vengeance, genocide, pogroms, gulags, and nuclear proliferation all testify to that. And, most ironically, segments of the Christian community came to embrace the sacrificial system that their Jewish brothers and sisters were repudiating. Christ's death, which was supposed to illuminate and end the sacrificial mentality, came to be seen as a sacrifice. The "Heavenly Father" whom Jesus proclaimed as making the rain to fall on the just and the unjust was twisted into a bloodthirsty tyrant who demanded an even more perfect and more bloody sacrifice than the Yahweh of the Hebrew Scriptures. Rather than proclaiming a Gospel that put an end to violence and sacrifice, segments of Christianity sacralized the most excruciating of sacrifices, thus intensifying the reign of death over humanity rather than liberating humanity and setting them free for a new life. In Girard's view, such a theology of Christ as sacrificial victim turns the Gospel upside down and rejects the offer of new life in order to continue the cycle of violence and death that Christ came to stop.

THE AMBIGUITY OF RELIGION

Girard's theory illustrates what I have elsewhere called "the ambiguity of religion"—that the same religion can articulate humankind's highest moral sensibilities and underwrite humankind's worst atrocities

(Jones, 2002). According to Girard, the religious desire for purification arises out of the scapegoating mechanism. But, as illustrated by the Hebrew prophets and the life of Jesus, religion can also disentangle itself from the scapegoating process and so provide ways for humankind to transcend the need for blood sacrifice and end the cycle of violence.

The accuracy of Girard's account of the origin of religion, of the message of the Hebrew prophets, and of the meaning of Jesus' life and death are not my primary concern here. However, Girard's theory intersects with my interests in several places. First his theory of the origin of religion, like that found in the Cain and Abel story or in Freud's *Totem and Taboo,* inextricably links religion and violence. So we should not be surprised that religions spawn terrorists and that the first terrorists (for example, the assassins or the zealots) were acting in the name of what they held sacred. Or that movements for spiritual renewal such as Aum Shinrikyo or The People's Temple so easily turn deadly. Wherever religion or spirituality calls, we should be on the lookout for violence and death. And the kind of Christian theologizing, which Girard seeks to unmask and reject, that makes Christ the epitome of sacrifice rather than the exposure and repudiation of the sacrificial mentality is exactly the kind of theology that we find throughout history in apocalyptic Christianity's texts of terror. But Girard also insists that religion is not only inevitably a part of the problem; it is also a necessary part of the solution. Prophetic and revelatory traditions and religious disciplines that connect us to a transcendental or sacred reality that critiques and relativizes our egotism and its acquisitive desires are the only way out of the mimetic cycle of rivalry and violence.

What, then, do we learn about religion from studying religiously motivated terrorism? Religiously motivated terrorists, groups like Aum Shinrikyo and the People's Temple and texts like the *Left Behind* series all illustrate the ambiguity of religion. Religion can bring into people's lives a sense hope, meaning, and purpose so necessary to human well-being. Religion can inspire great works of art, music, and literature. Religion can give rise to powerful movements for social justice and experiences of personal transformation. Here religion can do great good and enrich human life. Religion also strengthens feelings of shame and humiliation and the longing for revenge. Religion also plays upon people's needs for submission and authority. Religion also inculcates prejudices and the splitting of the world into a battle between the completely pure and the irredeemably evil. In this regard religion does great mischief and brings calamity upon the human species.

So a complete psychology of religion must include the psychology of religious violence. Such psychological processes as shame and humiliation, splitting, and seeing the world in black-and-white terms, along with the inability to tolerate ambivalence and the dynamic of projection and demonizing the other all contribute to violence and genocide apart from religion. But the history and psychology of religion make clear that such dynamics are not only central to the evocation of violence, they also lie close to the heart of much religious experience. By demanding submission to a deity, text, institution, group, or teacher that is experienced as wrathful, punitive, or rejecting, religions inevitably evoke or increase feelings of shame and humiliation that are major psychological causes of violent actions. By continually holding before the devotee an overly idealized institution, book, or leader, religions set up the psychodynamic basis for splitting and bifurcating experience. By teaching devotees that some groups are inferior, evil, satanic, or condemned by God, religions encourage the demonizing of others and their social death, making their slaughter seem inconsequential, justified, or even required. For these reasons any turn to violence is not accidental but is rather close to the heart of much of the religious life.

A RELIGIOUS COUNTERTERRORISM: THE RELIGIOUS CRITIQUE OF RELIGION

I have argued that religiously sponsored terrorism is, among other things, a religious phenomenon. Political, economic, class, and ethnic issues may all play central roles in acts of religiously motivated terrorism. But the ritualizing that often accompanies such actions, the prominent use of sacred texts in the justification of such actions, and the central role of ministers, priests, rabbis, imams, gurus, and other religiously sanctioned leaders in the organizations that support and encourage such actions all point to the essentially *religious* nature of these actions as well. If these actions are essentially religious as well as political, social, and cultural, then the response to them must be religious as well as political or military. Jessica Stern (2003) argues that, like many contemporary spiritual movements, religiously motivated terrorist organizations appeal to the "God-shaped hole in human consciousness that is a symptom of modernity" that "we have yet to create a technology for fixing" (289). So far in human history, only religious and spiritual groups can speak to that "infinite longing" or "longing for the infinite" within human consciousness. Thus part of the response to religious terrorism must be to speak to that infinite desire in a way that heals and transforms rather than increases our feelings of shame and humiliation, our need for hyperidealizations and splitting, and our drive to demonize the other. Such is the responsibility of religious leaders and thinkers rather than policymakers or military strategists.

Put another way, the war on terror is a war of ideas (Bin Hassan, 2006). Berman concludes his essay on Sayyid Qutb with this exhortation,

> It would be nice to think that, in the war against terror, our side too speaks of deep philosophical ideas—it would be nice to think that someone is arguing with the terrorists and with the readers of Sayyid Qutb. But here I have my worries. The followers of Qutb speak, in their wild fashion, of enormous human problems, and they urge one another to death and to murder. But the enemies of these people speak of what? The political leaders speak of United Nations resolutions, of unilateralism, of multilateralism, of weapons inspectors, of coercion and noncoercion. This is no answer to the terrorists. The terrorists speak insanely of deep things. The antiterrorists had better speak sanely of equally deep things. . . . Who will speak of the sacred and the secular, of the physical world and the spiritual world. . . . President George W. Bush, in his speech to congress a few days after the Sept. 11, 2001 attacks, announced that he was going to wage a war of ideas. He has done no such thing. He is not the man for that. Philosophers and religious leaders will have to do this. Armies are in motion, but are the philosophers and religious leaders, the liberal thinkers, likewise in motion? There is something to worry about here . . . possibly the greatest worry of all. (Berman, 2003: 71)

Indeed, in this war of ideas, most of the ideas are religious ones.

This study suggests some of the things that religious leaders and practitioners can do, from within their traditions, to work against the rise of religiously sponsored terrorism. They can locate resources within their traditions that articulate a different view of the divine—a transcendental reality of love and compassion rather than of abjection and condemnation. They can reject splitting and dichotomizing and speak out against the in-group/out-group pseudo-speciation of much religious fanaticism. They can teach and model compassion and empathy for the other, even the other who is hated and despised. They can reject terrorism. Those religious leaders such as Martin Luther King, Jr., Gandhi, and the Dalai Lama who have sought to transform humiliation into justice and peace have done precisely those things.

Most of this book has been taken up with illustrating some of the ways that religions partake in and reinforce the psychological processes associated with violence and genocide. But the world's religions also contain resources for critiquing and transcending those same inner dynamics. These theological resources can be used by religious leaders in critiquing and transforming the theological and psychological roots of religiously sponsored terrorism. This would require the end of any theology of the divine as an overpowering and coercive or abjecting force that evokes a "moral defense" in which we are tempted to debase ourselves in order to idealize another. Then the necessity for splitting would be reduced. When splitting and the moral defense have been overcome, then the possibility opens up for a recognition of and tolerance for ambiguity within a religious tradition. So combating religious terrorism may require the combined efforts of social scientists and theologians. Psychoanalysts, for example, can expose the connections between religious terrorism and patriarchal images of God as an overpowering authority and describe what personality transformations might be required to reduce the underlying splitting and dichotomizing. Theologians need to find other resources within their traditions to provide devotees with alternative images of God.

Buddhist texts, for example, are full of paradoxical sayings whose point is not to cling to or ultimately insist on any teachings, rituals or forms, even those most hallowed or traditional. Regarding the Buddha, the sage Nagarjuna says,

> It is not asserted that the Blessed One exists after his passing away; nor is it asserted that he does not exist, or that he both exists and does not exist, or that he neither exists nor does not exist. Even while he is living, it is not asserted that the Blessed One exists, nor is it asserted that he does not exist, both exists and does not exist, or neither exists nor does not exist. . . . Nowhere did the Buddha teach anything at all. (Strong, 1995: 154)

So the great teacher taught nothing. At least nothing that can be grasped in words and articulated. So the task of such discourses is to drive the mind beyond the limitations of discursive thought. This is the same goal as the practice of meditating on brief statements with no logical meaning called "koans" (e.g., "What is the sound of one hand clapping?" is a clichéd example) in Zen Buddhism. D. T. Suzuki (1969), in his description of Zen Buddhism, tells the following stories, which are really acted out koans: "When Yukasan was asked to give a lecture, he did not say a word, but instead came down from the pulpit and went off to his own room. Hyakujo merely walked a few steps, stood still, and opened his arms—which was his exposition of the great principle of Buddhism" (293).

"If you meet the Buddha on the road, kill him" is an oft-quoted Zen saying. And there is a common simile in Buddhism that compares the dharma (the Buddha's teaching) to a raft: you use the raft to cross the stream, but once you arrive on the other side (enlightenment) the raft is discarded. So the practices and teachings of the religion are to be regarded as tools, means to an end, not as ends in themselves. All of these examples from within the traditions of Buddhism provide ways that Buddhism can critique its own pretensions and those of other religions.

We have already seen another kind of religious critique of the absolutizing of sacred traditions and practices in the sayings of the Hebrew prophets. Through the prophet Amos, the Hebrew God rejects the Levitical sacrificial system that goes back to Moses.

> I hate, I despise your feasts
> I take no delight in your solemn assemblies.
> Even if you offer me your burnt offerings and cereal offerings,
> I will not accept them
> And the peace offerings of your fattened beasts
> I will not look upon. (Amos 5: 21–22)

Jeremiah warns his people not to keep intoning, "the Temple of the Lord, the Temple of the Lord" as though it were a magic charm that could ward off the coming calamity. This is the same temple whose construction Israelite tradition attributed to a divine commandment. In this way the prophetic voice in Israel worked against any tendency to absolutize the temple, the ritual practices, and other such objects of devotion. And God's destruction of the kingdom of biblical Israel by the Assyrians and Babylonians can be read as the clearest critique of ancient Israelite religion. For the promise of a kingdom had been central to Israelite faith since the days of Abraham, but the prophets said that God could and would bring an end to that most cherished ideal—their own land and government. The prophetic passages in the Hebrew scriptures and the destruction of the sacred kingdom of ancient Israel represent another major critique of the absolutizing and idealizing of hallowed religious beliefs and practices—a dynamic that is central to religious fanaticism and terrorism.

Jesus' statement that "the Sabbath was made for us, we were not made for the Sabbath" stands in the same tradition (Mark 2:27). According to the priestly tradition in Genesis chapter 1, the existence of the Sabbath on which God rested was the goal and culmination of the whole process of creation. In that sense the Sabbath stands for the entire divine order including Torah and temple. When Jesus says that humankind was not made to serve the Sabbath, the law and the temple but rather the other way around, this, too, was a radical deabsolutizing of religious teachings and traditions. The forms and institutions of religion, however divine their origin and sacred their significance—and there is no evidence Jesus questioned the divine origin of the Sabbath or the law—are not to be taken as ends in themselves. Rather they exist to serve humankind, not the other way around. By such sayings, as well as by breaking the Sabbath law in order to heal those who are suffering, Jesus makes it clear that human need must take precedence over hallowed religious traditions.

As portrayed in the Gospels, Jesus' actions were consistently focused on reaching out with compassion to the suffering, the outcasts, and the marginalized. The times when he is described as speaking in anger, it is always and only against the misuse of religion—for example, against those who lay on others heavy burdens that they refuse to carry themselves or against the promoters of sacrifices who turn the temple into a business instead of a house of prayer for all people. Jesus' actions are consistently actions of love, compassion, and forgiveness. The people he condemns are not the ritually impure, the traitors, and the prostitutes; rather, the people he condemns are the righteous and the religious leaders who misuse religion and judge others. "Judge not that you are not judged" is a maxim that directly contradicts those who proclaim the God of wrath and vengeance who is worshiped by religious terrorists around the world. The name of the accuser in Hebrew is Satan. While the purveyors of an apocalyptic Gospel of blood and judgment call those Christians "satanic" who preach compassion and forgiveness, the biblical text insists that it is the one who judges others that is doing the work of Satan.

A RELIGIOUS COUNTERTERRORISM: THE REALITY OF GOD

The most powerful critique of the forms and traditions of the world's religions comes from within those traditions themselves, often from the prophetic and mystical teachings and practices at their heart.

Islam speaks of the 99 names of God. The point is not that this is an exhaustive description of God. Just the reverse. By reciting or meditating on these 99 names, the Muslim realizes the inexpressible and inexhaustible grandeur of the divine. The very words *Islam* and *Muslim* come from the same Arabic root that means peace. The root letters *s, l,* and *m* are the same as the familiar Hebrew word for peace, *Shalom,* and the word *salem* found in "Jerusalem," the "City of Peace." So the meaning of being a Muslim can be read as the "one who is a bringer of peace" (Smith, 1965: 217).

Muslim leaders in Britain and America were quick to vigorously condemn terrorist atrocities perpetrated by their co-religionists in those two countries. Immediately after the 9/11 attacks, the Council on American Islamic Relations (2007) issued the following statement:

> We condemn in the strongest terms possible what are apparently vicious and cowardly acts of terrorism against innocent civilians. We join with all Americans in calling for the swift apprehension and punishment of the perpetrators. No cause could ever be assisted by such immoral acts. All members of the Muslim community are asked to offer whatever help they can to the victims and their families. Muslim medical professionals should go to the scenes of the attacks to offer aid and comfort to the victims.

Five days later the eight major Muslim organizations in the United States that represent virtually all the Muslims living in the country sent a letter to President Bush and took out a full-page ad in the *Washington Post* that said, "American Muslims, who unequivocally condemned today terrorist attacks on our nation, call on you to alert fellow citizens to the fact that now is a time for all of us to stand together in the face of this heinous crime." In addition to this statement, the website of the Council on American Islamic Relations (2007) lists page after page of direct, vigorous condemnations of terrorist actions by Islamic fundamentalists from Muslim groups around the world.

Likewise, immediately after the 2007 attempted car bombings in London and Scotland, the Muslim Council of Britain issued the following public statement:

> Muslims everywhere consider all acts of terrorism that aim to murder and maim innocent human beings utterly reprehensible and abhorrent. There is no theological basis whatsoever for such acts in our faith. The very meaning of the word "Islam" is peace. It rejects terror and promotes peace and harmony.
>
> The words in the Qur'an are clear:
>
> *If anyone kills a human being, unless it be (in punishment) for murder, or of spreading corruption in the land, it should be looked upon as though he had slain all mankind, and if anyone saves a life it should be regarded as though he had saved the lives of all mankind. (5:32).*

Thus Islam's very name, as well as its doctrine of the transcendence of God, implicitly contradicts the ideologies and actions of Islamic terrorists. And Islam contains both traditional teachings (reviewed in Khosrokavar, 2005; Kimball, 2002; Venkatraman, 2007) and a wealth of prophetic declarations by contemporary Muslim leaders that speak of peace and condemn terrorism.

In every tradition are mystics who insist that the divine reality is beyond all human categories and so can only be experienced as a *via negativa*, a way of negation. For example, the *Tao Te Ching* opens with the saying, "The Tao that can be named is not the eternal Tao." A westerner might also say, "the God that can be named is not the eternal God." In this tradition stands John of the Cross's description of the "dark night of the soul." Thomas Aquinas is reported to have said that in the face of a mystical experience all of his writings, the massive *Summa Theologica* and *Summa Contra Gentiles*, were like "straw."

At the end of the fifth century, an anonymous Christian author known as Dionysius the Areopagite wrote a brief essay called *Mystical Theology* premised on claim that all human categories are limited and finite (see Happold, 1975). To speak directly about God (either by affirming or denying God's existence) would limit God by treating God like an object in the concrete world. That is precisely what God is not. Because the divine is beyond all categories, God's existence can neither be affirmed nor denied.

> Neither is He darkness nor light, nor the false nor the true; nor can any affirmation or negation be applied to Him. . . . We can neither affirm nor deny Him . . . [the] Cause of all things transcends all affirmation, and the simple pre-eminence of His absolute nature is outside of every negation—free from every limitation and beyond them all. (Happold, 1975: 217)

Neither theism nor atheism can capture the truth about God, for "there is no contradiction between the affirmations and negations [of God] . . . being beyond all positive and negative distinctions" (Happold, 1975: 213). The divine reality cannot be described in propositions, pictured in art, or described in words. The truth about the One beyond conceptualization can only come through an experience that is beyond conceptualization. The fact that direct statements and attempts at literal description of the divine reality easily fall into contradictions and absurdities is not a telling argument against the reality of God. Paradoxically, just the reverse is true. The contradictions and absurdities that result from trying to contain the divine in prepositional form only point to the truthfulness of the insistence that divine reality is beyond finite comprehensions. The only purpose of discursive debate about God is—like the practice of meditating on a Zen koan—to drive the mind beyond itself and into the transcendental darkness that lights up the world.

In this same vein, the fourteenth-century English spiritual classic appropriately called *The Cloud of Unknowing* (Hodgson, 1944) says that to know God is to enter a cloud where all knowing ceases. Here all religious practices and beliefs, no matter how devout, must be put aside.

> If ever you shall come to this cloud, and stay and work in it as I bid you, just as this cloud of unknowing is above you, between you and your God, in the same way put a cloud of forgetting beneath you, between you and all the creatures that have ever been made . . . I make no exceptions, whether they are bodily creatures or spiritual . . . whether these be good or evil. (Hodgson, 1944: 24; my translation)

This applies not just to those objects unrelated to religion but even those considered most spiritual: "Therefore, though it is at times good to think of the kindness and worthiness of God in particular. And though this is a light and a part of contemplation, nevertheless, in this exercise, it shall be cast down and covered over with a cloud of forgetting" (Hodgson, 1944: 26; my translation). No matter how truthful or pious a thought or image or object is, it is to be put under foot as a distraction from the experience of that divine reality that is beyond all words and images and forms.

Religious creeds, practices, and traditions are built around certain images, ideas, or concepts that become idealized in the process of fully investing oneself in them. Each religious tradition is centered on specific core metaphors to which idealizing transferences are often attached as these claims are sacralized: "the ways of the Tao are effortless," or "reality is empty," or "the law of the Lord is just," or "God is love." Even the atheist clings to his or her concept of God whose nonexistence he or she passionately defends. Passing through "the cloud of unknowing" wrenches all these constructs away, leaving nothing to cling to, leaving no satisfactory way of speaking about, or arguing against, or grasping, any ultimate source of security. As Thomas Merton (1961) stated, "In the deepest darkness we most fully" find God (208). This is a powerful religious argument against absolutizing any religious forms.

Another argument against the divinizing of religious forms can be found in the Protestant Reformation in the sixteenth century in Europe that launched an increasingly bitter attack against the practices and beliefs of the late medieval Roman Catholic Church. The French lawyer turned reformer, John Calvin, rejected not only the authority of the Catholic Church but also many of its practices, especially those involving the use of statues, icons, church paintings, and other depictions of God. In his main work, the *Institutes of the Christian Religion,* Calvin (1536/1960) condemned any attempt to picture or describe God as idolatry. In doing so, Calvin went beyond simply condemning works of religious art to insisting on God's "incomprehensible essence" (102). God is infinite and that "ought to make us afraid to try to measure him by our own senses. Indeed his spiritual nature forbids our imagining anything earthly" applies to God (121). While Calvin clearly has in mind the statues and paintings so prominent in late medieval Catholic churches, here he articulates a more general principle that goes beyond simply rejecting physical forms. Calvin's basic principle is that "God's glory is corrupted by an impious falsehood whenever any form is attached to him" (100), not simply forms made of wood, stone, or paint, but also forms made of words, even pious words. In this view, not only attempting to picture God on canvas but even to describe God in words or to identify God with any earthly

constructs is to commit idolatry, which the twentieth-century disciple of
Calvin, Richard Niebuhr defined as "absolutizing the relative."

This Protestant polemic against idolatry was invoked again in response
to the 1933 resolution by the Lutheran bishops of Germany applauding
the "saving of our nation by our Leader Adolph Hitler as a gift from
God's hand" (Manschreck, 1964: 515). This embrace of Nazism by the
church appalled a young Swiss pastor named Karl Barth. Barth gathered
similarly minded colleagues together, and in 1934 they issued a declaration in which they condemned identifying the Christian faith with "some
dominant ideological or political convictions" (Manschreck, 1964: 532).
The intellectual basis for their fierce critique of using Christianity to bap-
tize nationalistic pretensions was laid in Barth's *Commentary on Paul's Letter to the Romans* (1918/1963).

In his commentary on Romans, Barth (1918/1963) made a strict
separation between any finite, human set of beliefs or categories, no matter how pious or traditional, and the transcendental truth about God.
"No human word, no word of Paul, is absolute truth," Barth wrote in his
uncompromising style (19). No finite, human, philosophical categories
or political platforms can encompass God, for "human experience and
human perception end where God begins" (120). God can be known;
but at the same time God remains unknown. "God reveals Himself inexo-
rably as the hidden God who can be apprehended only indirectly. . . . He
conceals himself utterly," Barth writes (136).

This paradoxical knowing of God goes beyond any human formula-
tion, and it implicitly judges and rejects the pretensions of religion to
speak of or for God. Such a transcendental reality has nothing to do with
religion. Rather, Barth asks, "Are we not compelled to set the [knowledge
of God] over against all religious and ecclesiastical being and having and
doing?" (Barth, 1918/1963: 127). All religions (including Christianity)
are finite human constructions. Made of human words, gestures, and
symbols, all religions partake in all the limitations of any human en-
deavor. Barth writes that

> [Seeking] to experience the infinite, all who venture upon its contempla-
> tion or description or representation—this is always transgression. When-
> ever men suppose themselves conscious of the emotion of nearness to God,
> whenever they speak and write of divine things, whenever sermon-making
> and temple-building are thought of as an ultimate human occupation,
> whenever men are aware of divine appointments and of being entrusted

with a divine mission, sin veritably abounds. . . . No human demeanour is more open to criticism, more doubtful, or more dangerous, than religious demeanour. (Barth, 1918/1963: 136)

Barth's book represents a searing attack upon any human, institutional pretension—no matter how traditional or devout—to identify its categories with the truth about God.

So centuries after Jesus, the Protestant reformers and their descendents continued to condemn what they saw as the idolatry and absolutizing of sacramental worship and claims of divine authority and later the pretensions of the twentieth-century nation-state and its religious supporters. This Protestant polemic against idolatry can be read as another critical force within Christianity in the tradition of the Hebrew prophets and Jesus' teachings. The history of Christianity from Jesus' disputes with the Pharisees of his day to the reformers' attacks upon the medieval church to Barth's vigorous repudiation of the identification of German bishops with the Nazi party are another example of the continual polemic from within religion itself against the pretensions and idealizations of the religious life.

In another vein, the twentieth-century Protestant philosopher and theologian Paul Tillich (1957) writes of a dialectic between doubt and faith. Faith is necessary to connect us to the universal, primal ground of our existence. Doubt is necessary, lest the relative, finite, human structures of faith be absolutized and put in the place of the universal God. According to Tillich, religious beliefs and practices grow out of an experience of connection with that ultimate source of our existence. This experience takes place in the deepest parts of our selfhood. Since it is direct and immediate, the experience itself is certain (Tillich, 1957: 19).

This direct experience, however, is both evoked by and expressed through the texts, symbols, and practices of the world's religions. But as a unique experience, it is not identical with those religious forms. Even though the experience itself is certain, doubt is inevitable because of the slippage between this immediate experience and the limited and human forms through which it is evoked and expressed. In the face of such a gap between the experience and its expression, it takes "courage" to affirm the significance of those texts, symbols, practices, and other forms and to commit oneself to them (Tillich, 1957: 19). A living religion requires some expression in texts, stories, beliefs, practices, and works of art. Some doubt that represents the gulf between immediate religious experience and its expression in finite cultural forms is a necessary part of religious faith and life. In contrast to the methodological doubt of the scientist and the cynical doubt of the skeptic, Tillich calls this doubt that is a part of the life of religion an "existential doubt" (23). It is an acknowledgment that the forms of religion can never adequately or fully express the experience of connection to the ultimate source of life. Aware of these ambiguities, it takes courage to commit oneself fully to the beliefs, practices, and patterns of life of a particular religious tradition.

TOLERATING AMBIGUITY

At this point we need to inquire about the psychodynamics of what Tillich calls courage—the ability to live freely and creatively and to make and keep commitments in the face of the inevitable limitations, disruptions, and doubts that accompany finite human life, including the life of religion. The theories of Fairbairn (1952) and Klein (1975b) underscore that a more nuanced and less dichotomized and fanatical approach to religious devotion depends on the capacity to tolerate ambivalence and ambiguity. This means that I do not have to split the world into opposing camps of the all-good and the all-evil, but I can tolerate the anxiety aroused by shades of gray and the uncertainty that can accompany them. I do not have to enhance my self-esteem by demonizing others or projecting my own aggression onto them. Thus I can wholeheartedly love another and commit myself to finite and imperfect human institutions, even religious ones. I do not have to overidealize them in order to feel secure or devoted. This less dichotomized stance requires the capacity for a mature and compassionate, not an emotionally desperate, way of being religious (Jones, 2002).

By suggesting that there is a doubt that is inevitably a part of faith, Tillich is pointing to something important in our discussion of the psychology of religion and religious terrorism. Religious fanatics tend to be those who crave or demand certainty in their religious beliefs. However, according to Tillich, as finite, limited, and fragile creatures we may wish for absolute certainty, but we must live with the limitations built into all our claims—even our religious ones—because of the finitude of our minds, our culturally relative cognitive schemas, and the impact of our unconscious conflicts. Absolute certainty in any area of human knowing—including religion—must remain a wish that will forever elude us in this limited world.

This need for certainty has an important psychological dimension. Feelings of certainty require repressing this fact of our human finitude and limitation. And we know clinically that repression almost always breeds anxiety, fear, and often aggression. The stronger the doubts, the stronger must be the force used to repress them. The reaction when this psychological certainty-system is threatened is equally forceful and often aggressive. It is probably not coincidence that religious groups composed of those who demand absolute certainty also tend to be those that are most fanatical and aggressive—aggressive in arguing with anyone who disagrees, aggressive in trying to convert others to their beliefs, aggressive in their visions of the end times, aggressive even to the point of advocating violence. Such absolute certainty is purchased at a psychological cost in the energy it takes to repress or deny the inevitable limitations on all human claims and beliefs. And often this denial can breed a violent reaction when that feeling of certainty is challenged and the uncertainty behind it exposed.

Religions must use finite human gestures, words, and artifacts to speak of what is infinite and beyond all words and gestures. All religions have at their heart this paradoxical affirmation: that there is a universal, sacred reality beyond the world of time and space, language and symbol, and yet this transcendental reality can be experienced in and through the finite words, gestures, and symbols of that religion. So religions must, at the same time, both affirm and negate language, gesture, and symbol. We can point to the infinite. We can experience the infinite in ecstatic moments. As Tillich (1957) points out, the word "ecstatic" means to stand outside ourselves. Ecstatic experiences push us beyond the boundaries of our ordinary understanding as Buddhism attempts to do with its Koans and paradoxical discourses and as is described in *The Cloud of Unknowing* and Barth's *Commentary on the Letter to the Romans*. But we cannot grasp the infinite or describe the infinite as though it were a concrete object.

Some devotees attempt to deny this paradox by claiming that their words, their gestures, their symbols really can describe the indescribable and grasp the ungraspable. Such an idea fits Barth's definition of idolatry—something finite put in the place of the infinite. This absolutizing of a finite set of beliefs, traditions, and practices ignores, and requires repressing, the fact that however inspired they may be, they are still finite and human words, symbols, and traditions. They may point us to the divine, but, existing as they do in the finite world, they are not themselves divine. Denying this reality requires repression and denial that, in turn, can lead to anxiety and aggression.

The point here is not to defend a particular position—say Tillich's existential philosophy, Buddhism's paradoxes, Dionysius's mysticism, or Barth's transcendental theology. The point they all agree on is the recognition that religious understanding is necessarily a profoundly paradoxical process. Religions contain elements that can exaggerate the holiness and divinity of their beliefs and practices and other elements that critique that same egoistic pretension to holiness and divinity on their own part.

There are myriad ways of being Christian, or Muslim, or Buddhist, or Jewish, or Hindu, or the follower of any other faith. Some of these ways promote and build upon the psychologies and theologies that sponsor violence and terrorism: they create humiliation, they overidealize their own traditions, they demand submission to a figure who shames them, they dichotomize the world, they demonize the other, they sanctify violence. Other trajectories within these same religions, often more ancient and traditional, serve to undercut these same dynamics: they transform humiliation into compassionate action, they critique the idolatry and pretensions of the human ego, they worship figures of compassion and forgiveness, they teach peace. In these ways they seek to transform not just the conscious beliefs that are central to religiously motivated terrorist groups, they also seek to transform the deeper psychological roots of religious terrorism: to replace shame and humiliation with realistic humility, to overcome splitting and demonization with an acknowledgment of human commonality, to evoke experiences of forgiveness and compassion rather than abjection and condemnation. Such religions enable their adherents to recognize and accept the ambivalences and ambiguities that inevitably accompany religious practice, to understand the complexities of human motivation, and to experience the continuities between people, rather than seeing the world through the radical discontinuity of apocalyptic thinking.

All the world's religions have advocated, supported, and sanctified violence and terrorism. All the world's religions also have teachings, practices, and examples that vigorously critique and reject without compromise not only terrorist actions but also the deeper psychological motivations for those actions. Will spokesmen and spokeswomen arise within all the traditions who can speak without compromise for a critique of their religion's pretensions and the rejection of the tactics of terror? Or will religions' most forceful and media-savvy spokespersons continue to be those who advocate the spilling of more and more blood upon the earth? Humankind's future may depend on the answer.

NOTES

Preface

1. A report of these discussions can be found in Hill, 2006.

Chapter 1

1. That is, these violent acts are not predictable as specific events. In most every case, and certainly in the case of 9/11, there was plenty of reason to think that something would occur, and steps could have been taken to lessen the chances or prevent it, such as stepping up airport security inspections or hardening and securely fastening cockpit doors. Nothing done after 9/11 could not have been before 9/11 and so may have prevented the attacks. Not being predictable does not necessarily mean not preventable. For more on the problematics of predicting specific terrorist actions, see Post, Ruby, and Saw (2002) and Sprinzak (1998b).

2. Post, Sprinzak, and Denny (2003) argue that this "fusion of the individual and the group" is central to understanding Palestinian suicide bombers, but the interviews they conducted indicate that much more complex motivational factors are involved. See also Miller (2004), for papers that both support and critique this singular situationalist perspective.

3. I am indebted to Scott Atran for pointing this out to me. See also Atran (2006b). Also, it was only after finishing writing this section in 2005 that I found Moghadam's (2005) critique of Pape's book that makes many of the same points I make here.

Chapter 2

1. Neutral designations are almost impossible here. Muslims, even those who reject the appeal to martyrdom, reject the designation of "suicide bombers" because these people have none of the psychological characteristics of those who commit suicide, and suicide is condemned in the Koran. While I personally regard them as terrorists, as hard as it is for me for personally, I feel that stance should not dominate a scholarly text. I will follow the convention of Raphael

Israeli and refer to them most frequently as "human bombers" (quoted in Strenski, 2003). See also Merari (1998).

2. As you will see from the next chapter, I have come to question Lifton's and Wessinger's claim that apocalyptic thinking was so central to the Aum's worldview and to the sarin attack. But Lifton is clearly correct that Asahara's teaching was becoming increasingly apocalyptic as he felt more and more threatened and that that move coincided with an increasing focus on violent actions. My only question is, what is cause and what is effect in the turn toward apocalypticism and violence?

3. In fairness we should note that Eric Rudolph does not simply blame the rise of abortions on moral degeneracy. Rather he notes that the need for abortions arises in many cases as the result of social policy and that the number of abortions could be reduced significantly by a more humane social policy. He writes: "This country that put a man on the moon, now will not provide enough sustenance to care for its own children. This country has enough food to feed the world, but not an ounce of milk to spare for another child" (Rudolph, 2005: 4). This is a sentiment that a confirmed pro-choice person can certainly endorse.

4. I am not suggesting that religion is the main cause of America's violent history. Many other factors, including immigration patterns and life on the frontier, have also contributed to violence in American life. Also, the idea of America's manifest destiny arising from America's religiously derived sense of being a special, elect nation, exempt from the usual conditions of national life, contributed to the violent extermination of the indigenous Americans, which, in turn, contributed to the legacy of violence in America. For background on the interplay of religion and violence in American history, see Lieven (2004), Taylor (2005), and Slotkin, (1998).

5. Examples of this assertion are found throughout Davis (2003) and Hassan (2001). Post et al. (2003) conclude that, in contrast to the West, in Middle Eastern Muslim communities "liberation and religious freedom are the values that define success, not necessarily academic or economic success" (175).

6. A related and potentially important topic is the subject of deconversion— leaving a religious group. Again, there is a fair amount of research on this topic, most of it done in the 1970s and 1980s regarding cults and new religious movements. It would be important to study those who left terrorist groups and renounced religious violence. One might learn something useful about facilitating such deconversions. A fine example of this research is Wright (1987).

CHAPTER 3

1. Again, I express my deepest gratitude to Professor Manabu Watanabe for making his expertise and knowledge so readily available to me, as well as for his friendship and hospitality. At its 2006 Annual Meeting, the American Academy of Religion sponsored a panel on Buddhism and violence, and I am grateful to Professors Derek Maher and Stephen Jenkins for sharing drafts of their papers with me.

2. Some commentators have compared Aum's devotion to Asahara with the worship of the divine emperor in Japan that is implicated in much of Japan's behavior in World War II, but this comparison is beyond the scope of this chapter.

3. Reader (2000) also speculates that the subway attack might have been a way for Aum to call attention to itself and gain a public awareness of its teachings that it had failed to achieve by more legitimate means. In this it certainly succeeded.

4. I am indebted to Professor Watanabe for this suggestion about the devotees' identification with Asahara's own humiliations.

5. There is one aspect of Aum that is striking to the researcher of religiously motivated violence: many of the participants in the murders and the sarin gas attacks later repented and turned against Aum (Lifton, 2000). I know of no other examples of this in contemporary religiously motivated violence. Former terrorists, who later reject violence as a political strategy, turn to more nonviolent and traditionally political methods to pursue their cause. But they do not usually repent of their previous actions and turn against their comrades, at least not on the scale that happened with Aum after Asahara and many leaders were arrested and brought to trial. Perhaps this points to some difference in the religious psychology behind Aum's deeds and that of other religiously motivated violent actions.

CHAPTER 4

1. I must begin by again thanking Kathleen Bishop, Chuck Strozier, and Mark Taylor, who brought their expertise and critical acumen to bear on their careful readings and helpful comments on this chapter. Their feedback and insights and ongoing discussions with them have considerably enriched this chapter. I also want to thank Jon Pahl, who graciously made his lecture notes on *Left Behind* available to me.

2. To state the obvious, the book does not start with a billionaire CEO committing stock fraud that results in his employees losing their life-savings and ending up impoverished or an insurance executive looting his company and taking off to the Cayman Islands, leaving thousands without access to health care.

3. While any commentary on the political implications of this series seems redundant, in addition to a general resistance to any worldwide or transnational organizations aimed at bringing peace or justice, two specific political/policy effects can be noted. First, concerning current (2006) Middle Eastern policy, as has been widely and accurately reported, apocalyptic Christians have been among the most powerful and active American supporters of the Likud policies in Israel and the insistence that no Israeli land, including any of the occupied territories, be ceded to the Palestinians for a Palestinian state. Premillennial dispensationalism requires that the Jews be able to return to a reconstituted "biblical Israel" as a precursor to Christ's second coming. This has extended to the American Ambassador Elliott Abrams meeting in the White House with representatives of dispensational theology to assure them that, while supporting Sharon's proposal (in 2005) for a Gaza withdrawal, the U.S. government

would never countenance an Israeli policy that would undermine the territorial integrity of "biblical Israel" for the sake of a Middle Eastern peace. Abrams reassured this group that "biblical Israel" would remain intact so that Christ's return would not be interfered with. The image of a high-ranking government official meeting in the White House to make foreign policy based on this theology speaks for itself (see Perlstein, 2004; Kaplan, 2004; Taylor, 2005). The second involves environmental policy. Hardrock mining for minerals has left Montana (not my home state of New Jersey) with the largest Superfund cleanup sites in the country. Mining companies have been exceptionally resistant to undertaking any cleanup, and the government has refused to prod them. One reason for this recalcitrance, in the words of one who has studied this issue, is because "the CEO and most of the officers of one of the major American mining companies are members of a church that teaches that God will soon arrive on Earth, hence if we can just postpone land reclamation for another 5 or 10 years it will then be irrelevant anyway" (Diamond, 2005, p. 462). All of this should not be too surprising since LaHaye is one of the most powerful leaders of the Christian right in America. I do not think that the *Left Behind* series is simplistically intended to be a coded, novelized version of the Christian right's political agenda, although no narrative opportunity is missed to push a clear antiabortion, antihomosexual, anti-women's rights message. Further discussion of the politics of the *Left Behind* series can be found in Urban (n.d.), Kristof (2004), Sullivan (2004), and Ungar (2005).

4. Here I must record a personal reaction: When I finished reading this carefully, I felt just sick. I am not a stranger to violence either in my own life or in books and movies. But the violence in the *Left Behind* series and especially in *Glorious Appearing* struck me as simply gratuitous and pornographic.

5. In the fall of 2006 I taught a seminar on the psychology of religious terrorism at Union Theological Seminary in New York. One of the students in the class, Gerald Williams, made a study of bloody imagery in Christian music, and I have drawn on that study in this paragraph.

6. For reviews, see Browne (2005) and Gaziano (2001). Gaziano concludes that "children of parents who feel powerless and who attempt to assert power through authoritarianism often grow up to have the same sense of powerlessness and other authoritarian characteristics, and they may be especially attracted to the portrayal of violent power options in mass media" (p. 240). Bushman and Anderson (2001) conclude that "since 1975, the scientific confidence and statistical magnitude of this link [between media violence and aggression] has been clearly positive and has consistently increased over time" (p. 478). See also Kiewitz and Weaver (2001).

7. Another example of the violence latent in American apocalyptic Christianity becoming manifest is the American televangelist Pat Robertson calling for assassination of the democratically elected president of Venezuela, Hugo Chavez, in 2005. "If he thinks we're trying to assassinate him, I think we really ought to go ahead and do it," Robertson said on his TV show *The 700 Club*. "We have the ability to take him out," Robertson went on to say, "and I think the time has

come to exercise that ability." Several evangelical leaders rejected Robertson's statements, but many national evangelical groups refused to comment. See Goodstein (2005).

CHAPTER 5

1. I am indebted to Ruth Stein for this observation.

2. The claim that early experience continues to exert an effect on our adult lives has been amply demonstrated by a variety of research projects in contemporary psychology, including research on attachment patterns, the development and functioning of cognitive schemas, and infant and early childhood development.

CHAPTER 6

1. There is a certain ambiguity in invoking the prophets at this juncture. Many of them attacked the ancient Israelite sacrificial and ritual systems in the name of God, thus undercutting any Jewish or Christian theology of God as a bloodthirsty tyrant—the theology often found in texts of religious terror. But much of the prophetic literature is a discourse of condemnation, thus reinforcing a theology of God as judge who condemns and metes out punishment on those he does not approve of—another theological theme also found in texts of religious terror. This reflects the psychological and moral ambiguity of righteous indignation. Righteous indignation has been a major motivation in movements of social reform, such as the civil rights movements of the 1960s; it has also been the source of much of the judgmentalism and narrow moralism that characterizes many religious people.

BIBLIOGRAPHY

Abi-Hashem. (2004). "Peace and War in the Middle East." In F. Moghaddam & A. Marsella (Eds.), *Understanding Terrorism* (pp. 69–90). Washington, DC: American Psychological Association Press.

Altemeyer, B., & Hunsberger, B. (1992). "Authoritarianism, Religious Fundamentalism, Quest, and Prejudice." *International Journal for the Psychology of Religion*, 2/2: 113–134.

Altemeyer, B., & Hunsberger, B. (2005). "Fundamentalism and Authoritarianism." In R. Paloutzian & C. Park (Eds.), *Handbook of the Psychology of Religion and Spirituality* (pp. 308–392). New York: Guilford Press.

Alexander, B. (2006). "The New Lies about Women's Health." *Glamour.* Available at www.glamour.com/features/healthandbody/060403fewohe (accessed May 28, 2006).

Ammerman, N. (1994). "Accounting for Christian Fundamentalism." In M. Marty & R. Appleby (Eds.), *Accounting for Fundamentalisms* (pp. 13–17). Chicago: University of Chicago Press.

Arena, M., & Arrigo, B. (2006). *The Terrorist Identity.* New York: New York University Press.

Armstrong, K. (2001). *The Battle for God.* New York: Ballantine Books.

Aryan Nation. Available at www.aryan-nations.org (accessed June 30, 2007).

Atran, S. (2003a). "Genesis of Suicide Terrorism." *Science*, 229/5612: 1534–1539.

Atran, S. (2003b). "The Strategic Threat from Suicide Terror." Publication 03–33. Washington, DC: AEI-Brookings Joint Center.

Atran, S. (2004). "Mishandling Suicide Terrorism." *The Washington Quarterly*, 27/3: 67–90.

Atran, S. (2005a). "The Emir: An Interview with Abu Bakar Ba'asyir." *Spotlight on Terror*, 3/9: 1–7.

Atran, S. (2005b). "The 'Virtual Hand' of Jihad." *Terrorism Monitor*, 3/10: 1–4.

Atran, S. (2005c). "Facing Catastrophe—Risk and Response: The 9/11 and 11-m Commissions' Blind Sides." Publication 05–05. Washington, DC: AEI-Brookings Joint Center.

Atran, S. (2006a). "A Failure of Imagination." *Studies in Conflict and Terrorism,* 29/3: 285–300.

Atran, S. (2006b). "The Moral Logic and Growth of Suicide Terrorism." *The Washington Quarterly,* 29/2: 127–147.

Atran, S. (2006c, February). "The Moral Logic of Martyrdom." Lecture presented at a conference on "The Psychology of Fundamentalism," Chicago Institute of Psychoanalysis, Chicago.

Atran, S., & Stern, J. (2005). "Small Groups Find Fatal Purpose through the Web." *Nature,* 437: 620–621.

Atta, M. (n.d.) "Last Letter." London: Reuters News Service.

Bagley, W. (2002). *Blood of the Prophets.* Norman, OK: University of Oklahoma Press.

Bailie, G. (1995). *Violence Unveiled.* New York: Crossroads.

Bandura, A. (1998). "Mechanisms of Moral Disengagement." In W. Reich (Ed.), *Origins of Terrorism* (pp. 161–191). Washington, DC: Woodrow Wilson Center Press.

Bandura, A. (2004). "The Role of Selective Moral Disengagement in Terrorism and Counterterrorism." In F. Moghaddam & A. Marsella (Eds.), *Understanding Terrorism* (pp. 121–150). Washington, DC: American Psychological Association Press.

Barkum, M. (1974). *Disaster and the Millennium.* New Haven, CT: Yale University Press.

Barth, K. (1963). *The Epistle of the Romans* (E. Hoskyns, Trans.). New York: Oxford University Press. (Original work published 1918).

Bass, T. (Ed.). (1999). *Obedience to Authority.* Mahwah, NJ : Erlbaum.

Batson, C., Schroenrade, P., & Ventis, W. (1993). *Religion and the Individual: A Social Psychological Perspective.* New York: Oxford University Press.

Baumeister, R., & Vohs, K. (2004). "Four Roots of Evil." In A. Miller (Ed.), *The Social Psychology of Good and Evil* (pp. 85–101). New York: Guilford Press.

Beier, M. (2006). "The Psychology of Violent Christian Fundamentalism." *The Psychoanalytic Review,* 93/2: 301–328.

Beit-Hallahmi, B. (2002). "Rebirth and Death: The Violent Potential of Apocalyptic Dreams." In C. Stout (Ed.), *The Psychology of Terrorism* (pp. 163–190). Westport, CT: Praeger.

Bergin, A. (1991). "Values and Religious Issues in Psychotherapy and Mental Health." *American Psychologist,* 46/4: 394–403.

Berman, P. (2003, May 23). "The Philosopher of Islamic Terror." *The New York Times Magazine,* pp. G24ff.

Bin Hassan, M. H. (2006). "Key Considerations in Counterideological Work against Terrorist Ideology." *Studies in Conflict and Terrorism,* 29/6: 531–558.

Borg, M., & Wright, N. T. (1998). *The Meaning of Jesus,* New York: Harper Collins.

Bray, M. (1994). *A Time to Kill.* Portland, OR: Advocates for Life.

Brokaw, B., & Edwards, K. (1994). "There Is a Relationship of God Image to Level of Object Relations Development." *Journal of Psychology and Theology,* 22/4: 352–371.

Browne, K., & Hamilton-Giachritsis, C. (2005). "The Influence of Violent Media on Children and Adolescents: A Public-Health Approach." *Lancet,* 366: 702–710.

Bushman, B., & Anderson, C. (2001). "Media Violence and the American Public: Scientific Facts versus Media Misinformation." *American Psychologist,* 56: 477–489.

Calvin, J. (1960). *Institutes of the Christian Religion* (F. L. Battles, Trans.). Library of Christian Classics, Vol. 1. Philadelphia: Westminster Press.

Canetti, D., & Pedahzur, A. (2002). "The Effects of Context and Psychological Variables on Extreme Right-Wing Sentiments." *Social Behavior and Personality,* 30/4: 317–334.

Christian Gallery. (2007, February). Available: www.christiangallery.com.

Clarkson, F. (1994, April 17). "Christian Reconstructionism: Theocratic Dominionism Gains Influence." Available: www.rfcse.com.

Club de Madrid. (2005). *International Summit on Democracy, Terrorism, and Security:* Vol. 1. *Addressing the Causes of Terrorism.* Madrid, Spain: Club de Madrid.

Collins, J. (Ed.). (1998). *The Encyclopedia of Apocalypticism.* New York: Continuum.

Council on American Islamic Relations. (2007, July). Available: www.cair.com.

Crenshaw, M. (1981). "The Causes of Terrorism." *Comparative Politics,* 13: 379–399.

Darr, R. (2006). *Spy of the Heart.* Louisville, KY: Fons Vitae.

Davis, J. (2003). *Martyrs: Innocence, Vengeance and Despair in the Middle East.* New York: Palgrave.

Davis, W. (2006). "Bible Says: The Psychology of Christian Fundamentalism." *The Psychoanalytic Review,* 93: 267–300.

Diamond, J. (2005). *Collapse.* New York: Viking Press.

Durham, W. (2007). "Former Bush surgeon general says he was muzzled." Reuters, 10, 2007. Available from www.Reuters.com (accessed Oct. 17, 2007).

Durkheim, E. (1902/1965). *The Elementary Forms of the Religious Life* (J. Swain, Trans.). New York: Free Press.

Eagelton, T. (2005). *Holy Terror.* New York: Oxford University Press.

Eidelson, R., & Eidelson, J. (2003). "Dangerous Ideas: Five Beliefs That Propel Groups Towards Conflict." *American Psychologist,* 58/3: 182–192.

Eigen, M. (2002). *Rage.* Middletown, CT: Wesleyan University Press.

Eisenberg, N., Valiente, C., & Champion, C. (2004). "Empathy-related Responding." In A. Miller (Ed.), *The Social Psychology of Good and Evil* (pp. 386–415). New York: Guilford Press.

Erikson, E. (1969) *Ghandi's Truth.* New York: Norton.

Erikson, E. (1975). *Life History and the Historical Moment*. New York: Norton.

Fairbairn, W. R. D. (1952). "The Repression and Return of Bad Objects." In *Psychoanalytic Studies of the Personality* (pp. 59–89). London: Tavistock.

Freud, S. (1913/1950). *Totem and Taboo*. (Trans. J. Strachey). New York: Norton.

Freud, S. (1930/1962). *Civilization and its Discontents*. (Trans. J. Strachey). New York: Norton.

Frykholm, A. J. (2004). *Rapture Culture: Left Behind in Evangelical America*. New York: Oxford University Press.

Galanter, M. (1989). *Cults: Faith, Healing, and Coercion*. New York: Oxford University Press.

Gaziano, C. (2001). "Toward a Broader Conceptual Framework for Research on Social Stratification, Childrearing Patterns, and Media Effects." *Mass Communication & Society*, 4(2): 219–244.

Gethin, R. (1998). *The Foundations of Buddhism*. London: Oxford University Press.

Ghent, E. (1990). "Masochism, Submission, and Surrender: Masochism as a Perversion of Surrender." *Contemporary Psychoanalysis*, 24: 108–136.

Giddens, A. (2000). *Runaway World*. New York: Routledge.

Gilligan, J. (1996). *Violence*. New York: Random House.

Girard, R. (1977). *Violence and the Sacred* (P. Gregory, Trans.). Baltimore, MD: Johns Hopkins Press.

Girard, R. (1987). *Things Hidden from the Foundation of the World*. Stanford, CA: Stanford University Press.

Girard, R. (1996). *The Girard Reader* (J. Williams, Ed.). New York: Crossroads.

Goodstein, L. (2005, August 24). "Robertson Suggests U.S. Kill Venezuela's Leader." *New York Times*. Available at www.nytimes.com/2005/08/24/politics/24robertson.html (accessed Oct. 31, 2007).

Grossman, K. (2006, September 11). "View of God Can Predict Values and Politics." *USA Today*. Available at www.usatoday.com/news/religion/2006–09–11-religion-survey_x.htm.

Hafez, M. (2006a). "Rationality, Culture, and Structure in the Making of Suicide Bombers." *Studies in Conflict and Terrorism*, 29/2: 165–185.

Hafez, M. (2006b). *Manufacturing Human Bombs: The Making of Palestinian Suicide Bombers*. Washington, DC: United States Institute of Peace.

Happold, F. (1975). *Mysticism*. New York: Penguin.

Hassan, N. (2001, November 19). "An Arsenal of Believers." *The New Yorker*, pp. 36–41.

Hedges, C. (2006). *American Fascists*. New York: Free Press.

Hedges, C. (2005). *Shield New York Against Nuclear and Biological Terrorism*. New York: Center on Terrorism, John Jay College.

Heisig, J., & Maraldo, J. (1994). *Rude Awakenings: Zen, the Kyoto School and the Question of Nationalism*. Honolulu: University of Hawaii Press.

Hill, D. (2006, April/May). "Psychoanalysis and Fundamentalism." *National Psychologist.*

Hill, P. (2003). "Mix My Blood with Blood of the Unborn." Available at www.armyofgod.com (accessed April 17, 2006).

Hill, P. (1997). "Why I Killed an Abortionist." Available at www.saltshaker.us (accessed April 17, 2006).

Hodgson, P. (Ed.). (1944). *Cloud of Unknowing* and *The Book of Privy Counseling.* The Early English Text Society. London: Oxford University Press.

Hoffman, B. (2007). "What Went Wrong?" *Studies in Conflict and Terrorism,* 30/1: 93–95.

Hoffman, B. (2006). *Inside Terrorism.* New York: Columbia University Press.

Hood, R., Hill, P., & Williamson, W. (2005). *The Psychology of Religious Fundamentalism.* New York: Guilford.

Hood, R., Spilka, B., Hunsberger, B., & Gorsuch, R. (1996). *The Psychology of Religion: An Empirical Approach.* New York: Guilford Press.

Horgan, J. (2006). *The Psychology of Terrorism.* London: Routledge Press.

Horsely, N. (n.d). "The Nuremburg Files." Available at www.christiangallery.com (accessed May 30, 2007).

Jenkins, S. (2006, November). "Making Merit Through Warfare." Paper presented at the American Academy of Religion annual meeting, panel on Buddhism and Violence, Washington, DC.

Jones, J. (1991). *Contemporary Psychoanalysis and Religion.* New Haven, CT: Yale University Press.

Jones, J. (1996). *Religion and Psychology in Transition: Psychoanalysis, Feminism, and Religion.* New Haven, CT: Yale University Press.

Jones, J. (2001). "The Sacred: A Relational Psychoanalytic Investigation." *Psyche en Geloof,* 12/3: 93–104.

Jones, J. (2002). *Terror and Transformation: The Ambiguity of Religion in Psychoanalytic Perspective.* London: Routledge.

Jones, J. (2006). "Why Does Religion Turn Violent? A Psychoanalytic Exploration of Religious Terrorism." *The Psychoanalytic Review,* 93/2: 167–190.

Jones, J. (2007, September). "Violence, Religion and Contemporary American Christianity—A Psychological Study." Paper presented at the conference on the Psychology of Religion and Spirituality, Prague.

Juergensmeyer, M. (2000). *Terror in the Mind of God.* Berkeley: University of California Press.

Kakar, S. (1982). *Shamans, Mystics, and Doctors.* Chicago: University of Chicago Press.

Kaplan, E. (2004). *With God on Their Side.* New York: The New Press.

Kellen, K. (1998). "Ideology and Rebellion: Terrorism in West Germany." In W. Reich (Ed.), *Origins of Terrorism* (pp. 43–58). Washington, DC: Woodrow Wilson Center Press.

Kent, D. (2006, November). "Onward Buddhist Soldiers: Sermons to Soldiers in the Sri Lankan Army." Paper presented at the American Academy of Religion annual meeting, panel on Buddhism and Violence, Washington, DC.

Khosrokhavar, F. (2005). *Suicide Bombers: Allah's New Martyrs* (D. Macey, Trans.). London: Pluto Press.

Kiewitz, J. W. (2001). "Trait Aggressiveness, Media Violence, and Perceptions of Interpersonal Conflict." *Personality & Individual Differences*, 31/6: 821–835.

Kimball, C. (2002). *When Religion Becomes Evil*. San Francisco: Harper.

Kippenberg, H., & Seidensticker, T. (2006). *The 9/11 Handbook*. London: Equinox.

Kirby, A. (2007). "The London Bombers as 'Self-Starters.'" *Studies in Conflict and Terrorism*, 30/5: 415–428.

Kirkpatrick, L., Hood., R., & Hartz, G. (1991). "Fundamentalist Religion Conceptualized in Terms of Rokeach's Theory of the Open and Closed Mind." *Research in the Social Scientific Study of Religion*, 3: 157–179.

Kisala, R., & Mullins, M. (2001). *Religion and Social Crisis in Japan: Understanding Japanese Society through the Aum Affair*. New York: Palgrave.

Klauck, H-J. (1992). "Sacrifice in the New Testament" (R. Fuller, Trans.). In *Anchor Bible Dictionary* (Vol. 5, pp. 886–891). New York: Doubleday.

Klein, M. (1975a). *Love, Guilt and Reparation, 1921–1945*. New York: The Free Press.

Klein, M. (1975b). *Envy and Gratitude, 1946–1963*. New York: The Free Press.

Koenigsburg, R. (1975). *Hitler's Ideology*. New York: The Library of Social Science.

Kohut, H. (1971). *The Analysis of the Self*. New York: International Universities Press.

Kohut, H. (1973). "Thoughts on Narcissism and Narcissistic Rage." In R. Eissler (Ed.), *The Psychoanalytic Study of the Child* (pp. 360–400). New York: Quadrangle Books.

Kohut, H. (1977). *The Restoration of the Self*. Madison, CT: International Universities Press.

Kohut, H. (1978). Remarks about the formation of the self. In P. Ornstein (Ed.), *The Search for the Self* (Vol. II, pp. 737–770). New York: International Universities Press.

Krakauer, J. (2004). *Under the Banner of Heaven: The Story of a Violent Faith*. New York: Random House.

Kristof, N. (2004, July 17). "Jesus and Jihad." *New York Times*. Available at http://query.nytimes.com/gst/fullpage.html?res=9C06E5D7153AF934A25754C0A9629C8B63 (accessed Oct. 31, 2007).

LaHaye. T. (1999). *Revelation Unveiled*. Grand Rapids, MI: Zondervan.

LaHaye, T., & Jenkins, J. (1995). *Left Behind* [the first book in the *Left Behind* series]. Wheaton, IL: Tyndale House.

LaHaye, T., & Jenkins, J. (2004). *Glorious Appearing* [the final book in the *Left Behind* series]. Wheaton, IL: Tyndale House.

Lawrence, B. (1989). *Defenders of God*. San Francisco: Harper & Row.

Lieven, A. (2004). *America Right or Wrong*. New York: Oxford University Press.

Lifton, R. (1979). *The Broken Connection*. New York: Basic Books.

Lifton, R. (2000). *Destroying the World to Save It*. New York: Henry Holt-Owl Books.

Lustick, I. (2006). *Trapped in the War on Terror*. Philadelphia: University of Pennsylvania Press.

Maekawa, M. (2001). "When prophecy fails: The response of Aum members to the crisis." In R. Kisala & M. Mullins (Eds), *Religion and Social Crisis in Japan: Understanding Japanese Society through the Aum Affair*. New York & London: Palgrave.

Maher, D. (2006, November). "The Rhetoric of War in Tibet: Towards a Buddhist Just War Theory." Paper presented at the American Academy of Religion annual meeting, panel on Buddhism and Violence, Washington, DC.

Manschreck, C. (1964). *A History of Christianity*. New York: Prentice-Hall.

Marsella, A. (2005, August). "Understanding Terrorism." Paper presented at the convention of the American Psychological Association, Washington, DC.

Marty, M., & R. Appleby. (1994). *Fundamentalisms Observed*. Chicago: University of Chicago Press.

McDermott, T. (2005). *Perfect Soldiers*. New York: HarperCollins.

McGinn, B. (2005). "Apocalypticism and Violence." In T. Heffernan & T. Burman (Eds.), *Scripture and Pluralism* (pp. 209–229). Leiden, the Netherlands: Brill.

McNish, J. (2004). *Transforming Shame*. Binghamton, NY: Haworth.

Merari, A. (1998). "The Readiness to Kill and Die: Suicide Terrorism in the Middle East." In W. Reich (Ed.), *Origins of Terrorism* (pp. 192–210). Washington, DC: Woodrow Wilson Center Press.

Merton, T. (1961). *New Seeds on Contemplation*. New York: New Directions.

Milgram, S. (1974). *Obedience to Authority*. New York: Harper & Row.

Militant Islam Monitor. Jihad Manifest letter found on the body of Theo Van Gogh. Available at www.militantislammonitor.org.

Miller, A. (2004). "What Can the Milgram Obedience Experiments Tell Us about the Holocaust?" In A. Miller (Ed.), *The Social Psychology of Good and Evil* (pp. 193–239). New York: Guilford Press.

Miller, A. (Ed.). (2004). *The Social Psychology of Good and Evil*. New York: Guilford Press.

Miller, W. (1993). *Humiliation and Other Essays on Honor, Social Discomfort, and Violence*. Ithaca, NY: Cornell University Press.

Mitton, C. (1962). "Atonement." In *Interpreter's Dictionary of the Bible* (Vol. 1, pp. 309–313). Nashville. TN: Abingdon Press.

Moghadam, A. (2006). "Suicide Terrorism, Occupation, and the Globalization of Martyrdom: A Critique of *Dying to Win*." *Studies in Conflict and Terrorism*, 29/8: 707–729.

Moghaddam, F. (2005). "The Staircase to Terrorism: A Psychological Exploration." *American Psychologist*, 60/2: 161–169.

Moghaddam, F., & Marsella, A. (2004). *Understanding Terrorism.* Washington, DC: American Psychological Association Press.

Mullins, M., Shimazono, S., & Swanson, P. (Eds.). (1993). *Religion and Society in Modern Japan.* Berkeley, CA: Asian Humanities Press.

Muslim Council of Britain (2007, July). Available: www.mcb.org.uk.

Nesser, P. (2006). "Jihadism in Western Europe after the Invasion of Iraq." *Studies in Conflict and Terrorism,* 29/4: 323–342.

Pahl, J. (2005). "What's Behind *Left Behind.*" Unpublished manuscript.

Paloutzian, R. (2005). "Religious Conversion and Spiritual Transformation." In R. Paloutzian & C. Park (Eds.), *Handbook of the Psychology of Religion and Spirituality* (pp. 331–347). New York: Guilford Press.

Paloutzian, R., & Park, C. (Eds.). (2005). *Handbook of the Psychology of Religion and Spirituality.* New York: Guilford Press.

Pape, R. (2005). *Dying to Win.* New York: Random House.

Parsons, W. (1999). *The Enigma of the Oceanic Feeling.* New York: Oxford University Press.

Pattison, S. (2000). *Shame: Theory, Therapy, Theology.* Cambridge: Cambridge University Press.

Perlstein, R. (2004, May 18). "The Jesus Launching Pad." *The Village Voice Online.* Available at http://www.villagevoice.com/news/0420,perlstein,53582,6.html (accessed Oct. 31, 2007).

Piscatori, J. (1994). "Accounting for Islamic Fundamentalism." In M. Marty & R. Appleby (Eds.), *Accounting for Fundamentalisms* (pp. 361–373). Chicago: University of Chicago Press.

Piven, J. (2006). "Narcissism, Sexuality, and Psyche in Terrorist Psychology." *The Psychoanalytic Review,* 93/2: 231–265.

Piven, J., Boyd, C., & Lawton, H. (Eds.). (2004). *Terrorism, Jihad, and Sacred Violence.* Giessen, Germany: Psychosocial-Verlag.

Post, J. (1984). "Notes on a Psychodynamic Theory of Terrorist Behavior." *Terrorism,* 7/3: 241–256.

Post, J. (1998). "Terrorist psycho-logic." In W. Reich (Ed.), *Origins of Terrorism* (pp. 25–40). Washington, DC: Woodrow Wilson Center Press.

Post, J., Ruby, K., & Shaw, F. (2002). "The Radical Group in Context." *Studies in Conflict and Terrorism,* 25/1: 73–100.

Post, J. Sprinzak, E., & Denny, (2003). "The terrorists in their own words: Interviews with 35 incarcerated middle eastern terrorists." *Terrorism and Political Violence,* 15/1: 171–184.

Powers, J. (1995). *Introduction to Tibetan Buddhism.* Ithaca, NY: Snow Lion Press.

Qutb, S. (1996). *Milestones.* Delhi, India: Ishaat-e-Islam Trust Publications.

Rambo, L. (1993). *Understanding Religious Conversion.* New Haven, CT: Yale University Press.

Rapoport, D. (1998). "Sacred Terror: A Contemporary Example from Islam." In W. Reich (Ed.), *Origins of Terrorism* (pp. 103–130). Washington, DC: Woodrow Wilson Press.

Reader, I. (1996). *A Poisonous Cocktail: Aum Shinrikyo's Path to Violence.* Copenhagen: Nias Publications.

Reader, I. (2000). *Religious Violence in Contemporary Japan: The Case of Aum Shinrikyo.* London: Curzon Press.

Reich, W. (Ed.). (1998). *Origins of Terrorism.* Washington, DC: Woodrow Wilson Center Press.

Religion and Ethics Newsweekly. (2004, April 16). "America's Evangelicals." PBS episode no. 733. Text available: www.pbs.org/wnet/religionandethics/week733/release.html.

Ritter, K., & O'Neill, C. (1996). *Righteous Religion.* New York: Haworth Press.

Roberts, M. (2005). "Tamil Tiger 'Martyrs.'" *Studies in Conflict and Terrorism,* 28/6: 493–514.

Robbins, T., & Anthony, D. (Ed.). (1995). *Armageddon in Waco.* Chicago: University of Chicago Press.

Robins, R., & Post, J. (1997). *Political Paranoia: The Psychopolitics of Hatred.* New Haven, CT: Yale University Press.

Rosenthal, J. (2006). *The French Path to Jihad.* Washington, DC: The Hoover Institution.

Roy, O. (2004). *Globalized Islam.* New York: Columbia University Press.

Rudolph, E. (n.d.) "Psalm 144: 1: Blessed be the LORD my strength which teacheth my hands to war, and my fingers to fight." Available at www.armyofgod.com (accessed April 17, 2006).

Rudolph, E. (2005). "Allocution to the Birmingham Court." Available: www.armyofgod.com (accessed April 17, 2006).

Sageman, M. (2004). *Understanding Terror Networks.* Philadelphia: University of Pennsylvania Press.

Sandeen, E. (1970). *The Roots of Fundamentalism.* Chicago: University of Chicago Press.

Shimazono, S. (2001). "The Evolution of Aum Shinrikyo as a Religious Movement." In R. Kisala & M. Mullins (Eds.), *Religion and Social Crisis in Japan* (pp. 19–52). New York: Palgrave.

Shorto, R, (2006, May 7). "Contra-contraception." *New York Times Magazine.* Available: www.nytimes.com/2006/05/07/magazine/07contraception.html.

Shupe, A. (1993). "Soka Gakkai and the Slippery Slope from Militancy to Accommodation." In M. Mullins, S. Shimazono, P. Swanson (Eds.), *Religion and Society in Modern Japan* (pp. 231–237). Berkeley, CA: Asian Humanities Press.

Silberman, I. (2005). "Religious Violence, Terrorism, and Peace." In R. Paloutzian & C. Park (Eds.), *Handbook of the Psychology of Religion and Spirituality* (pp. 529–549). New York: Guilford Press.

Slotkin, R. (1998). *Gunfighter Nation*. Norman, OK: University of Oklahoma Press.

Smith, H. (1965). *The Religions of Man*. New York: HarperCollins.

Spear, K. (1994). "Conscious and Pre-Conscious God Representations: An Object Relations Perspective." Unpublished doctoral dissertation, Fuller Theological Seminary, Pasadena, CA.

Sprinzak, E. (1998a). "The psychopolitical formation of extreme left terrorism." In W. Reich (Ed.), *Origins of Terrorism* (pp. 65–85). Washington, DC: Woodrow Wilson Center Press.

Sprinzak, E. (1998b). *From Theory to Practice: Developing Early Warning Indicators for Terrorism*. Washington DC: United States Institute of Peace.

Stanley, T. (2003). "Sayyid Qutb." PWHCE Middle East Project. Available at www.pwhce.org/qutb.html (accessed March 14, 2007).

Stein, R. (2006). "Fundamentalism, Father and Son and Vertical Desire." *The Psychoanalytic Review*, 93/2: 201–230.

Stein, R. (2002). "Evil as Love and as Liberation: The Mind of a Suicidal Religious Terrorist." *Psychoanalytical Dialogues*, 12/3: 393–420.

Stern, J. (2006, February 25). "Anatomy of Terror." Lecture presented at a conference on "The Psychology of Fundamentalism," Chicago Institute of Psychoanalysis, Chicago.

Stern, J. (2003). *Terror in the Name of God*. New York: Ecco Press.

Strenski, I. (2003). "Sacrifice, Gift, and the Social Logic of Muslim 'Human Bombers.'" *Terrorism and Political Violence*, 15/3: 1–34.

Strong, J. (1983). *The Legend of King Asoka*. Princeton, NJ: Princeton University Press.

Strong, J. (1995). *Experience of Buddhism*. New York: Wadsworth Publishing.

Strozier, C. (1994). *Apocalypse: On the Psychology of Fundamentalism in America*. Boston: Beacon.

Strozier, C. (1996). *Genocide, War, and Human Survival*. Lanham, MD: Rowman & Littlefield.

Sullivan, A. (2004, June). "Jesus Christ, Superstar." *Washington Monthly*. Available at http://findarticles.com/p/articles/mi_m1316/is_6_36/ai_n6137430 (accessed Oct. 31, 2007).

Sunday Week in Review. (2006, April 16). *New York Times*. Available at http://www.nytimes.com/2006/04/16/weekinreview/16luo.html?_r=1&oref=slogin (accessed Oct. 31, 2007).

Suzuki, D. T. (1969). "Zen Buddhism." In A. Frazier (Ed.), *Buddhism* (pp. 265–296). Philadelphia: Westminster Press.

Tambiah, S. (1976). *World Conqueror and World Renouncer*. London: Cambridge University Press.

Taylor, M. (2005). *Religion, Politics and the Christian Right*. Minneapolis, MN: Fortress Press.

Terman, D. (2007). *The Psychology of Fundamentalism.* Unpublished manuscript.

Tillich, P. (1957). *The Dynamics of Faith.* New York: Harper & Row.

Tisdale, T, (1997). *A Comparison of Jewish, Muslim, and Protestant Faith Groups on the Relationship Between Level of Object Relations Development and Experience of God and Self.* Unpublished doctoral dissertation, Rosemead Graduate School, LaMirada, CA.

Tobena, A. (2004). "Individual Factors in Suicide Terrorists: A Reply to S. Atran." *Science,* 304/5667: 47–49.

Ungar, C. (2005, December). "American Rapture." *Vanity Fair,* pp. 204–2005.

United Kingdom. House of Commons. (2006a). "Report of the Official Account of the Bombings in London on the 7th of July 2005." London: House of Commons Stationery Office.

United Kingdom. House of Commons. (2006b). "Intelligence and Security Committee Report into the London Terrorist Attacks on 7 July 2005." London: House of Commons Stationery Office.

United Nations. (2004). "Report of the High Level Panel on Threats, Challenges, and Change." Geneva: Author.

Urban, H. (n.d.). "Bush, the Neocons and Evangelical Christian Fiction." Available at www.isebrand.com/article_america_left-behind.htm (accessed October 31, 2007).

Venkatraman, A. (2007). "Religious Basis for Islamic Terrorism." *Studies in Conflict and Terrorism,* 30/3: 229–248.

Victoria, B. (1997). *Zen at War.* New York: Weatherhill.

Victoroff, J. (2005). "The Mind of the Terrorist: A Review and Critique of Psychological Approaches." *Journal of Conflict Resolution,* 49/1:3–42.

Waller, J. (2002). *Becoming Evil.* New York: Oxford University Press.

Watanabe, M. (1998). "Religion and Violence in Japan today: A Chronological and Doctrinal Analysis of Aum Shinrikyo." *Terrorism and Political Violence,* 10/4: 88–100.

Watanabe, M. (2005). "Aum Shinrikyo." In L. Jones (Ed.), *Encyclopedia of Religion* (2nd ed.). New York: Macmillan.

Watanabe, M. (n.d.). *Salvation and Violence: Two Kinds of Salvation in Aum Shinrikyo.* Unpublished manuscript.

Weimann, G. (2006). *Terror on the Internet.* Washington, DC: United States Institute of Peace.

Wessinger, C. (2000). *How the Millennium Comes Violently.* New York: Seven Bridges Press.

Winncott, D. W. (1971). *Playing and Reality.* New York: Routledge.

Williams, P. (1989). *Mahayana Buddhism.* New York: Routledge.

Wright, S. (1987). *Leaving Cults: The Dynamics of Defection.* Monograph no. 7. Washington, DC: Society for the Scientific Study of Religion.

Wulff, D. (1991). *Psychology of Religion*. New York: John Wiley.

Zimbardo, P. (2004). "A Situationalist Perspective on the Psychology of Evil." In A. Miller (Ed.), *The Social Psychology of Good and Evil* (pp. 21–50). New York: Guilford Press.

Zimbardo, P., Maslach, C., & Haney, C. (1999). "Reflections on the Stanford Prison Experiment." In T. Bass (Ed.), *Obedience to Authority* (pp. 193–237). Mahwah, NJ: Erlbaum.

INDEX